The Christian Communities of Jerusalem and the Holy Land

THE CHRISTIAN COMMUNITIES OF JERUSALEM AND THE HOLY LAND

STUDIES IN HISTORY, RELIGION AND POLITICS

Edited by
ANTHONY O'MAHONY

UNIVERSITY OF WALES PRESS
CARDIFF
2003

British Library Cataloguing-in-Publication Data
A catalogue record for this book is available from the British Library.

ISBN 0–7083–1772–3

Typeset by Mark Heslington, Scarborough, North Yorkshire
Printed in Great Britain by Bookcraft Ltd, Midsomer Norton, Avon

CONTENTS

CONTRIBUTORS

Thomas Hummel, Chair of Theology, Episcopal High School and Adjunct Professor of Church History at Virginia Theological Seminary. He is the author of *Patterns of the Sacred: English Protestant and Russian Orthodox Pilgrims of the Nineteenth Century* (London, 1995) and co-edited *Patterns of the Past and Prospects for the Future: The Christian Heritage in the Holy Land* (London, 1999).

Inger-Marie Okkenhaug, Department of History, University of Bergen. She is the author of *The Quality of Heroic Living, of High Endeavour and Adventure: Anglican Mission, Women and Education in Palestine, 1888–1948* (Leiden, 2002).

Anthony O'Mahony, Heythrop College, University of London. His publications include *Palestinian Christians: Religion, Politics and Society in the Holy Land* (London, 1999); *Christian and Muslim in the Commonwealth* (London, 2001); *Eastern Christianity: Studies in Religion, Politics and History* (London, 2003); *World Christianity: Politics, Theology and Dialogues* (London, 2003).

Sotiris Roussos, Panteion University, Athens. He has authored numerous studies and articles on eastern Christianity in the Middle East and has prepared a major study for publication entitled 'Greece and the Middle East: Greek Orthodox communities in Egypt, Palestine and Syria, 1919–1940'.

Ara Sanjian, Haigazian University, Beirut. He is the author of *Turkey and Her Arab Neighbours: Origins and Failure of the Baghdad Pact, 1953–1958* (London, 2000) and is working on a volume on the Armenian communities in the Middle East.

Kirsten Stoffregen Pedersen, Jerusalem, is a specialist on Ethiopian Christianity, especially the Ethiopian Church in the Holy Land and is a long-term resident of the Holy City. She has authored several books: *Traditional Ethiopian Exegesis of the Book of Psalms* (Wiesbaden: Harrassowitz Verlag, Äthiopistische Forschungen, 1995);*The History of the Ethiopian Community in the Holy Land: From the Time of Emperor Tewedros II till 1974* (Jerusalem, 1983) and *Les Éthiopiens* (Turnhout, 1990).

John Watson is an Anglican priest and a leading expert on contemporary Coptic Christianity and the author of *Among the Copts* (Brighton-Portland: Sussex Academic Press, 2000), 'The transfigured Cross: a study of Father Bishop Kamel (1931–1979)', *Coptic Church Review* (2000), and 'Abba Kyrillios: patriarch and solitary', *Coptic Church Review* (1996).

1

THE CHRISTIAN COMMUNITIES OF JERUSALEM AND THE HOLY LAND: A HISTORICAL AND POLITICAL SURVEY

Anthony O'Mahony

Introduction

Arguably as a sacred city, Jerusalem is the single most important place in the Middle East: for Muslims, the Haram al-Sharef is a symbol of victory; for Jews, the Wailing Wall a symbol of loss; and for Christians, the Holy Sepulchre a symbol of victory through loss. Religion and politics have interacted in every sacred story. Political theologies remain at least implicit in the histories of all major faith communities, and at the centre of every sacred story is at least one sacred place, which in turn carves out of the cosmos a space held to be inviolable and safe for believers, a sanctuary, the place where everything of ultimate significance has occurred. For the Christian community and in particular for the Christians of Jerusalem, the principal holy spaces are the church of the Nativity in Bethlehem, the churches and holy places in Nazareth and, especially, the church of the Holy Sepulchre in Jerusalem, which remains an important symbol of Christian presence and custodianship in Jerusalem. Christians have not always enjoyed the right of freedom to make pilgrimage to and worship in the Holy Sepulchre; however, access to the sanctuary has always remained a symbolic anchor for Christians in Jerusalem. Perhaps no single place speaks more eloquently of the diversity of Christianity in Jerusalem than the Holy Sepulchre, with multiple side chapels, belonging to Greeks, Armenians, Latins, Syrians, Copts, Ethiopians, competing liturgical rites and celebrations, and the aroma of many shades of incense upon the air.[1]

From the end of the crusader period onwards the Christian communities and churches of Jerusalem and Palestine have experienced a succession of political systems and states with no partiality to Christianity. At the same time, these churches were representatives of ecclesiastical traditions older than those states, indeed in many ways older than the ethnic identities that are now prevalent in the region.[2] This has meant that the involvement of Christians in politics has been a natural endeavour and a constant theme in the religious culture of Jerusalem. An expression of this relationship between religion and politics in its Palestinian monastic setting has been described by

John Binns in *Ascetics and Ambassadors of Christ: The Monasteries of Palestine 314–631*:

> The Monks were people who withdrew from the secular world of the city but also were conscious of belonging to it. This double vocation is shown most clearly in the contrast between the two best-known monks, Euthymius, who consistently sought the seclusion and silence of the desert, and Sabas, who, although a renowned ascetic, was involved in the life of the Church of Jerusalem to the extent of travelling to the imperial capital on two occasions to represent its interests.[3]

In many ways it is not difficult for the modern pilgrim or traveller to Jerusalem to imagine the naturally cosmopolitan character of what was Christian Palestine during its early centuries, where cultural and religious exchange had been woven into the very fabric of the landscape.[4] Christian Jerusalem would have been dominated by pilgrims and monastic houses bringing together people from east and west, south and north, from Africa, including Ethiopia, Nubia, Egypt and as far away as the western Atlantic coast of Africa; from Arabia, Armenia, Byzantium, Georgia, Central Asia, Persia and India in Asia; from all over Europe, from Ireland, Gaul, Spain, Britain, Scandinavia, Iceland and Russia.[5] The Judaean desert was populated with monks from all over the Christian world who, whilst acting as carriers of their own religious culture, would have known no identity other than their heavenly *civitas* or *polis*. The monks of Palestine, numbering approximately 3,000 during the Byzantine period, inhabited some sixty monastic settlements across the hills and plains of the Judaean desert.[6] The development of monasticism was made possible by economic prosperity and political stability, which characterized Palestine in that time,[7] and by the flow of pilgrims, which provided not only financial support, but also provided new members for monastic foundations.[8] It is during this time of expansion that the Judaean desert, a region delimited by Jerusalem, the Jordan river and the Dead Sea, is fully assimilated into the religious and monastic geography of the Holy Land. A modern expression of this long historical continuity in the complex make-up of Christianity in the Holy Land is that in Jerusalem today there are three patriarchs: Greek Orthodox, Armenian and Latin; five Catholic patriarchal vicars: Maronite, Greek Catholic, Armenian Catholic, Syrian Catholic and Chaldean Catholic; four archbishops: Assyrian, Syrian Orthodox, Coptic Orthodox and Ethiopian Orthodox; and two Protestant bishops: Anglican and Lutheran. These Christian communities have come under the rule of numerous political entities: Islamic, the Ottoman Empire, the British Mandatory Administration, and the modern states of Jordan and Israel. It is against this background that we will undertake a historical and political survey of the Christian communities of Jerusalem and Palestine and of church-state relations in the Holy Land.

Christianity in Jerusalem and Palestine: The Historical Background

Although characterized by plurality, the Christian Church was, in its earliest days, one undivided community; however, well before the time of the first Muslim conquest of Palestine in AD 638 the process of fission had commenced and a number of communities had come into being.[9] There was, however, as yet only one patriarch of Jerusalem and it was he who negotiated with the Muslim conquerors on behalf of all Christians in the area.[10] The Christian community of Palestine was heterogeneous by nature and was made up of a number of communities which had grown out of the theological turmoil which had beset the Christian world from the fourth century onwards. However, on the whole, available records indicate that from this date until the establishment of the crusading kingdoms relations between the various Christian communities in Jerusalem were good, in spite of the growing estrangement between Rome and Constantinople and between the oriental and Byzantine-Latin Christian worlds. The Muslim capture of Jerusalem in 638 ended the exclusive Christian hold over the city and transformed the political and religious context within which Christianity in Palestine lived and expressed itself.[11] A determined cultural shift took place during this early Islamic period; Christians learned how to pray in the language of their conquerors, they produced devotional and theological literature and translated the Gospels into Arabic. The monks in the monasteries of Palestine began to write theology and the saints' lives in Arabic, the language of the Qur'ān, and to translate the Bible, liturgical texts, hagiographies, patristic texts and other ecclesiastical works from Greek and Syriac into the lingua franca of the Islamic caliphate. During this early period after the Muslim conquest of Palestine, scholar-monks, such as Anastasius of Sinai[12] (d. c.700) and John of Damascus[13] (d. c.750), writing in Greek, the traditional ecclesiastical language of the Melkite patriarchates in the East, undertook to confront the religious challenge of Islam. This endeavour on behalf of the Christians took place principally within the Palestinian monasteries of Mar Sabas, Mar Chariton and St Catherine at Mount Sinai, which had long been known as important centres of Christian culture in the Holy Land. During this period, the Islamic authorities would attempt to induce the conquered peoples to join the new faith with the promise of political and social equality. During the first Abbasid century many Christian communities throughout the Islamic world gave expression to the Christian faith in Arabic, and by the second half of the eighth century these Melkite monastic centres in Palestine would themselves be producing the first Christian literature in Arabic.[14] As a response, the Christian communities in Palestine started to produce apologetic treatises in Arabic from the eighth century onwards by such figures as Theodore Abu Qurrah, Anthony David of Baghdad and Stephen of Ramlah. With their strong involvement with scholarship and as centres of learning and spirituality for the Melkite oriental patriarchates it is not surprising that the

Palestinian monastic communities would be one of the first to adopt Arabic as a mode of expression for Christian literature from the beginning of the Abbasid caliphate in 750 to the eve of the crusader period in 1050.[15]

However, with the capture of Jerusalem and the setting up of the Latin kingdoms, the cleavage between Latin and eastern elements in the Church became more pronounced, and the Latins, under a Latin patriarch, enjoyed a paramount status in all the holy places.[16] Since there was some doubt in eastern eyes about the validity of the appointment of the Latin patriarch, the eastern churches also elected a patriarch, but he moved to Constantinople for the duration of the crusading kingdoms. From about 1250 until about 1675 the Orthodox patriarchate returned to Jerusalem but then retired once more to Constantinople until the middle of the nineteenth century. After the demise of the crusading kingdoms the Latin patriarchate was based in Rome until its revival in 1847.

From the capture of Jerusalem by Saladin until its absorption into the Ottoman Empire, the Ayyubids and the Mamelukes of Egypt governed Jerusalem. The supremacy enjoyed by the Latins was maintained for almost a century after the fall of the city, although this period also saw the fall of the Latin church from its prominent position and the true beginning of the constant struggle between the Latin and the Orthodox churches for supremacy, particularly in connection with the ownership of and rights over the holy places.[17] The struggle was largely confined to three communities: the Armenians, the Orthodox church and the Latins. The other rites, although represented in the holy places, were generally too poor to be able to take any significant part in the struggle for authority. Nevertheless at some point after the fourteenth century several different communities had formed in and around the holy places: Latins,[18] Greeks,[19] Armenians,[20] Georgians,[21] Syrians,[22] Nubians,[23] Copts,[24] Ethiopians[25] and Maronites.[26] However, throughout the Mameluke period and the subsequent Ottoman period, the history of Jerusalem is primarily a history of continual change of status, of rights of ownership and of position among the various Christian communities in the holy places – although it should be noted that the majority of the Christian inhabitants of Jerusalem were eastern or oriental Christians, whatever happened in the holy places. The struggle for position arose not only out of the basic rivalry between the different communities, but also out of the Muslim concept of legal ownership of religious buildings and institutions. Muslim rulers held themselves to be the legal owners of all religious buildings and institutions within their dominions, no matter the faith to which they were devoted. They therefore claimed the right to allocate them, confiscate them or close them at will. Such buildings could not be repaired or rebuilt without permission, while the building of new churches was for obvious reasons forbidden by Islamic law. Thus Saladin closed the church of the Holy Sepulchre when he captured Jerusalem in 1187 until he had decided under whose jurisdiction he would place it. Similarly, the Franciscans, who had become established as official representatives in Jerusalem of the Holy See with the official title of Custodians of the Holy Land, were expelled by Ottoman decree from their headquarters in the cenacle on Mount Zion in 1552. They finally settled in the convent of St Saviour, which they acquired from the Orthodox patriarchate, which had itself acquired the convent from the Armenians.[27]

From about the beginning of the sixteenth century onwards the influence of the Orthodox church was generally greater than of the Latin, despite periods of reversion. This was a logical outcome of the conquest of Constantinople by the Ottoman Turks in 1453 and their subsequent capture of Jerusalem in 1517, since the Orthodox and the Armenian churches were the first recognized Christian *millets* or communities, while the Latins were usually supported by foreign states with which the Ottoman authorities were at war. The Ottoman period also saw the introduction of international politics into the controversies surrounding Jerusalem and the holy places. Thus France claimed the right to protect not only foreigners of Latin persuasion resident in the empire, but also Ottoman subjects who were members of the Latin or eastern and oriental Catholic communions. The Russians claimed a similar position in respect of Ottoman subjects with Orthodox beliefs following the Treaty of Kuchuk Kainardja in 1774.[28]

Christians under Ottoman Rule from the Fifteenth to the Nineteenth Centuries

With the capture of Constantinople in 1453 Mohammed II became the overlord of a numerous group of Christians at a time when the Orthodox church was without a leader.[29] The Sultan ordered the election of a patriarch to the vacant seat, and by assuming the functions of the defeated *basileus* he presented in person the *dekanikon*, the patriarchal crosier, to Gennadios II. This endowed the patriarch with an authority his predecessors had never enjoyed, for to the religious jurisdiction proper to his position the Ottoman authorities now added civil power over all Christians within the empire, which gave him much authority and equally great responsibilities.[30]

What remained after this settlement was an autonomous body under the direct rule in religious and civil affairs of an authority dependent solely on the Ottoman authorities, in effect a state within a state. The generic name given to such a system was *millet*. This system evolved out of Islamic tradition which tolerated non-Muslims who recognized their Scriptures as part of divine revelation – *ahl al-kitab* or the people of the book.[31] They were given the status of *dhimmis* or protected people, granted protection for their lives and liberties, albeit limited, and were allowed to practise their own forms of worship, provided that they accepted the domination of the Muslim rulers, paid special taxes – the *jizya* and the *kharaj*, the poll tax and the land tax – and suffered certain restrictions to mark their inferiority, such as the wearing of distinctive clothing and the prohibition against carrying arms and riding horses.[32]

The Ottoman government dealt with the dhimmis as members of the community rather than as individuals. This was a consequence partly of the general organization of Ottoman society and partly of the nature of Islamic practice and law, which did not recognize the differences and internal relations between the dhimmis. It was based on the concept that law was personal rather than territorial, and that religion rather than either domicile or political allegiance determined the law under which an individual lived. The term *millet* came to indicate over time religion, religious community, and/or nation. It was within these three basic meanings that the term was used in the Ottoman Empire concurrently until the Tanzimat reforms during the mid-nineteenth century. For administrative purposes the non-Muslim subjects of the Ottoman Empire were organized into autonomous religious communities or millets. The heads of the millets were chosen by the millet, but the choice was subject to the sultan's approval, communicated in the form of an imperial *berat*, which alone enabled the nominees to assume their offices and take possession of their temporalities. The heads of the millets had an important place in the official hierarchy of the state, of which they were regarded as functionaries. The heads of millets represented their communities in their general and personal affairs *vis-à-vis* the Sublime Porte. The autonomy of the millets was based on custom and practice, which was reinforced in the nineteenth century by specific edicts. Their affairs were conducted by the head of the millet, generally assisted by a council composed of both lay and clerical members. The millets were autonomous in spiritual matters and in certain administrative and judicial matters. Their jurisdiction embraced, in the religious sphere, clerical discipline; in the administrative sphere, the control of their properties, including cemeteries, educational institutions and churches; in the judicial sphere, marriage, dowries, divorce and alimony, and civil rights. Sentences pronounced by millet courts, if within their competence, were executed on their behalf by the state. In the case of millets composed of Christians whose spiritual heads resided outside the Ottoman Empire, the spiritual head recognized by the authorities had to be an Ottoman subject in possession of the imperial *berat*.[33]

For a few years following the Ottoman conquest of Constantinople, the head of the Orthodox millet, the patriarch, was more than the spiritual and temporal head of the Orthodox subjects of the empire, as the sultan's original *berat* gave out; he had jurisdiction over all Christians in the empire, whatever their church or rite. Eight years later, however, the Armenian church under an Armenian patriarch of Constantinople was recognized as a separate community, comprising not only the Armenian Christians, but also the Latins, the eastern and oriental Catholic communities, the Jacobites, the Nestorian-Assyrians and the Copts.[34]

The millet system and the whole Ottoman government framework served the empire well until its gradual decline towards the nineteenth century. However, the often fragile nature of the Ottoman Empire offered opportunities to the Great Powers of Europe for agitation and intrigue among the minorities who had become restive under the restrictions imposed by an Islamic system which did not correspond to the important contribution these communities made to civil society.[35] Pressure created by this situation was one of the major factors which induced the Ottoman government to carry out administrative reforms in the nineteenth century. The great Ottoman reform edicts of the Hatti Serif of 1839 and the Hatti Humayun of 1856 were an attempt to reconstruct Ottoman policy in a form which would enable non-Muslims to participate on a level of equality which they had been denied by Islamic practice and law, and foster their loyalty to the sultan.

The Hatti Humayun intended to reform the position of the non-Muslims in their relationship with the state as well as in the internal situation of their communities. Its first fruits were the promulgation of new constitutions for the major Christian communities: the Greek Orthodox (1862)[36] and the Armenian Orthodox (1863).[37] The new constitutions sought to diminish the influence of the higher clergy and promote the powerful interests of the lay community within the Christian millets. The new communal constitutions also stipulated a general representative assembly with two councils: one to deal with religious and clerical matters and the other with the education and welfare of the community. The reforms were carried out mainly within the Armenian and the Greek Orthodox community. The Ottoman reforms concerning the communal organization thus applied to these two major Christian communities but were not carried out in practice in the patriarchates of Jerusalem, owing to the strong resistance of the upper hierarchy of both patriarchates.

From the early expansion of the empire, the Ottomans recognized three principal communities only as millets: the Greek Orthodox,[38] the Armenian Orthodox[39] and the Jews.[40] Both through schisms and as a result of missionary activities, new communities emerged, principally from within the Greek Orthodox but also the Armenian millets. They were mostly awarded official recognition as millets only after a long struggle: the Syrian Catholics in 1743,[41] the Armenian Catholics in 1831,[42] and the Chaldean Catholics in 1843.[43] Officially the Armenians included and represented all other unclassified communities, such as the Assyrians, as well as the eastern and oriental Catholics, although in practice each community organized its affairs locally through its own ecclesiastical leaders. The Latins held a unique position as they were not regarded as a local community. They were represented by a special agent (vakil) and were granted special rights concerning judgement and internal administration.[44] Their status was strengthened through agreements with France, which acted as protector of all the Catholics within the empire.[45] The Protestants were organized as a separate group by virtue of orders of 1850 and 1853, but they too were not awarded recognition as a millet.

The Christian millets recognized by the Ottoman authorities at the end of the nineteenth century may be grouped as follows:

A. The eastern Orthodox churches
   1. The Greek Orthodox millet (the four Eastern Orthodox patriar-
      chates of Constantinople, Jerusalem, Alexandria and Antioch)
   2. The various Orthodox churches in the Balkans which had removed
      themselves from the jurisdiction of the Orthodox millet in the nine-
      teenth century
B. The oriental Orthodox churches
   3. The Armenian Orthodox
   4. The Assyrians
   5. The Syrian Orthodox (Jacobites)
C. Latin, eastern and oriental Catholic churches
   6. Roman Catholics (Latin Rite)
   7. Greek Catholics (Melkites)
   8. The Maronites
   9. The Syrian Catholics
   10. The Armenian Catholics
   11. The Chaldeans
D. Protestants
   12. The Protestants. In 1850 the sultan recognized the Protestants as a
      separate millet. However, no special jurisdiction was conferred.

Most of these communities would have had a presence in Jerusalem at some level from the beginning of the nineteenth century onwards, if not before. It is noteworthy that most of these millets were of comparatively recent origin. However, only the Orthodox millet, the Armenians, the Ethiopians and the Latins had any real standing in Jerusalem before the nineteenth century.[46]

Throughout the Ottoman period and until the early decades of the nineteenth century Jerusalem was regarded as an ordinary sanjak without any special significance.[47] On the whole, it was part of the province of *Sham* (Damascus) and subject to its governor. Its jurisdiction was limited to the Judaean hills. The coastal plains from Jaffa to Gaza formed administrative units of their own: the sanjaks of Gaza and Jaffa. The sanjaks of central and southern Palestine were, until the nineteenth century, considered of marginal importance by the Ottomans. In the eighteenth century, due to the decline of law and order in the empire, the sanjak went through a period of neglected and substantial decline. In the nineteenth century, however, this situation changed radically as new challenges facing the Ottoman government during that century aroused the need to strengthen Ottoman administrative rule in the region, which led to the sanjaks of Jerusalem and Gaza acquiring a greater importance for the Ottoman authorities.[48]

First of all, the international status of Jerusalem and indeed of Palestine as a whole began to rise. Religious revivals throughout the Christian world in the early nineteenth century resulted in a substantial growth in pilgrimage, the creation of religious institutions and missions in Jerusalem, and almost all the

European powers took part in the drive to establish a 'presence' in the country. Combined with this, archaeological enthusiasm and a desire to study ancient and biblical history led to a stream of scholars and travellers who exposed the Holy Land to the West. The use of steamships, moreover, made sea travel shorter and safer, and travelling became easier and cheaper. Consequently, curiosity and devotion brought yearly a constantly increasing number of pilgrims and visitors from many parts of the Christian world.[49] Interest manifested itself in the erection of new churches and restoration of the old ones, in the building of convents and especially in missionary activities which led to the establishment of schools and hospitals in Jerusalem and other towns.[50]

Although the nineteenth century witnessed this revival of interest in the Holy Land throughout the Christian world from Ethiopia[51] to the Americas,[52] from Russia[53] to Britain,[54] at the beginning of the century the Franciscans were the only representatives of Latin Christianity to be found in Jerusalem, and the Protestant communities hardly had a presence there at all. The various oriental churches were represented as they had been for centuries, but, with the exception of the Orthodox church and the Armenians, their following in Jerusalem was insignificant, apart from the inhabitants of the various convents and monasteries. This is, however, hardly surprising since the population of Jerusalem at the beginning of the nineteenth century was estimated to be no more than 12, 000.[55]

During the period between the end of the Crimean War and the beginning of the First World War, there was a general extension of all religious interests. The increase of Russian influence among the Orthodox was paralleled by a steady increase of French influence among the Latins and the eastern and oriental Catholic communities. In this connection the establishment of consuls in Jerusalem helped considerably, the first in the field being the British in 1838, followed by the French, Prussian and Sardinian consuls in 1843, the American in 1844, and the Austrians replacing the Sardinians in 1849. The Russians, however, were represented by an agent in Jerusalem dependent on their consulate-general in Beirut, which had been there since 1839. The Catholics established such foundations as the Ratisbonne Institute, the houses of the Sisters of Our Lady of Sion, the seminary in the church of St Anne, and by the end of the century had established throughout Palestine thirty orders, brotherhoods and associations, with twenty-nine convents, eighteen hospices, six higher schools, sixteen orphanages, four industrial schools and five hospitals. The Anglican church founded, in addition to the cathedral, the associated schools in Jerusalem; the Ophthalmic Hospital of the Order of St John was established; and the German Evangelical church administered the hospital of the German deaconesses, the Syrian Protestant Orphanage, the leper hospital in the German colony and the Lutheran church which was built on the site of the hospice of the Knights of St John. Similar work was undertaken by other Protestant churches which established themselves in Jerusalem and Palestine during the nineteenth century.

Modern historiography points to a connection between the rise of European presence and interests in the country and the decision of the Ottoman Government to separate the sanjak of Jerusalem from the province of Syria and to constitute it as an independent sanjak subject directly to Istanbul. Though there is a great deal to say in favour of these arguments, they are not the whole picture in determining the Ottoman authorities' wish to control directly the sanjak of Jerusalem.[56] But if the city of Jerusalem and its holy places started to acquire a prime importance in Ottoman eyes, the occupation of Syria by Muhammad Ali was a turning-point in Ottoman policy towards Syria as a whole and towards the sanjak of Jerusalem in particular. With the Ottoman restoration in 1841, the sanjak of Jerusalem began to enjoy a special status among the Palestinian sanjaks – long before foreign interests in Palestine became substantial. In spite of the fact that Jerusalem became an important administrative centre after 1841, the tendency at the Porte during the Tanzimat period was to keep it and its sanjak within the framework of the province of Damascus.[57]

However, the Christian communities and their institutions also played an important part in the emerging shape of the sanjak. The significance of Jerusalem and the Holy Land in Christianity is too well known to need discussion, but it should be emphasized that the status of the Holy Land found important institutional expression. The jurisdiction of the Greek Orthodox patriarchate of Jerusalem – possibly the oldest and most important Christian institution in Palestine – extended over western and eastern Palestine. It should be remembered that this patriarchate had existed without a break since the Roman period. The Latin patriarchate of Jerusalem, re-established in 1847, and the Anglican bishop of Jerusalem, first appointed at the end of 1841, also held authority over the whole of Palestine. It is not surprising, therefore, that among the Christian population, within this religious context, the political concept of Jerusalem and Palestine grew in significance and importance.

The existence of the sanjak of Jerusalem for almost two generations as a separate entity from the other regions of Ottoman Syria was of a tremendous importance for the emergence of Palestine some years later. It also did much to determine the character and future of Palestinian politics, and contributed to the emergence of Palestinian nationalism as distinct from Syrian-Arab nationalism.[58] But to be a separate administrative unit is not in itself sufficient to create an image with which the people identify. This image emerged as a result of a combination of factors – partly religious (both for Christians and Muslims), but, above all, owing to the character of the administrative reforms applied by the Ottomans in the Tanzimat period, to social changes and other factors.

The Christian Communities under Colonial Rule:
The British Mandate 1917–1948

The First World War and its immediate aftermath had disastrous consequences for the eastern and oriental Christian communities. Never since the capture of Constantinople (1453) and the disappearance of the Byzantine Empire had eastern Christianity suffered such damage to itself and its institutions. On the surface, nothing appeared to survive of the socio-political framework which, in the two opposing eastern empires, the Russian and the Ottoman, once sustained a Christianity closely bound up with the very structures of the two states. In Russia, the violent severance of the age-old and indissoluble links between the Church and the state following the Bolshevik revolution created a structural void to which was soon added an ideological opposition to the Church, whose consequences were incalculable. In the former Ottoman Empire, the Greek Orthodox community and the oriental Christians had to submit to another form of disintegration. The various communities emerged from the war weakened by long periods of famine and by repeated massacres, in Anatolia, in Armenia and Cilicia, in northern Mesopotamia and in northern Syria and Lebanon. The dissolution of the empire which followed the armistice of Mudros (30 October 1919) and the Allied occupation of Constantinople (1919–23), and after that the institution of the mandate regime, which gave Britain and France a privileged position in the Arab provinces in the Middle East, had important consequences for the Christian communities. Instead of dealing as in the past with a single Islamic authority, the post-war situation confronted the Christians of the region with a wide variety of regimes and forms of states. In addition, the Arab nationalist-inspired independence movements which developed confronted Christians, whether Copt, Melkite, Assyro-Chaldean, Syrian or Maronite, with new religious-political choices which in many cases split their confessional and ecclesial entity asunder between competing loyalties.[59]

The origins, declaration and implementation of the British mandate for Palestine have been the subject of intense and deep scholarly research and controversy.[60] The mandate for Palestine was to be very different from the other mandates which had been devised for other parts of the region, Iraq, Syria and Lebanon. The latter were considered to be Class A mandates, that is territories whose independence at some point in future had been provisionally recognized subject only to the administrative assistance of the mandatory. For Syria and Iraq, the mandatory power was obliged to draw up an organic law to provide for self-government and prepare the country for independence. The mandate for Palestine was formulated with different intentions. Palestine was given the status of a Class B mandate, and hence was not destined for independence; the idea was not even considered in the terms of the mandate. The British mandatory power in Palestine was charged with promoting the political, administrative and economic conditions to ensure the establishment of a national home for the Jewish people, while protecting the civil and religious rights of the rest of the population. Considering the terms of the mandate, it was inevitable that the British authorities found it difficult to accommodate the different aspirations of the Muslim, Christian and Jewish communities.[61]

In order to provide a basis for a consideration of subsequent developments, it is necessary to summarize the position of the Christian communities under the mandate. The mandate for Palestine was allotted by the League of Nations to Britain in 1920, the text of the mandate document was finally approved by the League in July 1922 and it came formally into effect in September 1923, two months after the signature of the Treaty of Lausanne. This document, together with the Palestine Order-in-Council 1922, as subsequently amended and modified by later Orders-in-Council and enactments of the government of Palestine, provided the framework within which the Christian communities in Jerusalem and in Palestine as a whole functioned.[62]

The fundamental rights of minorities were recognized by the mandate for Palestine. Article 2 guaranteed the civil and religious rights of all inhabitants of the country, whatever their race or religion. Article 13 of the mandate vested in the mandatory 'all responsibility in connection with the Holy Places and religious buildings or sites in Palestine, including that of preserving existing rights and securing free access to the Holy Places', while article 14 provided for the appointment of a special commission to 'study define and determine' rights and claims in connection with the holy places and the different religious communities in Palestine. Article 9 charged the mandatory with responsibility for ensuring a complete guarantee of their rights to all inhabitants of Palestine, whether nationals or foreigners, under the judicial system to be established in Palestine. It states: 'Respect for the personal status of the various peoples and communities and for their religious interests shall be fully guaranteed. In particular, the control and administration of *waqfs* shall be exercised in accordance with religious law and the dispositions of the founders'. Articles 15 and 16 enjoined the mandatory to ensure freedom of worship, the right of individual religious communities to maintain schools for the education of their own members and an absence of discrimination on grounds of race, religion or language, while allowing for such supervision of religious and charitable bodies of all faiths as was required for the maintenance of public order and good government. Finally, article 8 decreed that the privileges and immunities, including the benefits of consular jurisdiction and protection, formerly enjoyed under the terms of the Capitulations would not apply in Palestine during the period of the mandate.[63]

Although the position of the Christian communities was fairly closely defined by the mandate and the 1922 Order-in-Council, there was no legal provision for the continuation of the network of privileges and immunities which had accrued to the communities in general or to certain members of the communities in particular under Ottoman rule. Subject to the provisions of the mandate and the Order-in-Council, these privileges and immunities were generally maintained by the mandatory administration. It was, however, found necessary from time to time to enact ordinances to validate the continued enjoyment of the privileges, to provide further definitions of rights and jurisdiction, and to deal with anomalies which arose. The necessity for such legislation arose because the rights, privileges and immunities enjoyed by the religious communities were of two types. The several rights and privileges in connection with the holy places, as defined by Ottoman statutes, had been laid down in the Status Quo of 1757, and confirmed in 1852. During the mandate these rights and privileges were regulated by the 1757 and 1852 statutes, as extended by later decisions of the secular power based on the Status Quo principles. However, other rights, privileges and immunities enjoyed by some or all of the Christian communities and their charitable, education and medical institutions had never been satisfactorily defined or codified. To some extent they were covered by various Ottoman firmans and decrees, but in some cases the relevant firmans were contradictory, and in others an oral grant of a privilege was never confirmed in writing. The Palestine government, therefore, took the view that any community or organization could claim the right to enjoy a particular privilege if it could prove that it had enjoyed the privilege under the Ottomans. In addition, a number of discriminatory and contradictory firmans were regulated by ordinance.[64]

The British mandate for Palestine, whilst inheriting only part of the Ottoman Empire, would nonetheless inherit many Ottoman institutions and procedures, and in particular the millet system. The treatment of the Christians as a religious minority by the British mandate in Palestine represented the preservation and development of the Ottoman millet system.[65] The unparalleled character of the mandate for Palestine and its guaranteeing of the rights of the Christians as a religious minority on the one hand, and the existence of the holy places, sacred to the three great religions, on the other, would determine the continuation of the Ottoman millet system under the British mandate. The unique religious status of Palestine as the cradle of Christianity and the existence of the holy places focused upon it the eyes of the western religious institutions such as the Vatican and the Protestant churches, and of several European states such as France, Italy, Spain and indeed Greece, which sought to protect the privileges of the Greek Orthodox patriarchate of Jerusalem. Any legislative or administrative measure applying to the Christians in Palestine was liable to arouse a lively debate either from the rival Catholic powers, who did not fully accept the British holding of the mandate, or from Protestant or Orthodox bodies eager to promote their position under a government of their denomination. However, the civil and religious rights of the Christians were generally secured by the mandate for Palestine. The mandatory government was subject to international supervision by the League of Nations in executing these guarantees, as well as the remainder of the articles of the mandate. The status of the Christian communities in Palestine was determined by the unique nature and the terms of the

British mandate. The mandate articles provided for the continuance and development of the Ottoman millet system, with the innovation that no religion was to be the state religion. But whilst the Christian communities had been used to operating as a minority religious millet during the long centuries of Ottoman rule in Palestine, Christian communal organizations were in a very poor state and desperately needed reviving and reforming.

The basis for the continuation of the millet system as laid down by the terms of the mandate was extended and strengthened owing to political considerations. The autonomy allowed by the Ottoman millet system with regard to the dhimmis became the basis of the government's relationship with the Muslims, too. This continuation of the millet system in Palestine under the British mandate placed the Muslim community upon a completely different communal and political footing than under Ottoman administration. The Muslim community in Palestine had not been considered a separate community up until 1917, but as part of the general Islamic religious and political body which ruled the Ottoman Empire. Under the British mandate, the Muslim community came to resemble an Ottoman millet, which had previously been the status and organization of non-Muslim communities. The Muslim community in Palestine found itself severed from the Islamic environment which had traditionally given context and meaning to its religious, political and social status. Under the British mandate the Muslim community as the majority community found itself without a communal status and institutions, and at a disadvantage *vis-à-vis* the Christian and Jewish communities.[66]

The basis of recognition of religious communities by the British mandate was the continuation of autonomous rights obtained during the Ottoman period. The first list of recognized Christian communities under the British mandate can be found as a schedule to the Succession Ordinance 1923 and included the communities which had been officially recognized by the Ottoman government: Greek Orthodox, Latin, Armenian Orthodox, Armenian Catholic, Chaldean Catholic, Syrian Catholic. To these were added the Greek Catholic community recognized in 1923[67] and the Maronite community in 1924.[68] The amended Palestine Order-in-Council 1939 added to this list the Syrian Orthodox community, and altogether nine communities were recognized throughout the mandatory period. However, the Protestant church did not obtain the official status of a recognized community on the grounds that it had not obtained such a status during the Ottoman period.

Before the Muslim conquest, the population of Palestine was overwhelmingly Christian, albeit with a sizeable Jewish community. In the centuries following the conquest, the Christian population was arabized, and many converted to Islam, often under compulsion or social, economic and political pressure. Nonetheless, a significant minority remained Christian. During the Ottoman period, the largest Christian community was Greek Orthodox, with various pilgrim and holy-place Christian communities of a much smaller size.

Data extracted from the various Ottoman documents suggest that the Christian community moved from the rural environs towards the main urban centres between the Ottoman conquest in the sixteenth century and the early nineteenth century. Proportionately, there were 50 per cent fewer villages with a Christian rural population in the nineteenth century than in the sixteenth. What happened between the sixteenth and the beginning of the nineteenth centuries was a process of retraction of Christian rural presence in Palestine and its gradual movement from the periphery towards the centre, or rather the urban centres. The underlying motivation for this migration to larger urban concentrations with larger Christian populations may have been concern, real or imaginary, for their own safety, and perhaps for their proper communal and religious life. Many Christians were attracted by the holy places and the security that Jerusalem offered. This was a slow and gradual migration process that went on until the nineteenth century and the final result of it was a very limited Christian presence in the rural areas.[69] The Christian communities increased at a greater rate than the Muslim community, especially in the Jerusalem sanjak. In the case of the Orthodox, this increase can be explained by the fact that this community was generally more urban and less likely to reside in rural areas where mortality was high. The growth of the other Christian communities in the nineteenth century was primarily through conversion, more specifically conversion from the Greek Orthodox community.

In 1922, the first actual census was taken in Palestine. It was designed for a political purpose, the enumeration of the Palestinian population by religious groups as the basis for proportional voting for a projected Legislative Council. In the early period of the mandate the Christian population in Palestine comprised 9.6 per cent of the total population. In 1931 it had fallen to 8.8 per cent, although its absolute number increased. It has been estimated that the Christian community lost 13 per cent of its overall population during the First World War, mainly through migration out of Palestine and through a 4 per cent mortality rate. The reduction in the Christian proportion of the Arab Palestinian population was the outcome of their lower birth rate and a small amount of emigration. The Arab Christian birth-rate (37.2) was lower than that of the Muslim population (54.7) and approximated to that of the Jews (33.2) in 1922.[70]

Migration in search of economic opportunities and political-religious freedom from the Ottoman Empire to the Americas in the nineteenth century was particularly remarkable among the Christian communities of Palestine.[71] The first death among the emigrants to South America, recorded in the registers of the Latin parish priest's office in Bethlehem, however, goes back to 7 September 1796. The deceased emigrant's name was Andrea Francis Hanna Dawud from the Tarajmah quarter in Bethlehem.[72] In 1874, two brothers from the Zakhariya family from the same quarter in Bethlehem were among the first Arabs to arrive in Brazil. They sold mother-of-pearl curios such as rosaries, crosses and icons in the principal jewellers' street in Rio de Janeiro.[73] International exhibitions held in the United States played a pioneering role in attracting Palestinian Christian merchants. Many of them came to visit the Philadelphia Exhibition in 1876, the Chicago Exhibition in 1893 and the St Louis Exhibition in 1904, bringing with them Holy Land products, such as mother-of-pearl, olive wood and Nabi Moses stone, to exhibit and sell to the faithful and the curious. In time Chile became a main centre for emigrants from the two towns of Bethlehem and Bayt Jala. The first Palestinian Christian emigrant to arrive in Chile was Jubra'il D'eiq from the Tarajmah quarter in Bethlehem in 1880. During the first four decades of the twentieth century some families began to disappear gradually from local parish registers, resulting from the collective emigration of whole families. This pattern was most significant in these towns although the problem was evident throughout Palestine. With the coming of economic and, to a certain degree, political stability in Palestine under the British mandate, emigration from the Christian communities significantly decreased.[74]

The largest Christian centre of population in Palestine under the British mandate was the Jerusalem district, which included the towns of Bethlehem and Ramallah and the villages that surrounded them. Within this district all Christian denominations were represented. This was primarily due to the holy places in Jerusalem and Bethlehem. Second in size during this period was the Northern district, which included the towns of Haifa, Acre, Nazareth, Tiberias and Safad and the surrounding villages. The communities principally located in the northern district were the Greek Catholics, the Greek Orthodox and some Maronite villages along the Lebanese-Palestine border. Yet in none of the districts or subdistricts of British mandatory Palestine did the Arab Christian community constitute a majority of the population, and only in the Bethlehem subdistrict did the Christian population constitute as much as 45 per cent of the total population, according to the census of 1931. The Christians in Palestine were dispersed and formed an integral part of Arab Palestinian society as a whole. The 1922 census showed that 30,412 or approximately 41.5 per cent of the total Christian population were concentrated in the main towns of Jerusalem, Jaffa and Haifa. By 1931, the Christian population in these towns was 42,291 or 46.2 per cent of the total Christian population. The Christian community could also be found in the smaller towns of Palestine, such as Bethlehem, Bayt Jala, Ramallah, Nazareth and Shafa Amr, where in 1922 18,018 or 24.7 per cent of the Christian community lived. In 1931, the Christian population of these towns constituted 18,560 or 20.2 per cent of the total community. Christians lived in villages throughout Palestine, but the majority could be found in the villages surrounding Acre, Nazareth and Ramallah. As already mentioned there was a historical precedent: the drift of the Christian population away from isolated villages from the sixteenth century onwards was towards the larger settlements which traditionally had large Christian concentrations.

From the middle of the nineteenth century, the Palestinian Christian community was in a continual process of fragmentation and change. The majority Christian denomination, the Greek Orthodox community, was decimated by the continuing political and religious conflict between the Arab Orthodox community and the ethnically Greek hierarchy. This conflict, plus the important institutional and pastoral commitment offered by the other Christian communities in Palestine, attracted a great number of Arab Orthodox Christians to become Latin or eastern Catholics and, in some areas, Protestants. However, the largest Christian community, according to the British mandatory census, was the Greek Orthodox church. It declined in proportion to the Christian population, from 45.7 per cent (33,369) in 1922 to 43.5 per cent (39,727) in 1931. The Latin Catholic community increased its proportion of the total Christian population of Palestine from 19.5 per cent (14,245) in 1922 to 20 per cent (18,895) in 1931. The Latin Catholic community was especially strong in the central Christian belt, particularly in Jerusalem and Bethlehem, and in the coastal town of Jaffa. The proportion of the Greek Catholic community – which was predominantly found in the northern part of the country and which was historically an extension of that community in Lebanon and Syria – of the total Christian community fell from 15.3 per cent (11,191) in 1922 to 13.8 per cent (12,645) in 1931. The oriental Christian communities, which included the Maronites, the Armenians, the Syrians and the Chaldeans constituted 19.5 per cent (14,167) in 1922 and fell to 18.2 per cent (16,683) in 1931. The proportion of the Anglican community in Palestine also fell, from 6.2 per cent (4,553) in 1922 to 5.3 per cent (4,799) in 1931.

Palestinian Christians: Religion, Politics, Nationalism and Islam

One of the most important phenomena characterizing the political life of Palestine during the British mandate was the formation of a joint Muslim–Christian front within the emergence of the Palestinian Arab national movement.[75] This was something completely new and opposed to the long tradition of Christian isolation from public life. In the course of the process of reform in the Ottoman Empire in the nineteenth century the Ottoman government had attempted to improve the status of its Christian subjects and to give them equality with the Muslims, which on occasion had led to a violent backlash against the Christian community.[76] Palestinian Christian involvement in the emerging Arab national movement during the late Ottoman period may be understood as evidence that a marginal community's power to influence and shape the dominant community is greatest when the characteristic institutions are in a process of formation, radical modification or destruction which the marginal community is able to accelerate and focus.[77] Arab Christians actively participated in the emerging Arab national movement because they regarded it as the opportunity to break the yoke of their marginality and to create an ideology and community sufficiently broad to encompass them as full and equal participants. Christians later realized that although the Arab national movement was explicitly secular, the Arabs could not separate nationalism from Islam, as Turkish nationalism had done, following the ideas of European nationalism.[78] The influence of the Palestinian Arab Christians on the national movement in its formative stage was less marked than that of the Syrian Christians because the Palestinian Arab national movement appeared later on, in 1918, when the influence of Islam on the movement was already apparent.[79] Nevertheless, the early years of the Palestinian Arab movement were marked by the attempt to give Christians an equal position and to disregard religious affiliation. Both Muslims and Christians recognized the Islamic content of Arab history and culture, though the majority of national leaders, on the ideological level, carefully avoided giving an explicit definition of Arab nationalism in Islamic terms.[80] The political and religious dilemma of Arab Christian involvement in the national movement has been described in the following manner:

> In order to convince themselves – if not others – that they formed part of the Arab Nation they would have to reject what had governed the social arrangements of their community for countless generations and provided a sense of identity with their fathers and fathers' fathers. In the past they had been members of a religious community, and this membership at once defined their status and set the bounds of their public as of their private activity. Loyalty did not extend beyond the community, and traffic between communities was confined to an inescapable minimum of externals. But now this religion suddenly seemed a badge of servitude. Membership of the Arab nation had a price – which Muslims, being the majority and the rulers, did not have to pay. It meant the abandonment of communal organisation and the defiant assertion that religion was a private affair, that it could not be the constitutive principle of a society, that it had no political and little social significance. This radical change of view in a matter so intimate and so fundamental came abruptly, and if only because abrupt, it must also have been violent, creating a schism and discord within the community. When therefore, outside observers reported the solidarity of Christians with Muslims, were they not perhaps unwittingly echoing the claims and professions of the victorious party in a species of civil war which had raged inside the . . . Christian community.[81]

Another version of this dilemma was composed by the authors of the British official commission of Bertram and Young, reporting on the controversies between the Greek Orthodox patriarchate and the Arab Orthodox community:

> National consciousness is not a matter of what ought to be felt, but of what actually is felt. No amount of eloquent reasoning could persuade the inhabitants of Alsace-Lorraine that their true national consciousness is German. Similarly no amount of such reasoning would persuade the Orthodox congregation of Palestine that they are not Arabs . . . The dearest thought to every

young local Orthodox Christian is that he is an Arab, and his most cherished aspirations are those of Arab nationalism, which he shares with his Moslem fellow-countrymen.[82]

Arab Nationalism as an organized political movement with ideology and aims is a phenomenon of the twentieth century. Prior to the First World War it was confined to closed intellectual circles in Damascus, Beirut, Istanbul, Cairo and Paris, and was expressed through publication of newspapers and pamphlets and the formation of secret societies, the majority of which did not work for Arab independence and separation from the Ottoman Empire before the war.[83]

The Balfour Declaration aroused the apprehension and suspicion of the Arab population in Palestine, both Muslim and Christian, regarding Zionist aims and the political future of the country.[84] This gave rise to the emergence of a series of interconfessional political groupings: the Muslim–Christian associations. These newly formed Muslim–Christian associations were joined by notables, heads of prominent families, village shaykhs and Christian leaders. To the majority of the population these associations formed the first experience of political and public collaboration between Muslims and Christians, a unity which impressed many European observers. A few attempts to form common organizations had been made before 1914, but these applied to very small sections of the Muslim and Christian communities. In 1908, following the Young Turk revolution, several appeals were made to Christians by Muslims to overcome their confessional spirit and join them in the organizations for the benefit of the general population.[85]

The first Muslim–Christian association was established in March 1918 by the Arab population of the Jaffa–Ramallah district with a programme to combat growing Zionist influence and to impede the purchase of land by Jews. Several months later similar activity spread to Jerusalem which soon became the largest and best-organized centre of activity. Early in 1919 the statutes of the Muslim–Christian associations had already been laid down. They embodied two branches: one for the district of Jerusalem and the other for the whole of Palestine. The latter comprised four delegates from the Jerusalem branch – Jerusalem being the centre of the movement – and two delegates from each section of the general branch. By 1921, other associations had been established in Jaffa, Gaza, Nablus, Tul Karm and Hebron. Unsuccessful attempts were made to establish associations in Ramallah, Bethlehem and Haifa. Jerusalem was the only branch which had specific regulations regarding its internal organization. The Jerusalem Muslim–Christian association was set up as the representative body of the various sections and communities of the town in distinct groups. Its executive committee was composed of thirty members: ten representatives of the town's Muslims, five representatives of the Latin community, five representatives of the Greek Orthodox community, and ten representatives of the village mukhtars. Second to the Jerusalem Muslim–Christian association in activity stood the Jaffa association, which was concerned as much with economic and commercial issues and the general welfare of the Arab inhabitants as with the political situation.

Christian involvement in the early formative period of the Palestinian Arab national movement was not uniform in character or motives. Generally the Catholic communities, and particularly Barlassina, the Latin patriarch of Jerusalem, and Hajjar, the Greek-Catholic bishop of the Galilee, took a determined stand against the aspirations of the Zionist movement and took part in the Palestinian national movement on that basis. The stand taken by the Arab Orthodox community and the Greek Orthodox patriarchate was more complex. The Greek Orthodox patriarch was more fearful of the trend within the Arab Orthodox for a general arabization of the patriarchate than of the Zionist movement. The Greek Orthodox patriarchate and the traditional leadership of the community therefore tended to co-operate with the British government in Palestine from the start and opposed the trend towards unification with Hashemite Syria. In contrast to them stood the young, educated figures within the community, such as Khalil al-Sakakini, Yusuf al-'Isa and his brother 'Isa al-'Isa, leaders of the al-Nahdah al-Urthuduxiyyah (The Orthodox Revival), who were conspicuous by their Arab nationalist pro-unity stand and saw themselves as Arab in all respects and identified themselves with the Arab national movement. Nevertheless, the traditional leadership was not only more powerful, but also represented the majority of the community. Although Muslim–Christian solidarity was indeed real it was not total. The uniting factor was enmity to Zionism, but as far as the political future of the country was concerned there were great differences of opinion. The Christians were unceasingly torn between their communal loyalties and identity and the need to take part in the anti-Zionist struggle; while the Muslims for their part tried to restrain their anti-Christian sentiments with the passing of Ottoman rule, and did much to prevent the creation of a Christian question and a Christian front against them.[86]

However, Muslim–Christian unity and co-operation in the national movement came under stress as some Muslim leaders sought to emphasize the predominance of Islam in the formation and development of a Palestinian national identity. This led some figures in the Palestinian national movement to resort to poetry in order to express and illustrate the problems straining relations between Christian and Muslim within the national alliance, and to warn of the damage to the overall political goal, if the majority overrode the minority. When on 6 September 1930 Djamil al-Bahri, a Christian journalist and editor of *az-Zahra*, was murdered during a dispute between Muslims and Christians concerning a cemetery in Haifa, Wadi al-Bustani, an Arab Christian who had been involved in the formation of the national movement on the basis of Muslim–Christian co-operation, launched a poetic appeal:

> Not religion killed him
> And not the followers of religion.
> O you, who sow with the weapon of hostility
> Do not attribute this disgraceful deed
> To the religion of the Hanifen, you criminals.

Muslim symbolism in poetry stands alongside appeals to both Christians and Muslims, in the name of the fatherland, making the love of the fatherland a religion and hence undermining an exclusive religious claim. In 1929 Ibrahim Tuqan composed the following as part of a Palestinian poem:

> Our religion is love
> For this fatherland – whether open or secret.
> Tell of it, History,
> Be a witness of it, Time!
>
> The Christian is the brother of the Muslim,
> O Palestine, with heart and mouth
> Spread, Palestine, the love
> Of Christian and Muslim in your flag.
> Our sign is the arch
> Of Pleiads in our blood.

The Christian poets make statements which anticipate this special relationship between Christianity and Islam. An appropriate example of this is from Wadi al-Bustani:

> Yes, I am a Christian.
> Ask yesterday and ask tomorrow.
> But I am an Arab, who
> Loves Muhammad.[87]

Muslim–Christian relations were also strained by some Muslim leaders who considered that Islam, as the religion of the majority which had for centuries dominated and ruled over the dhimmi, should be venerated and even embraced by Christians, as Islam was the foundation of the Arab national movement.[88] Extreme Muslim leaders even made calls to the Palestinian Christians to embrace Islam. Many Palestinian Christians were forced into a position of apology and self-justification. Najib Nassar, the Christian editor of al-Karmil, responded to these calls. He divided the Arab nation into two groups: those who responded to the Prophet's call and joined Islam (fariq al-ijaba) and those who, while remaining true to their religion, accepted his gospel and biddings in everyday life, manners and national commands (fariq al-da'wa). Fariq al-da'wa were the brethren of fariq al-ijaba in language, race and habits. The article continued by praising the Prophet as the founder of Arab history who managed to gather the Arabs around him, and to whom the Arabs owed their common fate, heritage and culture. Therefore, since the establishment of Islam, the Arab Christians participated

together with the Muslims in celebrating the Prophet's birthday. He refuted
the claim that the Christians' celebration was not sincere because they had
not accepted Islam. Muhammad taught religious principles; he was also sent
to teach good manners, and whosoever did not accept both could not be
regarded as a true Arab and Muslim. The greatness of Muhammad and his
followers formed the basis of the Arab national emergence (*nahdat al-'Arab*)
and both Muslims and Christians should follow his way in order to achieve
this goal.[89]

The Arab Christians' desire to prove themselves as more perfect Arabs
found its strongest expression in a pamphlet written by an Orthodox
Christian, Khalil Iskandar al-Qubrusi. The pamphlet, bearing the title
Da'wat Nasara al-'Arab ila al-Dukhul fi al-Islam (A call to the Christian
Arabs to embrace Islam),[90] denounced European Christianity as a corrupt
religion which oppressed eastern Christianity, and European monks and
missionaries as sowing dissension between the Muslims and Christians of
Palestine. In contrast, it expressed its admiration of Islam as being a benevolent, egalitarian and democratic religion which formed the basis of Arab
nationalism and unity. Its conclusion was a call to embrace Islam: 'This is the
religion to which I call all Arab Christians without exception in order to free
them from the trivialities of the foreigners and to rid them of their corruption'.[91] Very few Arab Christians, if any, responded to this call. The majority
continued to identify themselves with the Muslim majority, preserving their
Christian communal identity. This offered a paradox, and most Christians
continued to live with it. They tried to prove good Arab nationalists, bearing
the stigma of their deficiency in being non-Muslims, which prevented them
from becoming fully accepted as equals.

The most obvious example is that of Khalil al-Sakakini, who was one of
most active Arab Christians at the Palestinian Arab National congresses; and
one of the few Arab Christians who supported Faysal's administration and
the idea of an independent united Arab state. He was perhaps one of the few
Christians accepted by Muslim national social circles beyond the common
membership of organizations. Nevertheless, he too came to realize the
awkward position of being a member of a minority religious group. An inner
glimpse of the insecurity and even bitterness which al-Sakakini, as an Arab
Christian nationalist, felt beyond the mask of expression of solidarity with
Arab nationalism and Islam is found in his letters to his son, Sari, who was
then studying in the United States. The son translated the letters and circu-
lated them among friends, adding a preface explaining his father's identity:

> He is a Christian but does not make a hullabaloo out of his being one . . . He
> never goes to church because he fears to come out of there rebellious and he
> fears to disturb the calm of his soul and the stability of his mind. Briefly, his
> Christianity is different from the Christianities I have so often come to know
> in this part of the world, because it makes him an open minded man and not
> a narrow minded hypocrite.[92]

In the first of these translated letters, Khalil al-Sakakini told of a lecture he had given, which had not been properly appreciated:

No matter how my standing may be in science and literature, no matter how sincere my patriotism is, no matter how much I do to revive this nation . . . as long as I am not a Moslem I am nought. If you desire to amount to anything, then be a Moslem and that will be peace.

If I enjoy any position in this land, if the people love me and respect me, it is because they think that I am nearer to Islam than to Christianity, because I am wealthy in the Arabic language, because they fancy that I am a conservative and will not depart from Oriental customs under any circumstances. But if I were to struggle with a Moslem who is less founded in knowledge and heritage than I, I would not doubt that they would prefer him to survive.

. . . whenever I think of your and your sisters' future I am alarmed for you . . . I only pray to God that your age will be better than mine; that you will not return to this country until it has changed, and when a man will be estimated by what he achieves and not according to how he preserves these outworn customs.[93]

As the years passed, al-Sakakini's recognition of Muslim domination over the national movement became more explicit. In 1935 he rejected appointment to the post of director of the Arabic department in the Palestine broadcasting service, explaining that a Muslim was preferable for the post. This was a symbolic gesture to those Arab Christian nationalists who had neglected their own communal identity in the hope of becoming totally amalgamated in a new secular identity which, they came to realize, could not be achieved. Although the Muslim–Christian association had been established in the form of a partnership between Muslim and Christian leaders and notables, the Christians realized the dominant role of the Muslims over the movement, which forced them into a marginal position. Christian participation was signified by individual activities among the leadership of the national movement, rather than among the rank and file. Yet they did not usually act as leaders in their own right, but as attachés to Muslim leaders, acting in their service. The Palestinian Arab national movement was dominated by large and leading Muslim families. The Christians did not have a part in this establishment, and without this it was impossible to gain leadership in their own right.

The Impact of the 1948 War on the Christian Communities in Jerusalem and Palestine

At its final session in 1946 the Assembly of the League of Nations adopted unanimously, with Egypt abstaining, a resolution which recognized that 'on the termination of the League's existence, its functions with respect to the mandated territories will come to an end, but notes that Chapters XI, XII and XIII of the Charter of the United Nations embody principles similar to those declared in Article 22 of the Covenant of the League'. These chapters provided for the establishment of an international trusteeship system for certain categories of territories, including territories held under mandate, but provided that the terms of individual trusteeship would be subject to individual agreement by the states concerned. In 1946 Britain agreed to conclude trusteeship agreements for all territories which it administered under the mandate system, with the exception of Palestine. Transjordan was also excepted on grounds that Britain intended to recognize her independence, which was subsequently done in the treaty of alliance signed on 22 March 1946.

With regard to Palestine, the British Government advised the United Nations in April 1947 that they intended to place the question of Palestine on the agenda of the next session of the General Assembly, and to ask the Assembly to make recommendations concerning the future government of Palestine, on the grounds that the mandate had become unworkable and they had no powers to alter its terms. In May, therefore, the United Nations set up a Special Committee on Palestine (UNSCOP) to examine the position and make recommendations. The UNSCOP report, submitted at the end of August 1947, was unanimous on a number of general points, and the majority report recommended the partition of Palestine into an Arab and a Jewish state, and the placing of Jerusalem under a special regime. The two states were to become fully independent, though bound together by an economic union, after a transitional period of two years under special arrangements. The UNSCOP proposals were adopted by the General Assembly on 29 November 1947. The proposals provided for freedom of conscience and worship, the continuance of existing provisions for the status of the various religious communities and religious or charitable bodies, the continuance of the right enjoyed by each religious community to maintain its own schools and other educational establishments, including those run by foreign bodies, on the basis of existing rights, subject to any requirements of a general nature the state might impose, and for the maintenance of existing rights in respect of holy places and religious buildings or sites, including exemption from taxation. The proposals for Jersualem provided for the establishment of a *corpus separatum* under an international regime, and laid down in some detail its administration. This included the maintenance of the existing rights of religious and charitable bodies along the lines indicated above. The UNSCOP proposals were accepted by the Jewish Agency, but rejected by the Arab states.

Fighting broke out in Palestine shortly after the United Nations had accepted the plans. This was to continue sporadically until armistice agreements had been signed early in 1949. In the meantime the mandate ended on 14 May 1948, the state of Israel was proclaimed, and Arab forces entered Palestine. In the course of the fighting, Israeli forces occupied west Jerusalem (the New City) and Transjordanian forces occupied east Jerusalem including the Old City. The *de facto* control exercised by the opposing forces formed the basis for the demarcation lines laid down in the armistice agreements. By the end of 1948, it was clear that both sides had completely rejected the idea of an international regime for the city of Jerusalem, and the Israelis told the United Nations that they would assume sovereignty over west Jerusalem and the strip connecting it with the Jewish state. The Transjordanian response was to state their intention to annex the West Bank, to appoint a new mufti of Jerusalem and to announce the intention of claiming east Jerusalem for Transjordan. In January 1950 Jerusalem was formally proclaimed the capital of Israel, and in April 1950, the West Bank, including east Jerusalem was offi- cially annexed to Jordan (as Transjordan was now known).

The division of Jerusalem into Jordanian and Israeli sectors was of consid- erable importance to the Christian communities in the city, since the Arab quarters of west Jerusalem which had been taken by the Israelis were almost entirely Christian Arab areas, and much of the centre of west Jerusalem was Christian church property on which the shrines and monasteries of east Jerusalem depended for their maintenance. In addition, the heads of the vari- ous communities lived and worked, almost without exception, in places which fell under Jordanian control. Whatever the legal issues, therefore, the Christian communities and their charitable, religious and educational institu- tions had to establish a working relationship with the authorities of both Israel and Jordan in order to continue with their functions. This included the question of the applicability or otherwise of relevant legislation to their prop- erties and functions. The armistice line set up after the 1948 war cut Jerusalem in half. The local Christian communities thus found themselves for the first time in many centuries under a native Arab government, a state moreover formed against the background of the demise of the Ottoman empire in 1917, the British mandatory administration and modern Arab nationalism, with Arab Christian backing, while other Christians found themselves in a radically changed political, religious and cultural environ- ment in that territory which became the state of Israel. However, Arab Christians played a far greater part in Arab political activity in the new state of Israel than their proportion in the total Arab population would have suggested. Enjoying a higher, more western education, they filled the socio- political vacuum created by the exodus of the predominantly Muslim Palestinian leadership during the 1948 war.[94] The proportion of Christians in the remaining Arab population increased from 10 per cent during the late mandatory period to 21 per cent in 1949.[95]

As a result of intrinsic international interest in Jerusalem, home to the sacred sites of Judaism, Christianity and Islam, Israeli policy towards the holy places was under constant scrutiny by the international community. Israel's treatment of these sites provided a barometer to measure the degree of the newly established state of Israel's commitment to its proclamation of inde- pendence pledge (14 May 1948) to safeguard the holy places of all religions. The issue was particularly pressing in light of the United Nations' emphasis on the Jerusalem issue in each of its resolutions concerning the Palestine–Israel conflict.[96]

The first Knesset, elected on 25 January 1949, was to have drafted and promulgated a constitution for Israel. However, it decided in June 1950 against such a course, and voted for the evolution over an unspecified period of a constitution in the shape of a series of basic laws. In the declaration of the establishment of the state of Israel, issued on 14 May 1948, a provisional Council of State was established, and freedom of religion, conscience, language, education and culture was guaranteed. The declaration further decreed that the law which existed in Palestine on 14 May 1948 would continue in force in the state of Israel insofar as such continuance in force was consistent with the provisions of the declaration, with any future laws and with the changes arising out of the establishment of Israel.

The legal position of the Christian communities in the early years of Israeli administration was, therefore, that the rights and privileges enjoyed by these communities and various organizations under their control, or loosely attached to them which were specifically embodied in Palestinian law, continued in force, and the communities recognized under the mandate for various purposes continued to be recognized. However, any rights, privileges or immunities enjoyed by the communities and by charitable and other organizations which were not so embodied would not necessarily continue.

Generally, Israeli legislation throughout the years since 1948 has provided for the continuance of the position of the Christian communities, although the competence of the religious courts concerning the creation of endowments appears to have been withdrawn. Israeli legislation concerning taxation and other financial matters did, on the whole, provide for continued exemption in whole or in part to religious, charitable, educational, social welfare and cultural bodies, but it normally included a provision that it was up to the authorities concerned to decide whether any given organization qualified for the exemption, whether or not such exemption had been enjoyed during the mandate. In other words, although the legislation provided for continuance of privileges, immunities and exemptions according to the strict letter of the law, the practical application of the law was such that erosion of these privileges and immunities was possible.

A matter of even greater concern for the religious communities was the Israeli attitude to the transfer of income and other funds from Israel to Jordan, since in most cases the bulk of the communities' income derived from property in Israel or west Jerusalem, while the bulk of their expenditure was in Jordan or east Jerusalem. Thus the Orthodox patriarchate owned property in Israeli-held territory which yielded an income of some $22,000 per annum, while its income from Arab-held areas totalled no more than $1,500 per annum. The patriarchate's monthly expenditure amounted to some $4,000, mainly disbursed in east Jerusalem. Generally, the Israelis were not disposed to allow free and unrestricted transfer of funds, and although the ruling was later relaxed to some extent, some Christian authorities found themselves in serious financial straits as a result of the Israeli attitude. The Israelis also tended to use this point as a means of applying further pressure on the authorities to sell or lease property.[97]

The kingdom of Transjordan, formerly under mandate, achieved full independence on 25 May 1946; the constitution, in many respects similar to the Organic Law of 1928, was promulgated on 7 December 1946 and amended in 1952 and 1954. Thus no special declaration was made by Jordan (the designation 'Hashemite Kingdom of the Jordan' was officially declared to be the only correct title for the state on 1 June 1949) on the termination of the mandate over Palestine, parallel to that put out by Israel when that state was created.

The position regarding the activities of the Christian communities in east Jerusalem was equally complex. The first formal step to regularize the legal position of the West Bank was the issue of Law no. 48 of 1949 concerning the administration of Palestine. The purpose of this law was to clarify and consolidate earlier enactments on the subject. It empowered the king of Jordan to assume all the powers previously vested in the British high commissioner and the Palestine government under the 1922 Order-in-Council, provided for the continuance in force of the law existing in Palestine at the termination of the mandate, and invalidated any subsequent enactments by the Jordanian authorities in respect of Palestine. Finally, the West Bank was formally incorporated in the kingdom of Jordan in April 1950.

The major Christian shrines of Jerusalem and Bethlehem subject to the Status Quo in the strict sense were Jordanian responsibility. During Jordan's military occupation of the West Bank the sanctuaries of Jerusalem were under the control of the governor of the city, who rigorously applied the Status Quo. After the formal incorporation of the territories in April 1950 the king decided that a special regime was necessary and in December of that year the post of Supervisor of the Haram al-Sharef and Supreme Custodian of the Holy Places was created.[98]

The first holder of the office, Ragheb Bey Nashashibi, died in April 1951, a few months after his appointment. The Latin patriarch had viewed the creation of the office with some disfavour, and on the death of Ragheb Bey Nashashibi the French and Italian representatives in Amman tried to prevent the nomination of a successor. The government, however, immediately appointed Dr Hussein El Khalidi, giving him instructions to examine and record precise details of the status quo in all its ramifications, translating all the relevant firmans and documents. The move provoked fresh démarches from the French and Italians. The high custodian's staff was small and the department inadequately financed; it is therefore probable that he had not proceeded far with this stupendous task before his resignation in 1952. This was caused by the government's overruling of the high custodian's decision in a dispute between the Orthodox, who wanted to replace oil lamps by electricity on a cross surmounting the church of the Nativity in Bethlehem, and the Latins and Armenians, who objected. The high custodian had ruled against the Orthodox, who at once appealed to the government and got the decision reversed. Dr Khalidi on 13 August 1952 summoned the representatives of the six Christian communities to announce his resignation on the ground that the royal decree of 16 April 1951 defining his duties was not completely valid under the constitutional law in force in the country. The office of the high custodian, though not formally abolished, has not since been filled, and its responsibilities have devolved on the overworked and understaffed governorship of Jerusalem. The governor has suggested setting up a holy places commission as proposed in the mandate.

The attitude of the Jordanian authorities to the Christian communities and their manifold activities was at least as important as, if not more important than, the attitude of the Israelis, since the heads of all the important Christian communities in Palestine are resident in Jordan or east Jerusalem, and most of their charitable and educational activities have been in east Jerusalem. Nothing in the Jordanian constitution or other legislative acts of the government specifically bound the Jordanian authorities to observe the corpus of rights, privileges and immunities except those specifically legislated for by the Palestinian government. Generally, however, the Jordanian authorities proved to be conscientious guardians of the holy places and other shrines of Christendom, and at that time to have taken a generally liberal attitude towards the non-religious activities of the churches, and have maintained and even extended the rights of the community courts.

The Six Day War in 1967 brought the whole of the old British mandate of Palestine under Israeli rule. However, the old armistice line of 1949 remained as the border between the civilian Israeli community and the occupied territories under military administration. The sole exception was east Jerusalem, which was annexed and integrated into the Israeli state. Thus a new border was created between the church leaderships within the new Israeli borders and the majority of the Christian population on the occupied West Bank. The border was not insignificant for matters of church administration, nor for the unity between Christians, their conditions for political and civic activities being vastly different.[99]

The Christians of Jerusalem have experienced profound political and social changes during the past century, which can only be compared with the conquest by Muslims in the seventh century, or the coming of the Ottomans in the sixteenth. The Christian communities, if not fully involved, have borne the consequences of the various political and military struggles which set Israel against the Arab states and which marked the various stages in the Israeli–Palestinian conflict. They have also experienced at first hand the difficult events which have marked the recent history of relations between Israel and the Palestinians inside the state of Israel, in the occupied territories and in the surrounding states. From 1948 the Christian communities found themselves partly inside the new state of Israel and partly in those territories of the West Bank that initially belonged to Jordan and were then occupied by Israel in 1967. The political events and wars that marked the creation of the state of Israel, the Palestinian trauma of defeat and the subsequent refugee crisis, the military and political stand-off between the neighbouring Arab states and Israel, the crisis over the status of Jerusalem and the non-implementation of the United Nations-sponsored internationalization of the Holy City all caused crucial changes to the religious, political and everyday lives of the Christians of the Holy Land.

Notes

[1] These opening thoughts owe much to John Renard's 'Theological perspectives on the Middle East', *American–Arab Affairs*, 34 (1990) 56–63.

[2] Samuel Rubenson, 'Church and state, communion and community: some issues in the recent ecclesiastical history of Jerusalem', in Heikki Palva and Knut S. Vikor (eds), *The Middle East: Unity and Diversity* (Copenhagen, 1993) 84–102.

[3] (Oxford, 1994), v.

[4] For an early Christian understanding of the Holy Land see Robert Wilken, *The Land Called Holy: Palestine in Christian History and Thought* (New Haven, 1992); *idem*, 'Byzantine Palestine: a Christian holy land', *Biblical Archaeologist*, 51 (1988) 214–37; *idem*, 'Christian pilgrimage to the Holy Land', (in N. Rosovsky (ed.), *City of the Great King: Jerusalem from David to the Present* (Cambridge, Mass., 1996), 117–35. For the development of the idea of Christian holy places see R. A. Markus, 'How on earth could places become holy? Origins of the Christian idea of holy places', *Journal of Early Christian Studies*, 2 (1994), 257–72, and P. W. L. Walker, *Holy City, Holy Places? Christian Attitudes to Jerusalem and the Holy Land in the Fourth Century* (Oxford, 1990). For an interesting cartographical expression see Catherine Delano Smith, 'Geography or Christianity? Maps of the Holy Land before AD 1000', *Journal of Theological Studies*, n.s. 42 (1991), 143–52.

[5] See G. Stroumsa, 'Religious contacts in Byzantine Palestine', *Numen*, 34 (1989), 16–42 and Pierre Maraval, *Lieux Saints et pèlerinages d'orient: histoire et géographie des origines à la conquête arabe* (Paris, 1985).

[6] Y. Hirschfeld, *The Judean Desert Monasteries in the Byzantine Period* (New Haven, 1992), 78–90, and *idem*, 'List of the Byzantine monasteries in the Judean desert', G. C. Bottini, L. Di Segni and E. Allata (eds), in *Christian Archaeology in the Holy Land* (Jerusalem, 1990), 1–90. See also Otto Meinardus, 'Notes on the laurae and monasteries of the Wilderness of Judea', *Liber Annus: Studii Biblici Fransciscani*, 15 (1964–5), 220–50; 16 (1965–6), 328–56; and 19 (1969), 305–27.

[7] P. W. L. Walker, 'Jerusalem and the Holy Land in the 4th century', in Anthony O'Mahony, Göran Gunner and Kevork Hintlian (eds), *The Christian Heritage in the Holy Land* (London, 1995) 22–34.

[8] See the work by Lorenzo Perrone, 'Monasticism in the Holy Land: from the beginnings to the crusaders', *Proche-Orient Chrétien*, 45 (1995), 31–63; 'Christian holy places and pilgrimage in an age of dogmatic conflicts: popular religion and confessional affliation in Byzantine Palestine (fifth to seventh centuries)', *POC*, 48 (1998), 5–37 and 'Aspects of Palestinian monasticism in Byzantine times: some comments and proposals', in Thomas Hummel, Kevork Hintlian and Ulf Carmesund (eds), *Patterns of the Past, Prospects for the Future: The Christian Heritage in the Holy Land* (London, 1999), 264–72.

[9] There is no good general history of Christianity in Jerusalem and the Holy Land;

however, see the following: S. P. Colbi, *A History of the Christian Presence in the Holy Land* (Lanham: University Press of America, 1988) and Friedrich Heyer, *Kirchengeschichte des Heiligens Landes* (Stuttgart, 1980). See also the remarks by L. Porreone, 'Per la storia della Palestina cristiana. La storia della chiesa di Terra Santa di Friedrich Heyer', *Cristianesimo nella Storia,* 7 (1986), 141–65.

[10] For a general survey of the situation of the Christian communities during this early Islamic period of Jerusalem's history see A. Linder, 'Christian communities in Jerusalem', in J. Prawer and H. Ben-Shammai (eds), *The History of Jerusalem: The Early Muslim Period 638–1099* (New York, 1996), 121–62 and Robert Schick, 'Fate of the Christians in Palestine during the Byzantine-Ummayyad transition 600–750 AD' (unpublished Ph.D., University of Chicago, 1987); *idem,* 'Christian life in Palestine during the early Islamic period', *Biblical Archaeologist,* 51 (1988); and *idem, The Christian Communities of Palestine from Byzantine to Islamic Rule: A Historical and Archaeological Study* (Princeton, 1995).

[11] For an account of the Christian communities in Palestine during this period see Moshe Gil, *A History of Palestine, 643–1099* (Cambridge, 1992), 430–89.

[12] Sidney H. Griffith, 'Anastasios of Sinai, the Hodegos and the Muslims', *Greek Orthodox Theological Review,* 32 (1987), 341–58.

[13] Daniel J. Sahas, *John of Damascus on Islam: The 'Heresy of the Ishmaelites'* (Leiden, 1972); *idem,* 'John of Damascus on Islam revisited', *Abr Nahrain,* 23 (1984–5), 104–18 and *idem,* 'The seventh century Byzantine–Muslim relations', *Islam and Christian–Muslim Relations,* 2, 1 (1991), 3–22.

[14] On Christian Arabic literature see Samir Khalid Samir and Jorgen S. Nielson (eds), *Christian Arabic Apologetics during the Abbasid Period (750–1258)* (Leiden, 1994).

[15] Sidney H. Griffith, *Arabic Christianity in the Monasteries of Ninth Century Palestine* (London, 1992); *idem,* 'The monks of Palestine and the growth of Christian literature in Arabic', The *Muslim World,* 78 (1988), 1–28; *idem,* 'Stephen of Ramlah and the Christian kerygma in Arabic in 9th century Palestine', *Journal of Ecclesiastical History,* 36 (1985), 23–45; *idem,* 'Anthony David of Baghdad, scribe and monk of Mar Sabas: Arabic in the monasteries of Palestine', *Church History,* 58 (1989), 7–19; and *idem,* 'The view of Islam from the monasteries of Palestine in the early Abbasid period: Theodore Abu Qurrah and the *Summa Theologiae Arabica*', *Islam and Muslim–Christian Relations,* 7, 1 (1996), 9–28.

[16] Bernard Hamilton, *The Latin Church in the Crusader States: The Secular Church* (London, 1980); and *idem,* 'The Latin church in the crusader states', in K. Ciggaar, A. Davids, H. Teule (eds), *East and West in the Crusader States: Context, Contacts, Confrontations* (Louvain, 1996), 1–20; Richard Rose, 'Pluralism in a medieval colonial society: the Frankish impact on the Melkite community during the first crusader kingdom of Jerusalem, 1099–1187' (unpublished Ph.D., University of California, Los Angeles, 1981); *idem,* 'The native Christians of Jerusalem, 1187–1260', in B. Z. Kedar (ed.), *The Horns of Hattin* (London, 1992), 239–49; and *idem,* 'The crusader period in the Holy Land and ecclesiology', in D. M. A. Jaeger (ed.), *Christianity in the Holy Land* (Jerusalem, 1981), 169–96.

[17] Donald F. Little, 'Communal strife in late Mamluk Jerusalem', *Islamic Law and Society,* 6, 3 (1999), 69–96, and 'Christians in Mamluk Jerusalem', in Yvonne Yazbeck Haddad and Wadi Z. Haddad (eds), *Christian–Muslim Encounters* (Gainesville, 1995), 210–20.

[18] For a general account of the Latin presence in Palestine see Charles A. Frazee, *Catholics and Sultans: The Church and the Ottoman Empire 1453–1923* (Cambridge, 1983), 59–63, 145–50, 214–19, 304–8.

[19] Speros Vryonis, 'The History of the Greek patriarchate of Jerusalem as reflected in Codex Patriarchicus no. 428, 1517–1805', *Byzantine and Modern Greek Studies,* 7 (1981), 29–53; and *idem,* 'The history of the Greek patriarchate of Jerusalem as reflected in Codex Patriarchicus no. 428, 1517–1805', The *Third International Conference on Bilad al-Sham* (University of Yarmouk/Jordan: Palestine), 1 (1983), 155–76.

[20] On the Armenian community in Jerusalem see Kevork Hintlian, *History of the Armenians in the Holy Land* (Jerusalem 1989, 2nd edition); Avedis K. Sanjian, *The Armenian Communities in Syria under Ottoman Dominion* (Cambridge, Mass., 1965); *idem*, 'The Armenians and the holy places in Jerusalem', *The Third International Conference on Bilad al-Sham: Palestine 19–24 April 1980* (Yarmouk University), 1, (1983), 127–44; and *idem*, 'The Armenians and the holy places in Jerusalem', *Bazmavep*, 139, 3–4 (1977), 649–84.

[21] For the Georgians see Gregory Peradze, 'An account of the Georgian monks and monasteries in Palestine', *Georgica*, 4–5 (1937), 181–246; Richard Rose, 'Jerusalem and Jihad: the devotion of the Iberian nation to Jerusalem: a footnote on the role of the Georgians in late medieval Jerusalem', *Proche-Orient Chrétien*, 41 (1991), 10–24; Butrus Abu-Manneh, 'The Georgians in Jerusalem in the Mamluk Period', in Ammon Cohen and Gabriel Baer (eds), *Egypt and Palestine: A Millennium of Association (868–1948)* (New York, 1984), 102–12.

[22] On the Syriac Christian community in Jerusalem see Andrew Palmer, 'The history of the Syrian Orthodox in Jerusalem', *Oriens Christianus*, 75 (1991), 16–43 and 76 (1992), 74–94; Y. Koriah-Karkenny, *The Syrian Orthodox Church in the Holy Land* (Jerusalem, 1976); G. Every, 'Syrian Christians in Palestine in the Middle Ages', *Eastern Churches Quarterly*, 6 (1945–6), 230–39; and *idem*, 'Syrian Christians in Jerusalem, 1183–1283', *Eastern Churches Quarterly*, 7 (1947), 363–72.

[23] Otto Meinardus, 'The Christian kingdoms of Nubia', *Cahiers d'Histoire Égyptienne*, X (1966), 133–64.

[24] Otto Meinardus, *The Copts in Jerusalem* (Cairo, 1960); *idem*, 'The Copts in Jerusalem and the question of the holy places', *Coptic Church Review*, 16 (1995), 9–25; and *idem*, 'The Copts in Jerusalem and the question of the holy places', in Anthony O'Mahony with Göran Gunner and Kevork Hintlian (eds), *The Christian Heritage in the Holy Land* (London, 1995), 112–28.

[25] For the Ethiopians see Anthony O'Mahony, 'Between Islam and Christendom: the Ethiopian community in Jerusalem before 1517', *Medieval Encounters: Jewish, Christian and Muslim Cultures in Confluence and Dialogue*, 2 (1996), 140–54.

[26] On the Maronites see Louis Wehbé, *L'église maronite* (Jerusalem, 1985).

[27] It is possible that its original owners had been the Georgian church in Jerusalem. For the whole affair see Ammon Cohen, 'The expulsion of the Franciscans from Mount Zion: old documents and new interpretations', *Turica*, XVIII (1986), 147–58. And for a general account of the Franciscan presence in Jerusalem see the following: M. Piccirillo (ed.), *La custodia di Terra Santa e l'Europa: i rapporti e l'attività culturale dei Francescani in Medio Oriente* (Jerusalem, 1983); *idem*, *Custodia di Terra Santa, 1342–1942* (Jerusalem, 1951); G. Golubovich, *Biblioteca bio-bibliografica della Terra Santa e dell'oriente francescano 1215–1400* (Rome, 1906–27) (5 vols); M. Roncaglia, 'The Sons of St Francis in the Holy Land: official entrance of the Franciscans as custodians of the basilica of the Nativity in Bethlehem', *Franciscan Studies*, X (1950), 257–85; and B. Pandzic: 'L'interesse della Sacrae Congregationis per la Terra Santa', in *Sacrae Congregationis de Propaganda Fide Memoria Rerum: 1622–1972* (Rome, 1976), vol. 2: *1700–1815*, 413–20; Leonhard Lemmens, *Biblioteca bio-bibliografica della Terra Santa e dell'oriente francescano II: Serie Documenti: Tomo I: Acta. S. Congregationis de Propaganda Fide pro Terra Santa, Parte I 1622–1720* (Rome, 1922); *idem*, *Tomo II: Acta S. Congregationis de Propaganda Fide pro Terra Santa Parte II: 1721–1847* (Rome, 1922); and *idem*, *Die Franziskaner im Heiligen Lande: die Franziskaner auf dem Sion 1336–1551* (Münster, 1925).

[28] Bernard Collin, *Le Problème juridique des Lieux-Saints* (Paris, 1956), 1–65; and Anton Odeh Issa, *Les Minorités chrétiennes de Palestine à travers les siècles. Étude historico-juridique et développement moderne international* (Jerusalem, 1976).

[29] Speros Vryonis, 'The Byzantine patriarchate and Turkish Islam', *Byzantino-Slavica*, LVII (1996), 69–111; and T. Halasi-Kun, 'Gennadios' confession of faith', *Archivum Ottomanicum*, XII (1987–92), 5–104.

[30] For the Orthodox church during the Ottoman period see Halil Inalcik, 'The Status of the Greek Orthodox patriarch under the Ottomans', *Turica*, 21–3 (1991), 407–37, and Kemal H. Karpet: 'Ottoman views and policies towards the Orthodox Christian church', *Greek Orthodox Theological Review*, 31 (1986), 131–55.

[31] For a general account of the Christians under Islamic rule see Bat Ye'or, *Le Dhimmi: Profil de l'opprimé en Orient et en Afrique du Nord depuis la conquête arabe* (Paris, 1980), translated into English as *The Dhimmi: Jews and Christians under Islam* (London, 1985); and *idem*, *Les Chrétientés d'orient entre jihad et dhimmitude* (Paris, 1991), translated into English as *The Decline of Eastern Christianity under Islam: From Jihad to Dhimmitude, Seventh–Twentieth Century* (London, 1996). See also Bat Ye'or, *Juifs et Chrétiens sous l'Islam. Les dhimmis face au défi intégriste* (Paris, 1994); and Alain Brissaud, *Islam et Chrétienté: treize siècles de cohabitation* (Paris, 1992).

[32] See also the following works on the evolution of the status of non-Muslims within the Islamic world: Antoine Fattal, *Le Statut légal des non-musulmans en pays d'Islam* (Beirut, 1958); *idem*, 'Comment les dhimmis étaient jugés en terre d'Islam', *Cahiers d'Histoire Égyptienne*, 3 (1951), 321–41; *idem*, 'La nature juridique du statut des dhimmis', *Annales de la Faculté de Droit*, Université de Saint-Joseph, Beirut (1956), 139–54; A. S. Tritton, *The Caliphs and their Non-Muslim Subjects: A Critical Study of the Covenant of Umar* (Oxford, 1930); and N. Edelby, 'L'autonomie législative des Chrétiens en terre d'Islam', *Archives d'Histoire du Droit Oriental*, 5 (1950–1), 307–51. See also the thoughtful and suggestive works by André Ferre: 'Muhammad a-t-il exclu de l'Arabie les Juifs et les Chrétiens?', *Islamochristiana*, 16 (1990), 43–65; and *idem*, 'Protégés ou citoyens?' *Islamochristiana*, 22 (1996), 79–117; and Jean-Marie Gaudeul, 'The correspondence between Leo and 'Umar: 'Umar's letter re-discovered?', *Islamochristiana*, 10 (1984), 109–57; and *La correspondance de 'Umar et Léon (vers 900)* (Présentation et notes par J.-M. Gaudeul) (Rome, 1995).

[33] B. Braude, 'Foundation myths of the *millet* system', in Braude and Lewis (eds), *Christians and Jews in the Ottoman Empire* (New York, 1982), 1, 69–88.

[34] Kevork B. Bardakjian, 'The rise of the Armenian patriarchate of Constantinople', in Braude and Lewis (eds), *Christians and Jews in the Ottoman Empire*, 1, 89–100.

[35] A. Groiss, 'Minorities in a modernizing society: secular vs. religious identities in Ottoman Syria 1840–1914', *Princeton Papers in Near Eastern Studies*, 3 (1994), 39–70.

[36] Alexis Alexandris, *The Greek Minority of Istanbul and Greek–Turkish Relations 1918–1974* (Athens, 1992), 25–30.

[37] Tiran Nersoyan, 'Laity in the administration of the Armenian church', *Kanon: Jahrbuch der Gesellschaft für das Recht der Ostkirchen*, 3 (1977), 96–119.

[38] Richard Clogg, 'The Greek *millet* in the Ottoman Empire', in Braude and Lewis (eds), *Christians and Jews in the Ottoman Empire*, 1, 185–207. See also now R. Clogg's important collection of reprinted studies: *Anatolica: Studies on the Greek East in the 18th and 19th Centuries* (London, 1996).

[39] Bardakjian, 'The rise of the Armenian patriarchate of Constantinople'.

[40] Stanford J. Shaw, *The Jews of the Ottoman Empire and the Turkish Republic* (London, 1991), 1–36.

[41] Ignace Zaide, 'Église syrienne', in *Dictionnaire de théologie catholique*, XIV, cols 3018–88).

[42] On the Armenian Catholic community in the Ottoman territories see Charles A. Frazee, 'The formation of the Armenian Catholic community in the Ottoman Empire', *Eastern Churches Review*, 7 (1975); 149–63; Mesrob J. Terzian, *Le patriarcat de Cilicie et les Arméniens catholiques (1740–1812)* (Beirut and Rome, 1955); and Vartan Tekeyan, *Le patriarcat arménien catholique de Cilicie: au temps de Grégoire Pierre VI (1812–1840)* (Beirut and Rome, 1954).

[43] Eugène Tisserant, 'Église chaldéenne', in *Dictionnaire de théologie catholique*, XI, cols 158–223.

[44] Livio Missir de Lusignan, 'La nation latine en territoire Ottoman: les précédents', *Revue d'Histoire Maghrébine*, 12, 37–8 (1985), 157–60; *idem*, 'Introduction à l'histoire

de la Latinité ottomane', in *XX Deutscher Orientalistentag* (Erlangen, 1977), 400–2; and *idem, Rome et les églises d'orient: vues par un Latin d'orient* (Paris, 1976).
[45] Alfred Schlicht, *Frankreich und die syrischen Christen (1799–1861): Minoritäten und europäischer Imperialismus im vorderen Orient* (Berlin, 1981).
[46] Georges Batch, *Statut personnel: introduction à l'étude de la condition juridique des Chrétiens de Palestine sous la domination ottomane (1517–1917)* (Rome, 1963). See also the study by A. Cohen on Ottoman policy towards the Christians in Jerusalem, 'The Ottoman approach to Christians and Christianity in sixteenth-century Jerusalem', *Islam and Christian–Muslim Relations*, 7 (1996), 205–12.
[47] Butrus Abu Mannah, 'The rise of the sanjak of Jerusalem in the late 19th century', in Gabriel Ben-Gor (ed.), *The Palestinians and the Middle East* (Ramat Gan, 1978), 21–32. For the history of sixteenth–eighteenth century Ottoman Palestine see Uriel Heyd, *Ottoman Documents on Palestine 1552–1615* (Oxford, 1960); Ammon Cohen, *Palestine in the 18th Century: Patterns of Government and Administration* (Jerusalem, 1973); *idem, Jewish life under Islam: Jerusalem in the Sixteenth Century* (Princeton, 1978); *idem, Economic Life in Ottoman Jerusalem* (Cambridge, 1989); Amy Singer, *Palestinian Peasants and Ottoman Officials: Rural Administration around 16th Century Jerusalem* (Cambridge, 1994); E. Toledano, 'The sanjaq of Jerusalem in the sixteenth century: aspects of topography and population', *Archivum Ottomanicum*, 9 (1984), 279–319; D. S. Powers: 'Revenues of public waqfs in sixteenth-century Jerusalem', *Archivum Ottomanicum*, 9 (1984), 163–202; and Adar Arnon, 'The quarters of Jerusalem during the Ottoman period', *Middle Eastern Studies*, 28, 1 (1992), 1–65.
[48] For the history of ninteenth-century Palestine and Jerusalem, see B. Abu Mannah, 'Jerusalem in the Tanzimat period: the new Ottoman administration and the notables', *Die Welt des Islams*, n.s. 30 (1990), 1–44; *idem*, 'The establishing and dismantling of the province of Syria 1865–1888', in J. P. Spagnolo (ed.), *Problems of the Modern Middle East in Historical Perspective*, (London, 1992), 7–26; Haim Gerber, *Ottoman Rule in Jerusalem, 1890–1914* (Berlin, 1985); *idem*, 'The Ottoman administration of the sanjak of Jerusalem 1890–1908', *Asian and African Studies*, XII (1978), 33–76; and *idem*, 'A new look at the Tanzimat: the case of the province of Jerusalem', in David Kushner (ed.), *Palestine in the Late Ottoman Period* (Leiden, 1986), 30–45.
[49] Naomi Sheppard, *The Zealous Intruders: The Western Rediscovery of Palestine* (San Francisco, 1987); Thomas Hummel, 'English Protestant pilgrims of the 19th Century', in A. O'Mahony with Göran Gunner and Kevork Hintlian (eds), *The Christian Heritage in the Holy Land* (London, 1995), 160–80; *idem, Patterns of the Sacred: English Protestant and Russian Orthodox Pilgrims in the Nineteenth Century* (London, 1995), and *idem*, 'The sacramentality of the Holy Land: two contrasting approaches', in David Brown and Ann Loades (eds), *The Sense of the Sacramental: Movement and Measure in Art and Music, Place and Time* (London, 1995), 78–100.
[50] For an overall survey of this activity see A. Carmel, 'Activities of the European Powers in Palestine, 1799–1914', *Asian and African Studies*, 19 (1985), 43–91.
[51] On the Ethiopian community in Jerusalem see Enrico Cerulli, *Etiopi in Palestina: storia della comunità etiopica di Gerusalemme*, 2 vols (Rome 1943–7).
[52] On American activity in late Ottoman Palestine see A. L. Tibawi, *American Interests in Syria 1800–1901* (Oxford, 1966); Ruth Kark, *American Consuls in the Holy Land* (Detroit, 1994); Caesar E. Farah, 'Protestantism and politics: the 19th century dimension in Syria', in D. Kushner (ed.), *Palestine in the Late Ottoman Period* (Leiden, 1986), 320–40; Joseph L. Grabill, *Protestant Diplomacy and the Near East: Missionary Influence on American Policy, 1810–1927* (Minneapolis, 1971); and Jacob M. Landau, 'The United States and the Holy Land in the nineteenth century', in M Sharon (ed.), *The Holy Land in History and Thought* (Leiden, 1988), 273–8. To date, very little has been published on American Catholic activities in Palestine, but see David E Klatzker, 'American Christian travellers to the Holy Land, 1821–1939' (Ph.D., Temple University, 1987); and *idem*, 'American Catholic travellers to the Holy Land, 1861–1929', *Catholic Historical Review*, 74 (1988), 55–74.

53 On the involvement of Russia in the nineteenth and early twentieth centuries in Palestine, see the following: Derek Hopwood, *The Russian Presence in Syria and Palestine 1843–1914: Church and Politics in the Near East* (Oxford, 1969); *idem*, ' "The resurrection of our eastern brothers" (Ignatiev): Russia and the Orthodox Arab nationalism in Jerusalem', in Moshe Ma'oz (ed.), *Studies on Palestine during the Ottoman Period* (Jerusalem, 1975), 394–407; Igor Smolitsch, 'Zur Geschichte der Beziehungen zwischen der russischen Kirche und dem Orthodoxen Osten: die russische kirchliche Mission in Jerusalem (1847–1914)', *Ostkirchliche Studien*, 5 (1956), 33–51 and 89–136; Theodore Stavrou, *Russian Interests in Palestine 1882–1914: A Study of Religious and Educational Enterprise* (Thessaloniki, 1963); Theodore Stavrou and Peter R. Weisensel, *Russian Travellers to the Christian East from the Twelfth to the Twentieth Century* (Columbus, OH, 1986); T. Stavrou, 'Russian policy in Constantinople and Mount Athos in the nineteenth century', in Lowell Lucas (ed.), *The Byzantine Legacy in Eastern Europe* (New York, 1988), 225–49.

54 For British religious and political activity in nineteenth-century Ottoman Palestine see Alexander Schölch, 'Britain in Palestine 1838–1882: the roots of the Balfour policy', *Journal of Palestine Studies*, 22 (1992), 39–56; and A. L. Tibawi, *British Interests in Palestine, 1800–1901* (Oxford, 1961).

55 For an important discussion regarding the demographic situation in Palestine see Justin McCarthy, *The Population of Palestine: Population History and Statistics of the Late Ottoman Period and Mandate* (New York, 1990).

56 Abu Mannah, *The Rise of the Sanjak of Jerusalem*, 1–7.

57 Abu Mannah, *The Rise of the Sanjak of Jerusalem*, 25. For Palestine in the late Ottoman period see 'Adel Manna', 'Continuity and change in the socio-political elite in Palestine during the late Ottoman period', in T. Phillipp (ed.), *The Syrian Lands in the 18th and 19th Century* (Stuttgart, 1992), 69–89; Miriam Hoexter, 'The role of the Qays and Yemen factions in local political divisions: Jabal Nablus compared with the Judean Hills in the first half of the nineteenth century', *Asian and African Studies,* IX (1973); and *eadem*, 'Egyptian involvement in the politics of notables of Palestine: Ibrahim Pasha in Jabal Nablus', in Ammon Cohen and Gabriel Baer (eds), *Egypt and Palestine: A Millennium of Association (863–1948)* (New York, 1984), 190–213; Thomas D. Phillipp, 'Social structure and political power in Acre in the 18th century', in T. Phillipp (ed.), *The Syrian Lands in the 18th and 19th century,* 91–108; and *idem*, 'The rise and the fall of Acre: population and economy between 1700 and 1850', *Revue du Monde Musulman et de la Méditerranée*, 55–6 (1990), 124–40; A. Schölch, *Palestine in Transformation, 1856–1882: Studies in Social, Economic and Political Development* (Washington, DC, 1992); and *idem*, 'Jerusalem in the 19th century (1831–1917)', in K. J. Asali (ed.), *Jerusalem in History* (London, 1989), 228–48; B. Doumani, 'Rediscovering Ottoman Palestine: writing Palestinians into history', *Journal of Palestine Studies*, 21, 2 (1992), 5–28; Shimon Shamir, 'Egyptian rule (1832–1840) and the beginning of the modern period in the history of Palestine', in Cohen and Baer (eds), *Egypt and Palestine*, 214–31.

58 Muhammad Muslih, 'Urban notables, Ottomanism, Arabism and the rise of Palestinian nationalism, 1864–1920' (Ph.D., Columbia University, 1986); *idem, The Origins of Palestinian Nationalism* (New York, 1988).

59 For the position of the Christian communities in the region after the end of Ottoman rule see Jean-Pierre Valognes, *Vie et mort des Chrétiens d'orient: des origines à nos jours* (Paris, 1994), 55–104.

60 Henry Laurens, 'Genèse de la Palestine mandataire', *Maghreb Machrek*, 140 (1993), 3–34; Charles D. Smith, *Palestine and the Arab–Israeli conflict* (New York, 2nd edn, 1992); Michael J. Cohen, *The Origins and Evolution of the Arab-Zionist Conflict* (Los Angeles, Calif., 1987); Isaiah Friedman, *The Question of Palestine: British–Jewish–Arab Relations, 1914–1918* (New Brunswick and London: 2nd expanded edn, 1992); see also Charles D. Smith's important critique of Friedman, 'The invention of a tradition: the question of Arab acceptance of the Zionist right to Palestine during World War I', *Journal of Palestine Studies*, XXII, 2, 48–61.

[61] Jacob Landau, 'Mandates', in *Encyclopaedia of Islam* (2nd edn).

[62] A. H. Hourani, *Minorities in the Middle East* (Oxford, 1947), 52–9.

[63] On British rule in Palestine see Bernard Wasserstein, *The British in Palestine: The Mandatory Government and the Arab–Jewish Conflict 1917–1929* (Oxford: 2nd edn, 1991). See also Gabriel Sheffer, 'Policy making and British policies towards Palestine 1929–1939' (D.Phil., Oxford, 1970); *idem*, 'The images of Arabs and Jews as a factor in British policy towards Palestine', *Zionism*, 1, 1 (1980), 105–28; and *idem*, 'British colonial policy making towards Palestine 1929–1939', *Middle Eastern Studies*, 14 (1978), 307–22.

[64] For a detailed description of legal arrangements in Palestine in the late Ottoman and early British period see Edoardo Vitta, *The Conflict of Laws in Matters of Personal Status in Palestine* (Tel Aviv, 1947); Frederic M. Goadby, *International Interreligious Private Law in Palestine* (Jerusalem, 1926); and F. M. Goadby, 'Religious communities and courts in Palestine', *Tulane Law Review*, 8, 2 (1934), 215–35.

[65] For the legal and administrative background of the Christian communities in Palestine see Daphne Tsimhoni, 'The status of the Arab Christians under the British mandate in Palestine', *Middle Eastern Studies*, 20, 4 (1984), 166–92.

[66] For the Islamic Community during the British mandate see Uri M. Kupferschmidt, *The Supreme Muslim Council: Islam under the British Mandate for Palestine* (Leiden, 1987), 1–16; Robert H. Eisenman, *Islamic Law in Palestine and Israel: A History of the Survival of Tanzimat and Sheri'a in the British Mandate and the Jewish State* (Leiden, 1978), 73–151; Michael Dumper, *Islam and Israel: Muslim Religious Endowments and the Jewish State* (Washington, DC, 1994), 7–24; and Roger Owen, 'Defining traditional: some implications of the use of the Ottoman law in mandatory Palestine', *Harvard Middle Eastern and Islamic Review*, 1, 2 (1994), 115–31.

[67] *Palestine Official Gazette*, 1 September 1923.

[68] *Palestine Official Gazette*, 1 September 1924.

[69] Amnon Cohen, 'The receding of the Christian presence in the Holy Land: a 19th century Sijill in the light of 16th century Tahrirs', in Thomas Phillipp, (ed.), *The Syrian Land in the 18th and 19th Century*, 333–40.

[70] *Palestine: Report and General Abstracts of the Census of 1922. Taken on the 23rd of October 1922*, compiled by Barron (Jerusalem, 1923). The 1922 census was taken for the purpose of general elections, and did not include social and economic data. The 1931 census included data on all aspects of life in Palestine: *The Census of Palestine, 1931*, compiled by E. Mills (Alexandria, 1933).

[71] Kamel Karpat, 'The Ottoman emigration to America', *International Journal of Middle East Studies*, 17 (1985) 175–209; and *idem*, *Ottoman Population 1830–1914: Demographic and Social Characteristics* (Madison, 1983).

[72] Mike George Salman, 'Emigration and its effect on the extinction of Bethlehem families', *Al-Liqa'* (Jerusalem), 1 (1989), 55.

[73] Adnan Musallam, 'The formative stages of Palestinian emigration to the Americas: until the eve of 1948', *Al-Liqa'* (Jerusalem), 2 (1992), 23.

[74] On Syrian Christian immigration to Egypt see Thomas Phillipp, *The Syrians in Egypt 1725–1975* (Stuttgart, 1985); and *idem*, 'Demographic patterns of Syrian immigration to Egypt in the nineteenth century', *Asian and African Studies*, XVI (1982), 128–41.

[75] Y. Porath, *The Emergence of the Palestinian-Arab National Movement, 1918–1929* (London, 1974), 293–303. See also the interesting study by Daphne Tsimhoni, 'The Arab Christians and the Palestinian Arab national movement during the formative stage', in Gabriel Ben-Gor (ed.), *The Palestinians and the Middle East* (Ramat Gan, 1978), 73–98.

[76] David Kushner, 'Intercommunal strife in Palestine during the late Ottoman period', *Asian and African Studies*, 18 (1984), 187–204. For a general view of relations see James A. Reilly, 'Inter-confessional relations in nineteenth century Syria', *Islam and Christian–Muslim Relations*, 7 (1996), 215–24)

[77] Robert Haddad, *Syrian Christians in Muslim Society: An Interpretation* (Princeton, 1970), 3.

[78] S. G. Haim, 'Islam in the theory of Arab nationalism', *Die Welt des Islams*, 4 (1955), 124–49; and *idem*, 'Islam and Arab nationalism', *Die Welt des Islams*, 3 (1954), 201–18. For the debate on the origins of Arab nationalism see Mahmoud Haddad, 'The rise of Arab nationalism reconsidered', *International Journal of Middle East Studies*, 26 (1994), 201–22; C. Ernest Dawn, *From Ottomanism to Arabism: Essays on the Origins of Arab Nationalism* (Urbana, 1973), 3–30; and Rashid Khalidi, 'Ottomanism and Arabism in Syria before 1914: a reassessment', in Rashid Khalidi et al. (eds), *The Origins of Arab Nationalism* (New York, 1991); and S. G. Haim, *Arab Nationalism: An Anthology* (Los Angeles, CA, 1962). For a survey of the political situation which confronted Islam see Jacob M. Landau, *The Politics of Pan-Islam: Ideology and Organization* (Oxford, 1990); and for the role of Islam in Palestinian nationalism see N. Johnson, *Islam and the Politics of Meaning in Palestinian Nationalism* (London, 1982).

[79] Philip Khoury, *Urban Notables and Arab Nationalism: The Politics of Damascus 1860–1920* (Cambridge, 1983), 95–6. For Christian involvement in the nineteenth-century Arab renaissance or *Nahda* see Khalil Samir, 'Rôle des Chrétiens dans les renaissances arabes', *Annales de Philosophie de l'Université Saint-Joseph* (Beirut), VI (1987), 1–31; and Antoine Makdissi, 'Les Chrétiens et la renaissance arabe', *Islamo-christiana*, 14 (1988), 107–26.

[80] For political Islam during the mandate see D. R. Irvine, 'Islamic culture and political practice in British mandated Palestine, 1918–1948', *Review of Politics*, 45 (1983), 71–93; and U. M. Kupferschmidt, 'Islam on the defensive: the Supreme Muslim Council's role in mandatory Palestine', *Asian and African Studies*, 17 (1983), 175–206.

[81] E. Kedourie, 'Religion and politics: the diaries of Khalil Sakakini', in *The Chatham Version and other Middle Eastern Studies* (Hanover, NH, 1984), 317–50, p. 319.

[82] A. Bertram and J. W. A. Young, *Report of the Commission Appointed by the Government of Palestine to Inquire and Report upon certain Controversies between the Orthodox Patriarchate of Jerusalem and the Arab Orthodox Community* (Oxford, 1926), 57–8

[83] E. Tauber, *The Emergence of the Arab Movements* (London, 1993); and *idem*, *The Arab Movements in World War I* (London, 1993)

[84] For the background to the development of the Palestinian Arab national movement see Ann Mosely Lesch, *Arab Politics in Palestine, 1917–1939: The Frustration of a Nationalist Movement* (Ithaca, 1979); and *eadem*, 'The Palestine Arab nationalist movement under the mandate', in William B. Quandt (ed.), *The Politics of Palestinian Nationalism* (Los Angeles, CA, 1973), 5–42; Y. Porath, 'The political awakening of the Palestinian Arabs and their leadership towards the end of the Ottoman period', in M. Ma'oz (ed.), *Studies on Palestine during the Ottoman period* (Jerusalem, 1975), 351–83; and *idem*, 'The social aspects of the emergence of the Palestinian Arab national movement', in M. Milson (ed.), *Society and Political Structure in the Arab World* (New York, 1973), 93–144.

[85] Khalil al-Sakákini, *Kadhá Aná Yá Dunyá* (The Diaries of Khalil al-Sakakini), ed. Hála at Sakakini (Jerusalem, 1955), p. 38

[86] Porath, *The Emergence of the Palestinian-Arab National Movement*, 295f.

[87] On Arab Christians and the development of Palestinian literature during the mandate period see Stefan Wild, 'Judentum, Christentum und Islam in der Palästinensischen Poesie', *Die Welt des Islams*, n.s. XXIII–XXIV (1984), 259–97.

[88] On the dilemma of the Arab Christians in regard to the secularism of the national movement see Hourani, *Minorities in the Middle East*, 295ff.

[89] *Al-Karmil*, 21 October 1923.

[90] It was published in Cairo, 1931 by the Muslim newspaper *al-Fath*, in which it had previously appeared as a series of articles. See the translation of the pamphlet in Kedourie, *Religion and Politics*, 343–50; a discussion of its contents can be found in Haim, *Arab Nationalism*, 58–61. According to Yusuf Ayyub Haddad, in his study *Khalilal-Sakákini: Hayatuhu Mawqifuhu wa Atharuhu* (Khalil al-Sakakini: His Life, Attitudes and Works) (Beirut, 1981), al-Sakakini published the text of Khalil Iskandar

al-Qubrusi's *Da'wat Nasara al-'Arab ila al-Dukhul fi al-Islam* in a newspaper called *Jaridat al-Adahiin,* in November 1930 and January 1931, which when compared proved to be the same. If Haddad is correct, then the true author of this booklet was none other than Khalil al-Sakakini.

[91] Kedourie, *Religion and Politics*, 343–44.

[92] The translated letters and Sari al-Sakakini's preface to them, Israel State Archives (ISA) 65–2646.

[93] Al-Sakakini's letter to his son, 12 December 1932, ISA 65–2646.

[94] Charles Kamen, 'After the catastrophe: the Arabs in Israel 1948–1951', *Middle Eastern Studies*, 23, 4 (1987), 453–95, and 24, 1 (1988), 68–109. See also Benny Morris, *The Birth of the Palestinian Refugee Problem 1947–1949* (Cambridge, 1988); and *idem*, *1948 and After: Israel and the Palestinians* (Oxford, 1990)

[95] Jean-Pierre Valognes, *Vie et mort des Chrétiens d'orient*, 566–613; and A. Kapeliouk, 'Les Arabes chrétiens en Israel (1948–1967)' (thèse de doctorat, l'Université de Paris Sorbonne, 1968); and *idem*, 'L'état social, économique, culturel et juridique des Arabes chrétiéns en Israel', *Asian and African Studies*, V (1969), 51–95. For Muslim–Christian relations see Chad F. Emmett, *Beyond the Basilica: Christians and Muslims in Nazareth* (Chicago, 1995).

[96] Alisa Rubin Peled, 'The crystallization of an Israeli policy towards Muslim and Christian holy places, 1948–1955', *The Muslim World*, 94 (1994), 95–125.

[97] For material on these developments see Daphne Tsimhoni, 'Between the hammer and anvil: the national dilemma of the Christian minority in Jerusalem and the West Bank', *Orient*, 24 (1983), 637–44; 'The demographic trends of the Christian population in Jerusalem and the West Bank, 1948–1978', *Middle East Journal*, 37 (1983), 65–88; 'Continuity and change in communal autonomy: the Christian communal organizations in Jerusalem, 1948–80', *Middle Eastern Studies*, 22 (1986), 398–417; and *Christian Communities in Jerusalem and the West Bank since 1948: An Historical, Social and Political Study* (Westport, Conn., 1993).

[98] Jean-Pierre Valognes, 'Les Chrétiens de Jordanie', in *Vie et mort des Chrétiens d'orient*, 614–35.

[99] Michael Dumper, 'Church–state relations in Jerusalem since 1948', in O'Mahony, Gunner and Hintlian (eds), *Christian Heritage in the Holy Land*, 266–87; and 'Faith and statecraft: church–state relations in Jerusalem after 1948', in A. O'Mahoney (ed.), *Palestinian Christians: Religion, Politics and Society in the Holy Land*, 56–81; *The Politics of Jerusalem since 1967* (New York, 1997), 160–206.

2

THE GREEK ORTHODOX PATRIARCHATE AND COMMUNITY OF JERUSALEM: CHURCH, STATE AND IDENTITY

Sotiris Roussos

Introduction

The history of the patriarchate of Jerusalem from the seventh century onwards was dominated by the Church's effort to secure the highest degree of autonomy from the state, Christian or Muslim, Arab, Ottoman, British or Israeli. A brief overview of the patriarchate's early history reveals that the Church preferred to co-operate with state policies in order to maintain its domain intact and to avoid any state interference in its internal affairs. In the case of the Greek Orthodox patriarchate, its domain was, and still is, its rights as custodian of most of the Christian holy places in Jerusalem.

The monastic character of the patriarchate precluded decisive participation of the laity in the administration of the church of Jerusalem. The Confraternity of the Holy Sepulchre managed the affairs of the patriarchate with the patriarch of Jerusalem as the abbot of the confraternity. As series of documents reveal, these two main traditional characteristics are deeply rooted in the early history of the patriarchate, particularly in the periods of Islamic rule.

The *ahitname* of Omar-Khattap to Patriarch Sophronios in 638 undertakes, as Speros Vryonis argued, 'to assure the Greek Patriarchate of three things: tax immunity for the clergy, possession of churches and property, and precedence over the other nations in the shrines'.[1] According to the same *ahitname*, 'it will remove from them those causes of troubles according to the submission and obedience which they have shown'.

The Ottoman conquest of Jerusalem by Selim I did not alter the privileged status of the patriarchate. On the contrary, the decree of Sultan Selim stated clearly the precise possessions and rights of the patriarchate not only in Jerusalem but also in the whole of Palestine. It acknowledged, at the same time, the leading role of the Orthodox patriarchate among the Ethiopians[2] and the Serbs[3] who were, according to the same decree, 'subservient to the Orthodox Patriarchate'.[4] Another new element in Selim's document was the protection of the patriarchate from any interference by local, religious or military Ottoman authority.

Thus, in exchange for obedience to the Ottoman Porte, the patriarchate acquired a series of privileges and a high degree of internal autonomy from local authorities.[5] A series of decrees issued by Sultan Murad IV in 1631 and Mahmud, son of Ibrahim, made it clear that only the Sublime Porte could determine the status of the Greek Orthodox patriarchate of Jerusalem and that any intervention by local authorities in disputes with other churches or over collection of taxes must be stopped immediately.

The decree of Murad IV restored the possession of certain holy places to the Greek Orthodox patriarchate. These had been given to the Catholics (Franks, as they were called in the documents) by the local authorities in Palestine. The decree noted that 'the race of the Frank . . . having become one with the judges, they took the possession by force.'[6]

On the other hand the *hatt-i-sheriff* of Mahmud in 1651 contains a petition by the patriarchate, and particularly the Confraternity of the Holy Sepulchre, against fiscal rapacity and extortion by the provincial Ottoman administration. It is clear that, after the move of the patriarch's residence from Jerusalem to Constantinople in the mid-sixteenth century, the patriarchate relied heavily on its connections with the bureaucracy of the Sublime Porte. The gradual weakening of the central Ottoman administration and the strengthening of the provincial authorities[7] inaugurated a period of fiscal extortion for the patriarchate, but the patriarchate could rely on its connection with the Sublime Porte.

A succession of decrees throughout the seventeenth century reveals the institutionalization of the provincial government's rapacity against the Patriarchate of Jerusalem as well as the rising power of the local administration at the expense of the Sublime Porte. In these documents, the local Ottoman authorities in Palestine are shown questioning the validity of past decrees and asking for confirmation by the Sublime Porte.

Throughout the struggle between the central and the provincial administration, the patriarchate stood firmly with the former. The patriarch of Jerusalem resided in Constantinople and remained closely linked to the Greek elite of the Ottoman bureaucracy, the phanariots.[8] It also became evident that the Franciscans had managed to acquire the support of the local administration by giving them more in taxes and other revenues than the Greek Orthodox patriarchate. Probably the Franciscans tried to rely on the provincial Ottoman officials, while the patriarchate counted on the Sublime Porte. This, however, cannot be taken as a rule in church–state relations in Palestine, as alliances and connections easily shifted.

The connection of the patriarchate with the Sublime Porte thwarted diplomatic efforts by France, Austria and Venice to curtail Greek Orthodox rights and possessions in the holy places in favour of the Franciscans. The Capitulations of 1604, 1673 and 1740 gave the Catholics the possession of several holy places and a preponderant role in Jerusalem. Concerning the holy places, the Franco-Ottoman treaty of 1740 accorded several rights in the church of the Holy Sepulchre.[9] The Greek Orthodox patriarchate managed to resume control over those holy places in 1757.[10] It is clear that the patriarchate knew the mechanism of Ottoman decision-making and exploited the Sublime Porte's suspicions of European attempts to meddle in Christian affairs in the Ottoman Empire.

The close links between the patriarchate and the phanariots and the patriarch of Constantinople[11] enabled it to pursue a policy of fund-raising throughout the Orthdodox world. The patriarchate had to cover the maintenance costs of monasteries, churches and holy places, and take care of pilgrims and the members of the Confraternity of the Holy Sepulchre. The phanariot governors of the semi-autonomous principalities of Moldavia and Wallachia granted the patriarchate of Jerusalem twenty-one monasteries with all their lands and revenues.[12]

On the other hand, the ecumenical patriarch issued several synodical letters to all the Orthodox, in Greek, Turkish, Wallachian and Slavic, calling on them to support the fund-raising of the patriarchate of Jerusalem.[13] A large number of monks travelled in the Ottoman Empire calling for financial support for the patriarchate. This custom of travelling and fund-raising for the Holy Sepulchre was inaugurated by Patriarch Germanos in the mid-sixteenth century, and was followed throughout the Ottoman period. Donations were not always in money but included land, houses, estates and shares in ship-ownership.

The nineteenth century found the patriarchate pursuing this traditional policy. While the phanariots and the patriarchate of Constantinople continued to intervene in the election of the patriarchs of Jerusalem,[14] the monasteries in the principalities of Moldavia and Wallachia were providing life-giving revenues to the patriarchate of Jerusalem. Nearly half of the revenues collected in 1831 in the Orthodox communities of the Ottoman Empire, Russia and the Habsburg territories came from the principalities of Romania and Bessarabia. [15]

This brief account of the patriarchate's connection with the central Ottoman administration, and particularly the Greek Orthodox elite of the Ottoman bureacracy, by no means leads to the conclusion that the phenomena of that earlier period are the same as or similiar to those in modern times. It reveals, however, a tradition of co-operation with state policies in exchange for internal administrative and financial autonomy. It is this tradition that shaped church attitudes and policies towards the state in the nineteenth century, as it confronted the end of the empires and the new political circumstances of the modern Middle East.[16]

Russian Enterprise and the Formation
of the Arab Orthodox Identity

The weakening of the Ottoman Empire brought new players into the Near East. Russia had dreamed of becoming the new centre of the Orthodox faith, the 'Third Rome' of Christianity and Orthodoxy, since the time of Peter the Great. From the Treaty of Kuchuk Kainardja in 1774,[17] Russia had already assumed the role of protector of the Orthodox population in the Ottoman Empire, but the way to the 'Third Rome' passed through the Greek Orthodox patriarchates and particularly the weak churches of Antioch and Jerusalem. The aspiration to create a 'Third Rome' was part of a greater vision. The Slavophiles in Russia dreamed of a great Graeco-Russian Orthodox Empire where all Orthodox nations would praise God in Hagia Sophia.[18] For the Russian priest, on the other hand, the Holy Sepulchre was the mother shrine of the whole church, and Palestine symbolized Orthodox Christendom.[19]

From 1843, Russian influence in the affairs of the patriarchate of Jerusalem became evident. In 1845, Cyrillos, a Russian protégé, was elected patriarch of Jerusalem despite strong opposition from the phanariots and the patriarchate of Constantinople. It was the first, but not a decisive, victory of Russian diplomacy in a long-standing conflict between Russian churchmen and diplomats on one hand and the phanariots and the Greek hierarchy in Jerusalem and Constantinople on the other.

In the eyes of the Greeks, the Russian enterprise was to do in the Levant what the Slavonic Benevolent Society had been doing in the Balkans since 1859, that is, to assist Orthodox Christians to develop national religious and educational institutions. Initially the Panslavist element represented only a small fraction of the founders of the Imperial Palestine Society, which became the vehicle of the Russian enterprise in Palestine after 1882. By the 1890s, however, the Panslavists dominated the society, intensifying their struggle against Greek pre-eminence in the patriarchates of Jerusalem and Antioch.[20]

The Greek hierarchy in Jerusalem and Constantinople followed their well-trodden path. Their links with the Ottoman bureaucracy and the Sublime Porte were still useful, albeit weaker, after the eruption of nationalism in the Balkans and the decline of the ecumenical patriarch's influence among the Orthodox population.[21] The Ottomans, nonetheless, did not welcome the advance of Russian ecclesiastical and political influence in the Levant, and assisted the senior Greek clergy in the Orthodox patriarchates in its territories to consolidate their position and defy Russian pressure. In 1872, when the supposedly Russophile patriarch of Jerusalem, Cyrillos, refused to condemn the autonomy of the Bulgarian church from Constantinople, the Greek hierarchy in Jerusalem managed to depose him, relying on its connection with the Porte.[22]

The other pole of Hellenism, the Greek state, showed no particular interest in helping the senior Greek clergy in Jerusalem or in interfering in the matters of the Levant. In 1899 a group of Greek nationalists headed by the professor

of history at the University of Athens, Paulos Carolides,[23] urged the foundation of a Greek Palestine Society along with a Greek Society for Mount
Athos. However, the Greek state, showing signs of secularism and probably
unable to help, ignored the issue.[24]

The Russian enterprise, on the other hand, found allies among the Arab
Orthodox population who had been neglected by the senior Greek clergy in
Syria and Palestine. The Arabs in Palestine were virtually excluded from the
Confraternity of the Holy Sepulchre, and consequently could not advance to
the higher levels of the clergy. They accused the patriarchate of ignoring their
needs for education and the welfare of the poor.[25]

The deposition of Cyrillos in 1872 met with a strong reaction from the
Arab Orthodox who saw it as one more victory for the Greek hierarchy. An
Arab Orthodox delegation went to Constantinople to present their demands.
They asked for a constitution for the Greek Orthodox Church of Jerusalem
providing for the formation of a mixed council of lay and clerical members to
manage the finances of the patriarchate, lay participation in the patriarchal
election,[26] admission of Arab Orthodox to the Confraternity of the Holy
Sepulchre, and improvement of their education and welfare. These demands
were to remain the principal elements in contention between the Arab
Orthodox community and the Greek clergy who dominated the Jerusalem
patriarchate for more than a century.

The elction of Prokopios, a staunch supporter of Greek supremacy, to the
patriarchate met with a furious Arab reaction. The Russian diplomatic
mission in Jerusalem saw it as an opportunity to assist the Arabs and
dethrone the Greek senior clergy. Russian pressure was becoming more effective because of the patriarchate's urgent need for financial assistance. On the
other hand, the traditional ally of the Greek hierarchy, the Porte, kept a
watchful eye on the efforts of the Greek clergy to sustain its leading role in
the holy places. The situation in the Ottoman Empire was not the same as a
century earlier. Balkan nationalism, and particularly the Greek national
revival in the early nineteenth century, posed a threat to the integrity of the
empire, and the Church did not always follow the path of co-operation with
the Ottoman authorities, the patriarchate giving members a greater say in
church administration and finances. However, Patriarch Prokopios was
deposed by Russian pressure and was succeeded by Ierotheos. Despite his
promises, the concessions to the Arab Orthodox were never made owing to
Ottoman inconsistency and successful Greek manœuvring.

The Cyrillos affair and the subsequent ill-fated constitution sparked off an
intellectual and cultural movement among the Arab Orthodox who were
searching for national identity, and this would strongly influence the concep-
tion of Arabism. After the establishment of the Imperial Orthodox Palestine
Society in 1882, the Russians began a great educational operation. The society opened schools to train local teachers for the Arab Orthodox population.
In 1886 they opened a women's teacher training college in Bayt Jala, and in

1889 a men's college in Nazareth. By 1898 over 6,500 pupils attended the society's schools.[27]

The society thus achieved the main task of alienating the laity from the Greek Orthodox patriarchate. As E. Kedourie points out, 'it was Russian efforts which made the quarrel between laity and clergy a definite and inevitable quarrel between Arabs and Greeks.'[28] The demand for church constitutionalism was now transformed into church nationalism. The young Arab Orthodox elite, educated in the society's schools, was ready to break its ties with the tradition represented by the Greek hierarchy. The phenomenon was not unique. At the same time the ascent of an Arab patriarch to the see of Antioch led to the formation of a Greek national identity among the Greek-speaking Orthodox population of Cilicia in Asia Minor.[29]

The Young Turk revolution in 1908 gave this new generation an opportunity to demand a greater Arab share in the affairs of the patriarchate of Jerusalem. The constitution of 1908 provided for the setting-up of communal councils to supervise communal property and revenues. Patriarch Damianos refused the establishment of a mixed clerical and lay council to administer the patriarchate's finances, and demonstrations against the Patriarch's high-handed conduct erupted in Jerusalem, Jaffa and Bethlehem. In response to these events, the grand vizier Kamil Pasha directed a local investigation.[30]

To counter these new developments and radical trends in the Arab Orthodox community, the patriarchate sought to use its centuries-long connection with the Ottoman central administration to intervene in its favour. The governor of Jerusalem, Ali Ekrem Bey, reflecting wider Ottoman concerns, showed a bias against Russian initiatives and Arab Orthodox concerns. He was suspicious of the increase in Russian influence in Palestine and ready to use any means to curtail its activity. To reinforce this, he installed the Greek metropolitan at Acre against Russian and Arab wishes.[31]

The Greek hierarchy in the Jerusalem patriarchate, fearful that Damianos had some sympathy with Arab aims, adopted a hard-core position and rejected all compromise with the community. Even so, the patriarch continued to meet respresentatives of the Arab Orthodox. This was intolerable to the majority of the senior Greek clergy, and the Confraternity of the Holy Sepulchre used the meetings as a pretext for the deposition of the patriarch. However, personal feuds among the hierarchy were as much behind his dethronement as his attitude to Arab demands. Using their connections with the Porte and the patriarchate of Constantinople, the Confraternity brought the question of Damianos' deposition to the Porte. The news that the deposition had been recognized reached Jerusalem and led to furious demonstrations in the streets and occupation of the patriarchate by Arab crowds. Violent incidents became numerous, the Ottoman authorities had to rethink their position, and in February 1908 Damianos was returned to his throne and a mixed council was created to supervise the community's finances and welfare. This gave the Arab Orthodox a greater say in the patriarchate's administration and in future elections of the patriarch. However, in practice the mixed council never functioned. Further obstacles and disputes between the two sides prevented the realization of the 1909 agreement.[32]

The British Mandate, 1917–1948: Years of Uncertainty

British political hegemony in Palestine and the dissolution of the Ottoman and Russian empires created a greatly changed situtation and uncertainty for the Greek Orthodox patriarchate of Jerusalem and the Arab Orthodox community. The war also brought serious financial difficulties for the patriarchate, which had lost its vast endowment of properties in Romania, Bessarabia and Russia, and the numerous Russian pilgrims stopped coming after the Bolshevik Revolution.

The strong Greek upper clergy sensed that its only remaining ally was the Greek state, which had been carved out of the Ottoman Empire in the early part of the nineteenth century. It should be noted that after the Greek War of Independence in 1821 and the creation of the Greek state there were two rival poles of the Greek nation, the secular in Athens and the church-communal one in Constantinople. The end of the First World War strengthened the secular pole, transforming Greece into a regional power.[33] The patriarchate of Jerusalem had always turned to Constantinople, but now it had to seek Greek state help. Hence the majority of the Holy Synod asked on 3 May 1918 for moral and material help from the Greek government.[34] In addition the majority of the Holy Synod exploited the power vacuum in Palestine in order to depose Patriarch Damianos and avenge the failure of the coup in 1908.

Palestine and the Greek Orthodox patriarchate of Jerusalem were not the priorities of Greek policy at that period. Nonetheless the government of Eleutherios Venizelos supported the initiatives of the Greek upper clergy and promised much-needed financial help through a loan from the Greek National Bank. Although there were no political motives behind the Greek government's attitude, the British would not tolerate any foreign meddling in Palestinian affairs. They knew that there was a long and fierce diplomatic struggle ahead for the protection of the holy places as well as possible reforms in the status quo. They, therefore, did not wish to allow a precedent of foreign intervention, Greek or any other.

The British saw the majority of the Holy Synod as a mere instrument of Greek policy in Palestine and, as a result, they supported Damianos in securing his throne and becoming the indisputable head of the Greek Orthodox church in the Holy Land. Most of his opponents left Palestine for a self-styled exile at the patriarchate of Alexandria in Egypt. The British also thwarted Greek plans for financial support of the patriarchate, viewing it as one more vehicle of Greek influence in Palestine.

The Arab Orthodox community, on the other hand, suspected the manœuvring of the Greek upper clergy and their connection with the Greek government and particularly the Greek consul in Jerusalem. The community feared that a victory of the majority of the Holy Synod over Damianos' party would further harm the Arab Orthodox position. In defining the community's policy towards this development, its leadership was split into two main groups: those pursuing a traditional moderate policy, stressing the communal character of their claims; and radicals, who advocated the 'arabization' of the patriarchate. It seems that the traditional leadership prevailed and put forward demands for the reinstitution of the mixed council, better Orthodox education and welfare, and admission of Arab Orthodox to the Confraternity of the Holy Sepulchre.[35]

Responding to these disturbing developments, the British appointed a commission of inquiry in order to study the matter and propose solutions. Sir A. Bertram and H. C. Luke, prominent judges and men of experience in colonial matters, were appointed members of the commission. Their findings and proposals were in accordance with the general guidelines of British policy in Palestine. They did not accept any form of Greek interference, including arbitration by a joint committee of the patriarchates of Constantinople and Alexandria and the churches of Greece and Cyprus.

Regarding Arab Orthodox grievances, the commission urged the patriarchate to take care of the Arab Orthodox community, but did not provide the means. As a result, the Greek upper clergy, regardless of whether Damianos or his adversaries held power, continued to dominate the patriarchate and manage its property and revenues.

At the same time the British had to face a diplomatic struggle over the question of the holy places. The Catholic powers, notably France and Italy, and especially the Vatican, asked for a dominant role for Catholics in the holy places. The Catholics in Rome and Jerusalem expected that the victory of the Allies over the Turks would lead to Catholic supremacy in the Holy Land at the expense of Greek Orthodox rights.[36] The Catholics wished to play the leading role in the proposed commission for the holy places, and suggested that they alone should vote in the commission, leaving the other denominations only a consultative role. In June 1919, the patriarchate of Jerusalem responded with a memorandum advancing the *ab antiquo* rights of the Greek patriarchate over the holy places according to international agreements from the Byzantine era to the firman of 1852, which settled the matter of the Christian holy places.

The British tried to prevent Catholic interference, and consequently supported the rights of other churches in Palestine, particularly the Orthodox interests. Greece was not at that time a member of the League of Nations Council, and thus could not represent the rights of the Orthodox. Both British policy and rivalry among the Catholic powers prevented the setting up of the commission for the holy places, and Britain, as the mandatory power, undertook the preservation of the status quo until a permanent settlement of the question was agreed.

In Palestine, the patriarchate faced huge debts and a worrying lack of revenues. The British authorities established a committee to supervise the patriarchate's finances, and took all necessary measures to relieve the patriarchate of its debts. Even so the patriarchate was obliged to sell land to anyone who had enough money to buy it, notably the Jewish land development companies, and in 1923 the Palestine Land Development Company, enraging the Arab Orthodox farmers who used to cultivate this fertile land.[37]

The selling of patriarchate land to the Zionists, and, above all, the continuing neglect of Arab Orthodox education and welfare, infuriated the community, which now put forward radical demands for the 'arabization' of the patriarchate. Leading members of the community had already begun advocating Palestinian Arab nationalism.

From 1908 onwards, the Arab Orthodox community produced important pioneer founders of Arabic newspapers and magazines. Najib Nassar is considered the father of nationalist journalism in Palestine. In 1908 he founded the newspaper *al-Karmil*, and he was one of the first to see a threat in Zionism and Jewish settlement in Palestine.[38]

Another leading Arab Orthodox newspaper was *Filastin*, founded by the al-Isa brothers in Jaffa. It became the leading advocate of Palestinian Arab nationalism and the main forum of Arab nationalist intellectuals. *Filastin* was also an advocate of Palestinian geographical and political unity, defining the country as the area under the authority of the patriarchate of Jerusalem, the Christian Holy Land.[39] This anti-Zionist trend also prevailed in *Filastin* journalism. It was much easier for European anti-Semitic literature to reach Arab Christians through their western education and general cultural influence. On the other hand the largely urban Arab Christian elites saw Jewish immigrants as a threat to their material existence.

In contrast, the patriarchate, and Patriarch Damianos himself, co-operated with the mandate's policy of facilitating the establishment of a Jewish national home. In 1922 the bishop of Nazareth, Cleopas, urged Arab participation in the elections for the Legislative Council, while Arab nationalists boycotted the elections. The patriarch seemed to entertain the same views.[40] The centuries-long tradition of co-operating with the state was still present despite the change of circumstances, both internal and regional.

The response of the Arab Orthodox was expressed by the first Arab Orthodox congress, which called for decisive participation by the Arab Orthodox community in the management of Orthodox education and welfare as well as of the patriarchate's property and revenues. They also called for the admission of Arab Orthodox to the Confraternity and for participation by the lay community in the patriarch's election. The British could not afford yet another cause of tension in Palestine, and in 1925 they set up a commission headed by A. Bertram and J. W. A. Young to investigate the dispute and propose remedies.

The Bertram–Young commission met the uncompromising line of

Damianos. The patriarch, who in 1908 saved his throne thanks to his lenient policy towards the Arab Orthodox community, was now the hardliner. The commission did not accept radical Arab Orthodox claims but proposed admission of the Arab Orthodox to the Confraternity and greater lay participation in the management of the patriarchate's finances.

The British, bound as they were to preserve the status quo in the holy places, did not press for radical reforms in the patriarchate. They feared that any serious alteration in the status quo would bring the matter to the League of Nations, inviting other powers, namely France and Italy, to exploit the matter. They also turned down fresh Greek government proposals for Greek loans to the patriarchate. The Greek government, and particularly the Greek consul in Jerusalem, did not oppose the main proposals of the commission. Nonetheless the absence of a clear policy on the part of Greece gave the patriarch a free hand to reject any compromise.

The 40,000-strong Arab Orthodox community were disappointed by the findings of the Bertram–Young commission. Besides, there was a permanent split between the traditional leadership, which stressed communal identity and put forward demands mainly regarding education and welfare, and the radical young generation, which stressed its Arab identity. Radical leaders became leading figures in Muslim–Christian associations. This radical group called for the 'arabization' of the Greek Orthodox patriarchate following the ill-fated example of the Turkish Orthodox Church under the Kemalist regime.[41] This division continued to split the community throughout the 1930s.[42]

In 1931, the death of Patriarch Damianos signalled a new round of controversy between the Arab Orthodox community, represented by the second Arab Orthodox congress, and the Greek upper clergy. The Arab Orthodox maintained the same demands as thirty years before. The Greek government, on the one hand, supported the election of a highly qualified prelate who could successfully face the new circumstances, namely the patriarch of Alexandria, Meletios Metaxakis. On the other, they suspected that the British in Palestine would support Arab Orthodox demands in order to gain Arab Orthodox support for major British policies in Palestine. It seems that leading members of the community were supporters of the moderate Nashashibi Party and clearly backed British policies. Nonetheless neither Greek government plans nor Arab Orthodox claims came to an end. In 1937 the Greek upper clergy in Jerusalem managed to elect their favourite, Timotheos, as the new patriarch, and there were no substantial reforms in the regulation of the patriarchate.

The Volatile Period: Under Jordanian and Israeli Rule

The end of the Second World War and the termination of the British mandate again raised the issue of Jerusalem. The UN resolution of 29 November 1947 provided for an international regime for the city of Jerusalem, a *corpus separatum*, as it was called. The question of the 'internationalization of Jerusalem' had been a major issue in European diplomacy from 1852 onwards. As early as 1841 the Prussians had suggested an international agreement on Jerusalem, Bethlehem and Nazareth.[43]

Many, among them the Jewish Agency, thought that the internationalization should be vested in the Vatican, with its predominant influence in the Holy Land.[44] This view was not shared by the Greek Orthodox patriarchate. It is evident that its reservations were deeply rooted in mistrust of the Catholics and the Vatican. The Greek state, on the other hand, supported the plan. In the midst of its civil war, it could not afford a disagreement with its allies against the communists. Hence it had to follow British policy on the matter.

The views of the patriarchate reflected its fear of the role of the Vatican and the Catholic powers in an internationalized Jerusalem.[45] Regarding the nationality of the high commissioner, the patriarchate noted that he could not be either an Israeli or an Arab, that is, a member of the indigenous communities. They feared that a Catholic commissioner would favour Catholic claims to the holy places. The composition of the international court which would have ultimate jurisdiction in disputes over the holy places was another source of anxiety. Neither Israelis nor Arabs could be members of the court, and in the eyes of the patriarchate there was a considerable possibility of a pro-Catholic majority.

For the Greek Orthodox church in Jerusalem, Constantinople and Athens, the internationalization plan could transform Jerusalem into 'un centre d'intrigues internationales'. In his letter to the UN, the patriarch of Jerusalem, Timotheos, urged full representation of the Greek Orthodox church in decisions regarding the holy places. The patriarchate's view was thus closer to the Jewish dislike of a *corpus separatum* in Jerusalem.[46]

At that point, the siege of the walled city of Jerusalem in 1948 revealed the leading role of the patriarchate as an ancient communal centre. Hundreds of people, Arabs and non-Arabs, Orthodox and non-Orthodox, took refuge behind the opened gates of the patriarchate and its numerous buildings in the Old City. Despite heavy Jewish bombardment, which inflicted extensive damage on holy shrines and indeed on the dome of the Holy Sepulchre, the patriarchate continued to offer much-needed help to the terrified refugees.[47]

On 27 May 1948, King Abdullah paid an unofficial visit to Jerusalem to pray at his father's tomb in the Omar Mosque and to visit the church of the Holy Sepulchre. That visit revealed the close links between the patriarchate and the Hashemite dynasty. However, the death of Patriarch Timotheos in 1955 brought about a new round of internal strife between the Arab Orthodox community and the Greek hierarchy of the patriarchate.

The Arab Orthodox community, particularly the Amman association, organized a series of assemblies calling on King Husayn to promulgate a new set of regulations. The fourth Arab Orthodox congress convened in Jerusalem in March 1956. More than 300 delegates of the communities of Jordan, headed by a member of the Jordanian Parliament, Antun Attalah, participated. Support for Arab Orthodox demands also came from prominent political figures, namely the secretary of the National Socialist Party, Sulayman al-Nabulsi, and the secretary of the Ba'ath Party, Abdallah Rimawi.[48]

The Arab Orthodox claims were by no means new. They asked for the re-establishment of a mixed council with a clear Arab Orthodox lay majority, participation in the management of the patriarchate's properties and revenues, and in the preparation of its budget. The Arab Orthodox laity wanted a greater say in patriarchal elections, and that Arab Orthodox should be admitted to the Confraternity, with foreign members acquiring Jordanian citizenship. Orthodox higher education should also be provided.

This programme was a victory for the moderate wing of Arab Orthodox notables, who put forward minimal demands and did not seek for the nationalization of the patriarchate. The radical view, however, was expressed in a pamphlet published by a Syrian journalist, Husayn al-Hudhayfi, calling on King Husayn's Arab government to liberate the Arab Orthodox from the foreign hierarchy.[49]

The deadlock in the negotiations was broken by al-Nabulsi's nationalist government which clearly yielded to Arab Orthodox demands. Most of these, particularly the role of the laity in leading the community, in managing the Church's revenues and in electing the patriarch and two Arab bishops as members of the Holy Synod of the patriarchate, were agreed. The regulations had nearly passed the Senate when political instability in Jordan, the abortive armed coup and the change of government enabled the newly elected patriarch, Benedictos, to ask the king to reconsider the regulations.

In March 1958, the government of Ibrahim al-Hashim brought in a new set of regulations. It endeavoured to reach a compromise between the Arab Orthodox community and the Greek upper clergy.[50] The patriarchate retained its Greek character and the upper clergy continued to dominate the patriarchate's affairs. The compromise, however, provided for the appointment of an Arab bishop in August 1960 and the establishment of a mixed council. The elections for the council's lay members were boycotted by the Arab Orthodox communities in Bethlehem and elsewhere. In Greece the new regulations were seen as a result of the friendly relations between King Husayn and Greece, the fruit of Patriarch Benedictos's influence on the Jordanian king.[51]

The 1967 Arab–Israeli war and the Israeli occupation of east Jerusalem, the West Bank and Gaza strip created a new situation. The patriarchate followed its well-worn path of co-operating with state policy in order to maintain its dominant position in the holy places. However, the structure, aims and methods of the Israeli state apparatus were different from those confronted by the patriarchate in the past.

The patriarchate had now to deal with a state policy of definite intentions, priorities and plans. It was clear from the beginning that Israel would do everything to promote the Jewish character of the city, and consequently would take every step to facilitate Jewish pilgrimage and to protect Jewish holy places, which were ignored during the Ottoman and mandate arrangements under the Status Quo.[52] On the other hand, the Israeli authorities tried to reaffirm their commitment to the rights and privileges of the various Christian churches in the holy places.[53] It was probably understood that any confrontation over the Status Quo would inevitably lead to a Christian front both inside and outside Israel.

As for the Arab Orthodox community, the period after 1967 had similar characteristics regarding nation-building and national versus communal identification to those of the mandate period. Under Israeli occupation and turbulent relations with Arab regimes, the Palestinians, and more importantly Christian Palestinians, redefined their position, raising the banner of secular nationalism over communal identification and sectarianism. Middle-class Christian Palestinians became leading advocates of nationalism, secularization and radicalization of the Palestinian national struggle. In general, the political terminology, slogans and methods of the post-1967 Palestinian groups indicate a break with domination by the traditional elites. Several leaders of militant leftist groups were middle-class Christian Palestinians. They also gained commanding positions in the inner councils of the national movement.[54]

The culmination of the Palestinian national struggle on the one hand, and Israeli efforts to purchase patriarchate land in order to facilitate settlement planning on the other, intensified the antagonism between the Greek upper clergy and the Arab Orthodox community. Although there are no details concerning the scale of land sales and the circumstances under which they were taking place, the perception that the patriarchate was selling large areas of land to Israelis was very strong in the Arab Orthodox community.

Israeli occupation led to the social and economic dislocation of Christian Palestinians, and Orthodox Palestinians in particular. In his most interesting study of Palestinian Christian demography, Bernard Sabella demonstrated how vulnerable they are to emigration pressure. Until 1991, the estimated number of Christians who emigrated was 18,000, or 40 per cent of the present Christian population in the West Bank including east Jerusalem.[55] In 1922 more than half of Jerusalem's population were Christians, whereas in 1991 they constituted only 10 per cent of the population in roughly the same territory.[56] In Israel, the Christians were estimated in 1949 at 21.3 per cent of the non-Jewish population, but by 1990 they were about 12 per cent.[57]

In 1996, there were 26,473 Greek Orthodox Palestinians out of approximately 50,000 Christians in east Jerusalem, West Bank and Gaza. In 1992 the total faithful of the patriarchate of Jerusalem were estimated at 145,000 in the occupied territories, Israel and Jordan.[58] Greek Orthodox Palestinians, like the whole of the Palestinian Christian community, fit the model of a migrant community. High educational qualifications acquired in western schools, relatively high living standards and ties with relatives abroad are the main characteristics of Christian Palestinians. Moreover, in 1992 Church institutions could employ only 26.5 per cent of them and Christian unemployment reached almost 35 per cent of heads of households.[59]

The election of the Likud coalition in 1977 passed power over to policy-makers whose main priority was to facilitate the programmes of Jewish settlements in and around Jerusalem and to ensure Israeli predominance in Jerusalem. This change of focus tended to ignore or underestimate the position and interests of the various churches in the Holy Land.[60] In the case of the Greek Orthodox patriarchate, it has been argued that the Israeli authorities interfered in the patriarchal election in 1980, trying to thwart the election of Diodoros because of his alleged ties with Amman. Diodoros was, however, elected and tried to establish good relations with the Israeli authorities and especially the mayor of Jerusalem.[61]

The start of the Intifada, in 1987, changed the situation for Palestinian Christians, and for Greek Orthodox Palestinians in particular. The national struggle against Israeli rule strengthened the radicals of the community. Now demands for 'nationalization' of the church were included in the national agenda. Church land was part of the land of Palestine, and any tampering with this land was to be considered national treason. The Arab Orthodox Initiative Committee in 1992 revived the old demands and claims on the patriarchate.[62] Beliefs about the usurpation of Arab Orthodox rights by the Greek upper clergy again became prevalent in the community.[63]

Both pressure by the Palestinian Intifada and the change of Israeli priorities and policy-making led the patriarchate to a major break with its tradition of co-operating with state policy for internal autonomy. In April 1987, Patriarch Diodoros joined other heads of churches in signing a statement expressing concern and anxiety about the state of affairs in the occupied territories, and actually condemning Israeli policy on the matter. There is no adequate evidence whether the signing of the document was merely tactical and manœuvring but the patriarchate always officially maintained its concern about the Palestinian issue and its support for the Palestinians.[64]

The housing policies of the Likud government encouraged settler groups like Ateret-Kohanim to take over houses in the Muslim quarter of the Old City. On 11 April 1990, a few days before Easter, the same group took over the St John Hospice, which belonged to the Greek Orthodox patriarchate, putting more pressure on the relations of the patriarchate with the Israeli authorities. The patriarch condemned the incident and himself went to the hospice to reaffirm Greek Orthodox control. He ran into physical confrontation with the settlers, the police and Israeli soldiers, and was violently pushed to the ground.

The hospice's takeover led to a joint statement by the heads of the

Christian and Muslim communities. Feeling that there was no room for co-operation with the Likud government, Patriarch Diodoros went to Amman and presented the issue to the Jordanian government. Returning from Jordan, the patriarch managed to build an all-Christian front against the settlers.

Greece again became the political mainstay of the patriarchate abroad. Diodoros visited Athens, accompanied by members of the Greek hierarchy and the Greek consul in Jerusalem. The delegation held several meetings with the prime minister, C. Mitsotakis, and the foreign minister, A. Samaras. Greece was at the time negotiating the establishment of full diplomatic relations with Israel and was the only member-state of the European Union that had yet to recognize Israel. The St John Hospice incident came to disrupt the negotiating process.[65]

Establishing full diplomatic relations with Israel was, however, an aim of Greek policy, and the foreign ministry could not stop the process. Samaras expressed support for the patriarchate and assured the patriarch that he would take all necessary steps with his Israeli counterpart. Expressions of support, however, were not followed by appropriate diplomatic steps. On the contrary, the patriarchate was under the impression that the Greek government did not approve the patriarch's plans for the presentation of his case to the European Parliament in Strasbourg.[66]

The visit was not cancelled. The patriarch managed to meet most of the heads of the European Parliament's political groups as well as the high-ranking officials who dealt with relations between the EU and Israel. The visit coincided with the racist violation and desecration of a Jewish cemetery in France. This climate was not favourable to an anti-Israel campaign. Despite these adverse circumstances, the European Parliament approved on 16 May 1990 a statement in favour of the patriarchate, condemning at the same time the racist vandalism.

The visit of Diodoros to Syria and his meeting with President Assad was another major break with the centuries-long tradition of co-operating with state policies. The patriarch's mission in Europe and the Middle East was not part of a general plan for patriarchal representation abroad. It was a more or less ad hoc reaction to an immediate threat to patriarchal property. It is not yet certain whether this break with the traditional attitude signalled a major change in relations with the state. It was more a balancing act and bargaining lever than the start of a new era of relations between Israel and the Greek Orthodox patriarchate.

Conclusions

The centuries-long history of the Greek Orthodox patriarchate under Islamic rule led to the formation of a certain attitude to Church–state relations among the members of the Greek Orthodox upper clergy. The patriarchate co-operated with state policies in the political, social and economic spheres in exchange for church autonomy in its internal affairs. The millet system of the Ottoman Empire institutionalized this behaviour, which became the main guideline of the patriarchate's policy towards the state. This policy of co-operation enabled the patriarchate to face up to west European penetration in the holy places, maintaining its predominance among the churches in the Holy Land. In the fierce competition for control of the holy places, the patriarchate managed to exploit the Greek-phanariot connection with the central Ottoman administration and to enlist Ottoman support.

In the nineteenth century, the Greek Orthodox patriarchate was caught in the middle of Russo–Turkish conflict in the Levant. The Greek upper clergy's policies of co-operation with the Ottomans and exploitation of Ottoman suspicion of Russian plans in the Near East were the tools for maintaining Greek control of the patriarchate. At the same time, Russian educational enterprise and the continued Greek control of the hierarchy led to the formation of an Arab Orthodox identity among the Orthodox population in Palestine.

After the Second World War the creation of the state of Israel and the Arab–Israeli conflict changed the situation. The multi-ethnic empires were replaced by nation-states. The Palestinian struggle for self-determination and statehood now included the antagonism between laity and Greek upper clergy. For Greek Orthodox Palestinians who participate in the national struggle, nationalizing the hierarchy and church land are part of the national agenda.

Israeli priorities, on the other hand, overrode church autonomy in order to pursue a programme of a strong Israeli presence in Jerusalem. Policies of co-operation did not prove sufficient to safeguard the patriarchate's rights. As a result, we can see breaks in the tradition of co-operation. There are, however, no signs of a policy reversal.[67]

Notes

[1] S. Vryonis Jr, 'The history of the Greek patriarchate of Jerusalem as reflected in Codex Patriarchicus no. 428, 1517–1805', *Byzantine and Modern Greek Studies*, 7 (1981), 38–9. See also Nicolaos J. Pantazopoulos, *Church and Law in the Balkan Peninsula during the Ottoman Rule* (Thessaloniki, 1967); and T. H. Papadopoulos, *Studies and Documents relating to the History of the Greek Church and People under Turkish Domination* (Brussels, 1952).

[2] Anthony O'Mahony, 'Between Islam and Christendom: the Ethiopian community in Jerusalem before 1517', *Medieval Encounters: Jewish, Christian and Muslim Culture in Confluence and Dialogue*, 2 (1996), 140–54.

[3] Athanasios Angelopoulos, 'The relations between the ecumenical patriarchate and the Church of Serbia during the period 1885–1912', *Balkan Studies*, 13 (1972), 119–27.

[4] Ibid., 40–1.

[5] Halil Inalcik, 'The status of the Greek Orthodox patriarch under the Ottomans', *Turica. Revue d'études turques*, 21–3 (1991), 407–36; and Kemal H. Karpat, 'Ottoman views and policies towards the Orthodox Christian church', *Greek Orthodox Theological Review*, 31 (1986), 131–55.

6 Ibid., 43.

7 B. Cvetkova, 'The evolution of the Turkish feudal regime from the end of the 16th to the mid-18th century', in S. Asdrachas (ed.), *The Economic Structure of the Balkans under Ottoman Rule 15th–19th Centuries* (Athens, 1979) (in Greek).

8 Richard Clogg, 'The Greek millet in the Ottoman Empire', in B. Braude and B. Lewis (eds), *Christians and Jews in the Ottoman Empire* (New York, 1982), 1, 185–208; *idem*, 'The Greek mercantile bourgeoisie: progressive or revolutionary', in R. Clogg (ed.), *Balkan Society in the Age of Greek Independence* (London, 1981), 85–110.

9 W. Zander, *Israel and the Holy Places of Christendom* (London, 1971), 46–7.

10 R. Heacock, 'Jerusalem and the holy places in the European diplomacy', in A. O'Mahony, with Kevork Hintlian and Göran Gunner (eds), *The Christian Heritage in the Holy Land* (London, 1995), 201–2.

11 For the position of the ecumenical patriarch in the Orthodox world see the following studies: G. Arnakis, 'The Greek church of Constantinople and the Ottoman Empire', *Journal of Modern History*, XXIV (1952), 235–50; Vasili T. Istavridis, 'The authority of the ecumenical patriarch in the life of the Orthodox church', *Nicolas*, 18 (1991), 141–60; Maxime de Sardes, *Le patriarcat oecuménique dans l'Église Orthodoxe. Étude historique et canonique* (Paris, 1975); Richard Potz, *Patriarch und Synode in Konstantinopel. Das verfassungsrecht des ökumenischen Patriarchates* (Vienna, 1971).

12 'Memorandum on the lands of the Fraternity of the Holy Sepulchre in Bessarabia', in *Report of the Commission Appointed by the Government of Palestine to Inquire into the Affairs of the Orthodox Patriarchate of Jerusalem*, by the commissioners, Sir Anton Bertram and Harry Charles Luke (Oxford, 1921), 314–25.

13 Booklet of Chrysanthos, *Patriarch of Jerusalem* (Bucharest, 1768) (in Greek).

14 The patriarch of Constantinople, Agathagelos, tried to intervene in the election of the successor of Polycarpos who died in Istanbul in 1827. M. I. Gedeon, *Lists of Patriarchs* (Athens, 1996; 1st edn 1886), 703 (in Greek).

15 Ibid., 728–9.

16 See my 'The Greek Orthodox patriarchate and community in Jerusalem', in O'Mahony, with Hintlian and Gunner (eds), *The Christian Heritage in the Holy Land*, 211–24.

17 I. Parvev, 'Russia, Orthodoxy in the Ottoman Empire and the Peace of Kuchuk Kainardja, 1774', *Bulgarian Historical Review*, 18 (1990), 20–9.

18 D. Hopwood, *The Russian Presence in Syria and Palestine 1843–1914* (Oxford, 1969), 7.

19 *The Life of Protopapas Abakoum* (Athens, 1976) (Greek translation), 116.

20 T. Stavrou, *Russian Interests in Palestine 1882–1914: A Study of Religious and Educational Enterprise* (Thessaloniki, 1963), 206–10.

21 G. Arnakis, 'The role of religion in the development of Balkan nationalism', in C. and B. Jelavich (eds), *The Balkans in Transition: Essays on the Development of Balkan Life and Politics since the Eighteenth Century* (Berkeley, 1963), 115–44; and S. Vryonis, 'The Greeks under Turkish rule', in N. P. Diamandouros et al. (eds), *Hellenism and the First Greek War of Liberation (1821–1830)* (Thessaloniki, 1976), 45–58.

22 Evangelos Kofos, 'Attempts at mending the Greek–Bulgarian ecclesiastical schism (1875–1902)', *Balkan Studies*, 25 (1984), 347–75.

23 Prof. Paulos Carolides had advanced the theory that the Arab Orthodox of Palestine were originally Greeks who had been 'arabized' and had forgotten their Greek language.

24 T. Stavrou, *Russian Interests*, 156.

25 Anthony O'Mahony, 'Palestinian-Arab Orthodox Christians: religion, politics and church–state relations in Jerusalem, c. 1908–1925', *Chronos*, 3 (2000), 61–91.

26 During the mid-nineteenth century, a general trend of church 'constitutionalism' had already dominated the attitude of the laity in various eastern churches, and had advanced lay participation in the affairs of the patriarchate of Constantinople in the 1850s and later in the Coptic church. See R. Clogg, 'The Greek millet in the Ottoman Empire', in Braude and Lewis (eds), *Christians and Jews in the Ottoman Empire*.

[27] E. Kedourie, 'Religion and Politics', in *The Chatham House Version and Other Middle Eastern Studies* (London, 1984), 328.

[28] Ibid., 330.

[29] X. Exertzoglou, 'Diffusion of national identity in the Orthodox communities of Cilicia', *Deltio: Centre for Asia Minor Studies* (Athens), 11 (1995–6), 181–238.

[30] A. Bertram and H. C. Luke, *Report of the Commission appointed by the Government of Palestine into the Affairs of the Orthodox Patriarchate of Jerusalem* (Oxford, 1921), 253.

[31] D. Kushner, 'Ali Ekrem Bey, governor of Jerusalem', *International Journal of Middle East Studies*, 28 (1996), 352–3.

[32] Bertram and Luke, *Report*, 264–73.

[33] Roger Just, 'Anti-clericalism and national identity: attitudes towards the Orthodox Church in Greece', in Wendy James and Douglas H. Johnson (eds), *Vernacular Christianity* (Oxford, 1988), 15–30.

[34] The account of the period of the British mandate is based on my unpublished doctoral thesis, 'Greece and the Arab Middle East: The Greek Orthodox communities in Egypt, Palestine and Syria, 1919–1940' (School of Oriental and African Studies, University of London, 1994), 142–211.

[35] D. Tsimhoni, 'The Greek Orthodox patriarchate of Jerusalem during the formative years of the British mandate in Palestine', *Asian and African Studies*, 12 (1978), 77–122.

[36] Zander, *Israel and the Holy Places of Christendom*, 55–6.

[37] Memorandum on the Financial Committee of the Greek Orthodox patriarchate of Jerusalem, archives of the patriarchate of Alexandria, file 336, 20 December 1923.

[38] Q. Shomali, 'Palestinian Christians: politics, press and religious identity 1900–1948', in O'Mahony, Hintlian and Gunner (eds), *Christian Heritage in the Holy Land*, 228–9.

[39] Y. Porath, 'The awakening of the Palestinian Arabs', in M. Ma'oz (ed.), *Studies on Palestine during the Ottoman Period* (Jerusalem, 1975), 358–60, 380–1.

[40] F. H. Kisch, *Palestine Diary* (London, 1938), 39.

[41] Kedourie, *The Chatham House Version*, 318; S. Khuri and N. Khuri, *Khulasat ta'rikyh kanisant Urshalim al-urthuduksiya* (Jerusalem, 1925).

[42] 'Visit of the Arab Orthodox executive committee to high commissioner', Greek consul, 17 June 1932, file 7103, B/36, AYE, Greek Foreign Ministry Archives.

[43] Zander, *Israel and the Holy Places of Christendom*, 72.

[44] S. Slonim, 'Israeli policy on Jerusalem at the United Nations, 1948', *Middle Eastern Studies*, 20 (1994), 579–90.

[45] B. Papadopoulos, 'Brief note on the draft statute of the Jerusalem district', *Nea Sion*, 44 (1949), 199–211 (in Greek).

[46] A. Nachmani, *Israel, Turkey and Greece: Uneasy relations in the Eastern Mediterranean* (London, 1987), 108–10; S. Slonim, *Israeli Policy on Jerusalem*, 587.

[47] P. J. Vatikiotis, 'The siege of the walled city of Jerusalem, 14 May–15 December, 1948', *Middle Eastern Studies*, 31 (1995), 138–45.

[48] D. Tsimhoni, *Christian Communities in Jerusalem and the West Bank since 1948* (London, 1993), 38. See also D. Tsimhoni, 'The Greek Orthodox community in Jerusalem and the West Bank, 1948–1978: a profile of a religious minority in a national state', *Orient*, 23 (1982), 281–98; and eadem, 'Between the hammer and the anvil: the national dilemma of the Christian minority in Jerusalem and the West Bank', *Orient*, 24 (1983), 637–44.

[49] Ibid., 39.

[50] S. Colbi, *Christianity in the Holy Land, Past and Present* (Tel Aviv, 1969), 148–9.

[51] Quoted from the Greek newspaper, *To Vema*, 12 April 1959, in T. Psarakes, *Anthology of Jerusalem* (Athens, 1994), 53–7 (in Greek).

[52] M. Dumper, 'Church–state relations in Jerusalem since 1948', in O'Mahony, Hintlian and Gunner (eds), *Christian Heritage in the Holy Land*, 272–3.

[53] The Israeli Knesset passed the Protection of the Holy Places Law in June, 1967.

⁵⁴ Don Peretz, 'Palestinian social stratification: the political implications, *Journal of Palestine Studies*, 7 (1997), 70–1.

⁵⁵ Bernard Sabella, 'Palestinian Christian emigration from the Holy Land', *Proche-Orient Chrétien*, 41 (1991), 75.

⁵⁶ N. B. Williams, Jr., 'In Mideast: a Christian exodus', *Los Angeles Times*, 10 August, 1991.

⁵⁷ S. Geraisy, 'Socio-demographic characteristics: reality, problems and aspirations within Israel', in M. Prior and W. Taylor (eds), *The Christians in the Holy Land* (London, 1994), 47–8.

⁵⁸ Y. Courbage and P. Fargues, *Chrétiens et Juifs dans l'Islam arabe et turc* (Paris, 1992), 328.

⁵⁹ B. Sabella, *Palestinian Christians*, 76.

⁶⁰ M. Dumper, *Church–State Relations in Jerusalem*, 285; and P. Cockburn, 'Christians squeezed in the struggle for the Holy Land', *Independent*, 14 May, 1995.

⁶¹ D. Tsimhoni, *Christian Communities*, 44–6.

⁶² M. Dumper, *Church–State Relations in Jerusalem*, 278.

⁶³ See G. Bowman, 'Nationalising the sacred: shrines and shifting identities in the Israeli occupied territories', *Man*, 28 (1993), 1–30; S. K. Aburish, *The Forgotten Faithful: The Christians in the Holy Land* (London, 1993); and R. Beeston, 'Palestinians want the Greek out of Orthodox', *The Times*, 3 October 1992.

⁶⁴ S. K. Aburish, *The Forgotten Faithful*, 107–9.

⁶⁵ 'Brief account of the St John Hospice's capture by Israeli fanatics', *Nea Sion*, 83 (1991), 141–55 (in Greek).

⁶⁶ Ibid., 164.

⁶⁷ See my 'The Greek Orthodox community in Jerusalem in international politics: international solutions for Jerusalem and the Greek Orthodox community in the nineteenth and twentieth centuries', in Lee I. Levine (ed.), *Jerusalem, Its Sancity and Centrality to Judaism, Christianity and Islam* (New York, 1991), 482–95.

3

THE ARMENIAN CHURCH AND COMMUNITY OF JERUSALEM

Ara Sanjian

For Armenians, who take pride in reminding that theirs is the oldest state in the world to have proclaimed Christianity as its official religion, the Holy City of Jerusalem has long been an important focus of attention, perhaps second only to the Holy See of Etchmiadzin in Armenia.[1] The Armenian Apostolic church, organized around the Brotherhood of St James and headed by a patriarch, is, despite its relatively small size, and on a par with the much larger Greek Orthodox and Latins (Roman Catholics), one of the three custodians of the holy places and has waged a long struggle to maintain a presence there.

For lay Armenians, tattoos on the arm recording the year of their pilgrimage above the Jerusalem cross remain to date a permanent certification of that exalted journey. The Armenian clergy in Jerusalem has encouraged pilgrimage and has sought to provide the necessary facilities for pilgrims because the latter have always been its major source of income. It is probably due to the legacy of pilgrimage as well that the Armenian monastery of St James houses today the second-largest collection in the world – after that of the Institute of Ancient Manuscripts (Matenadaran) in Yerevan – of medieval Armenian manuscripts, nearly 4,000 in number, as well as other precious works of art. Although the Armenian clergy in Jerusalem has not distinguished itself in the fields of learning and scholarship, many emissaries sent to various parts of the world to encourage pilgrimage, as well as the pilgrims themselves, have brought with them many unique ecclesiastical vestments, ornaments and gifts that make up part of the patriarchate's present treasury.

The development of a resident lay Armenian community in Jerusalem is also intimately intertwined with pilgrimage. The Armenian church, like the other Christian churches in Palestine, was interested in having such a community in Jerusalem to buttress its claims for control of the holy places. However, since, unlike other churches, it did not engage in proselytizing and limited its followers to those who were Armenians, the Armenian church attempted to fulfil that task by encouraging many Armenian pilgrims to stay in Jerusalem permanently, and, whenever the number of Armenian laymen in Jerusalem fell to dangerously low levels, it asked Armenian feudal rulers to send scores of subjects and dependants to settle in Jerusalem and regenerate the secular community.

Until the years of the First World War, apart from pilgrims and visitors, no lay person was allowed to live permanently within the Armenian convent compound. Pilgrims who decided to stay on in Jerusalem were given houses owned by the Armenian church just outside the monastery, and gradually what became known as the Armenian quarter evolved. It is today one of the four principal quarters of the Old City, occupying roughly 120,000 square metres or one-sixth of the area within the Old City walls. It houses the Cathedral of St James and the monastery compound, surrounded by walls with several small streets. All the properties within this quarter belong to the Armenian church, which also owns much property beyond it, both inside and outside the Old City. That property is rented to businesses and government agencies, and most tenants are non-Armenians.

Armenians in Jerusalem and the Holy Land: The Early Period

Armenians were among the first pilgrims and monks to arrive in Palestine soon after the discovery of the holy places in the fourth century AD. Some pilgrims did not return to Armenia and stayed in the proximity of the sanctuaries in and around Jerusalem. Armenian monks were among the founders of desert monasticism in the Holy Land. Indisputable evidence of considerable Armenian presence in Jerusalem at the time is provided in the form of archaeological finds consisting of seven mosaic pavements, with inscriptions in Armenian, spread over a vast area on the Mount of Olives, with another near the Damascus Gate, as well as one with a Greek inscription which mentions an Armenian. These pavements could be as early as the fifth century.[2] The last of them was discovered in 1991, and similar finds may very well recur in the future. Further evidence is provided by tombs, dating from the early sixth century, and pottery vessels, all inscribed with Armenian letters. In Nazareth, old Armenian inscriptions, dating from the first half of the fifth century, that is, only two to three decades after the invention of the Armenian alphabet, have also been found.[3] The earliest ritual traditions of Armenia, too, owe much to those of Palestine. The first lectionary of Palestine, the oldest known document in the world to include the corpus of feasts, sites and dates in the Holy Land, was translated from Greek into Armenian and was used both in Jerusalem and in Armenia. The Greek original has been lost and survives only in the Armenian translation.

At first, the Armenian monks and ascetics in the Holy Land worshipped with monks and pilgrims of other nationalities in common chapels, each using its own liturgy and language. They also shared hostels and monasteries. All Christians were united under the authority of the bishop of Jerusalem. By the middle of the sixth century, however, the breach occasioned by the christological decisions of the Council of Chalcedon (AD 451) began to affect seriously religious harmony among those communities. The Byzantine emperors, being staunch adherents of the Chalcedonian creed, initiated persecutions of monophysites, Armenians included. The latter were warned that unless they adhered to the Chalcedonian doctrine they would not be permitted to stay in Jerusalem. Armenians lost some of their religious institutions to the Greeks. Many Armenian monks preferred to abandon their monasteries and leave for Caesarea in Palestine and for Egypt, rather than make doctrinal concessions. Others, however, remained in their institutions despite the persecutions meted out to them by the authorities.

On the other hand, this controversy helped crystallize, in the seventh century, a separate identity for the Armenian church in Jerusalem. The Armenian clergy built their own institutions and monastic establishments and severed their ties with the hierarchy of Jerusalem. The see of Jerusalem was split into a Greek patriarchate exercising jurisdiction over the dyophysite Christians, and an independent Armenian hierarchy having authority over the other monophysite Jacobite Syrian, Coptic and Ethiopian communities as well.

Byzantine pressure on Armenians in Jerusalem was cut short by the Arab conquest of the city in AD 638. The victors allowed their Christian subjects to pursue their religious beliefs freely and hold services in the dominical sanctuaries. Armenian sources claim that three separate charters issued by the Prophet Muhammad, and Caliphs 'Umar and 'Ali safeguarded the life and property of Armenians living in Jerusalem and recognized their rights over all religious sanctuaries under their control. Modern scholars doubt the authenticity of these (and similar Greek) documents, which could have been fabricated at a later period to support rival claims to the Christian sanctuaries. However, their validity was accepted by later Muslim rulers like Salah al-Din and the Ottoman Sultan Selim I as bases for conferring rights on the holy places to rival Christian churches.

With the Arab conquest the Armenian see of Jerusalem attained a stature which perhaps equalled that of the Greek patriarchate. Although the Armenians in Jerusalem numbered fewer than the Greeks, they enjoyed better relations with the Arabs, who were suspicious of the associations of the Greek church with the Byzantine Empire. Documentation is thin for this period, but there is reason to believe that the Christians of Palestine were generally treated fairly until the beginning of the eighth century. Later, however, they suffered some humiliating restrictions and discriminatory practices. The Fatimid ruler, al-Hakim (996–1021), destroyed many Christian churches throughout his dominions, including the Holy Sepulchre at Jerusalem. After his death, however, there was a reaction in favour of religious tolerance, and the period of Fatimid dominion is seen today as a period of tolerance. Armenians were in special favour in Egypt at the time, as many high offices there were frequently held by Armenians. The latter aided and supported their brethren in Jerusalem in all respects, and were helpful in promoting Christian interests in general. By the time the crusaders came to Jerusalem, there was already a sizeable resident Armenian lay population in

Palestine, and the boundaries of the present Armenian quarter in the south-western corner of the Old City were fairly well established.[4] Still, because of the excessive taxes imposed by successive Arab rulers and the failure of the catholici and princes to dispatch the revenues from endowments in Armenia, the Armenian clergy in Jerusalem had lost a substantial number of their private possessions and holdings. Their rights to free access to the common dominical sanctuaries had also been seriously curtailed. A number of Armenian monastic institutions had fallen into ruins; others had been left without administrators and occupied by the Greeks.[5]

The Armenian Church and Community in the Medieval Period

During the crusader period (1099–1187), the Armenian church secured important privileges in Jerusalem, guaranteeing the continued prosperity of the institutions which it already possessed, and was also able to increase the number of its monasteries and hostels. Its separate identity in Jerusalem was greatly strengthened, especially with the acquisition from the Georgians in the twelfth century of its present headquarters, the cathedral of St James and the adjoining buildings. This cathedral is believed to stand at the site where James the Less, the first bishop of Jerusalem, lived and was buried. It is also believed that the head of St James the Great, the brother of John the Evangelist, was buried at the same place after he was beheaded by Herod Agrippa.[6] St James's became the heart of Jerusalem's Armenian community, and its accommodations were considerably enlarged for the benefit of the local monastics and for the countless Armenian pilgrims and visiting merchants who annually arrived in Jerusalem and stayed there for some time – some even for years. Its limits were also extended through the acquisition or purchase of lands, and the whole complex now occupies a dominating position on Mount Zion. A monastic brotherhood bearing the same name was established, becoming the guardian of the Armenian-controlled holy places and protecting the interests of other monophysite churches, when their members were expelled from Jerusalem for short periods because of friction caused by theological discrepancies with the then predominant Latin church.[7]

The important position which the Armenian church held in Jerusalem during crusader times may be attributed to the friendly ties which the Armenian kingdom in Cilicia had with the Frankish states of the Levant. The Latin kingdom of Jerusalem, for example, had in its service an infantry corps of Armenians. Intermarriage was common between the Frankish and Cilician Armenian nobility. The first three crusader queens of Jerusalem and a substantial number of the princesses were of Armenian descent, and several privileges were bestowed upon the local Armenian community through their beneficence. There were also occasional visits from Cilicia by members of the Armenian royal family and high-ranking Armenian clergy. The former provided generously for the needs of the Armenians in Jerusalem, and this patronage helped pave the way for a constant flow of learned clerics into Jerusalem from both Armenia and Cilicia. Many lay Armenians also flocked to Jerusalem from Antioch, Edessa, Tarsus, Cilicia and Cappadocia. King Baldwin II granted the Armenians and other Christians trade privileges, tax exemptions and other incentives to promote their settlement in Jerusalem. Some indeed established permanent residence, acquiring a number of private hostels or inns, and occupying several new quarters, one of which was known as Ruga Armenorum. Among them were many skilled craftsmen and traders, and it seems that the Armenians had a market of their own. Armenians were also found in Caesarea, Acre, Tyre, Gaza, Bethlehem, Salt, Nablus and Kerak.[8]

In 1187, when Salah al-Din captured Jerusalem, over 1,500 Armenian resided in the city, and the conqueror adopted a very positive attitude towards the latter, perhaps to use them as a leverage against the Latins and Greeks. He considered the Armenian population of the city as indigenous and absolved them of the poll tax and ransom money he demanded from the other Christians, who had arrived with the crusaders. He also recognized the religious freedom of the Armenians and their monophysite dependants, and reconfirmed the integrity of their possessions and prerogatives in the holy places and other privately owned institutions and sanctuaries throughout his entire domains. Moreover, Armenians had the opportunity to acquire the church of the Holy Sepulchre, which was kept closed until 1192.

Following Salah al-Din's death, Palestine as a whole suffered from a long period of political instability, until the Mamelukes of Egypt managed to make the region their dependency. Despite these troubled times, however, it seems that Armenian pilgrimages continued unabated, and Armenians continued to enjoy overall a prominent position in the Holy Land. They had exclusive ownership of the Calvary, and their prominence is also testified by the carved Armenian doors to the basilica of the church of the Nativity in Bethlehem.

It is not clear when the head of the Armenian church in Jerusalem was elevated to the rank of patriarch. The edict of Caliph 'Umar in the seventh century AD refers to Bishop Abraham as such. Some modern scholars suggest, however, that this might simply be a general term used by Muslims for all heads of Christian churches, and point out that there is no mention of the title of patriarch for the successors of Abraham who headed the Armenian church in Jerusalem until the beginning of the fourteenth century.[9]

In Avedis K. Sanjian's view, the patriarchate originated in the second half of the sixth century with the separation of the Armenian clergy from the authority of the Chalcedonian Greek patriarch and the establishment of a distinct episcopal hierarchy. He argues that the incumbents of the see of Jerusalem were not designated as patriarchs for a long time only because they did not wish it to appear as if they had established a hierarchy independent of the supreme pontificate of the Armenian church. For all practical purposes, however, the role and function of their leaders was that of a patriarch, although their authority stemmed from their position as deputies of the Armenian pontificate.[10]

Most scholars, however, favour another point of view, according to which the patriarchate was established in 1311, when the St James Brotherhood refused to accept the pro-Latin policies of the Supreme Catholicosate, then based at Sis (Cilicia) and, in order to assert its independence, proclaimed its head, Bishop Sargis, as patriarch and guardian of the Armenian-controlled holy places. Sargis secured an edict from Sultan Nasr Muhammad of Egypt recognizing him as an independent patriarch and religious leader of Armenian communities and other eastern Christians in communion with them, as well as the actual owner and custodian of the holy sanctuaries and chief administrator of Armenian monastic institutions within Egyptian domains.[11]

Despite this breach, the patriarchate of Jerusalem remained within the framework of the see of Sis, and the Armenian bishops of Jerusalem continued to be ordained by the catholicos at Sis. When the hierarchical seat of the Armenian church was transferred from Sis in 1441 back to Etchmiadzin, the see of Jerusalem, too, came under the latter's jurisdiction, without breaking its cordial links with the separate catholicosate of Sis created in 1446.

During the 200 years of Mameluke rule, Armenians and their monophysite communicants in Jerusalem enjoyed relative freedom in exercising their religious rites. They were able, through the special privileges they were granted, to preserve and extend their sanctuaries, monasteries and other possessions, after due payment, of course, of regular taxes and bribes. In the first half of the thirteenth century, in particular, they succeeded in restoring their long-neglected sanctuaries and institutions and constructed new edifices through the generous contributions of the Armenian royal house of Cilicia and pilgrims, who came to the Holy Land in ever-increasing numbers.

The Mameluke administration of the Holy Land, however, did not always exhibit a spirit of tolerance towards Armenians and other Christians. Tax collectors constantly harassed and coerced the monasteries, demanding lawful and illegitimate levies. Ecclesiastical edifices ultimately lost their splendour because permits for construction and restoration were withheld. The Armenian clergy in Jerusalem was persecuted, and some were murdered in 1367 during the Mameluke reprisals against Christians for attacks by Franks on Alexandria (1365–9). Moreover, Mameluke sultans used the Christian holy sanctuaries as a pawn to enrich their coffers at the expense of the contending parties. The Georgians, who had family links with the Mamelukes, were the main beneficiaries. Armenians successfully withstood several Georgian attempts to retake the cathedral of St James, but had to relinquish the Calvary at Golgotha within the compound of the Holy Sepulchre. They acquired in its stead the Triforium, which was converted into a church in 1439 and named the Second Golgotha.

The Armenian Community after the
Ottoman Conquest of Palestine

Following the capture of Jerusalem by the Ottoman Sultan Selim I in 1517, the Armenian patriarch continued to be recognized as the ecclesiastical and spiritual head of the Armenian religious and lay communities in Jerusalem and the dependent dioceses of Transjordan, Damascus, Latakia, Beirut and Egypt. After 1775, the spiritual leaders of the Cypriot Armenian community were also, in the main, appointed by the patriarchate of Jerusalem. The Ottomans institutionalized the dependence on the Armenian patriarchate of other monophysite churches and religious communities in Jerusalem. This dependence is maintained today only at a symbolic level, as in the traditional visit paid to the Armenian patriarch by the heads of the Coptic, Ethiopian and Syrian Jacobite churches during Easter celebrations in which they offer him their respective bundles of Holy Fire candles.

The Ottoman government forced all Armenian sees within its political boundaries to obey the newly established Armenian patriarchate of Constantinople. The patriarchate of Jerusalem adapted itself to this new situation, acknowledging its subordination to Constantinople in administrative functions, but without recognizing the latter's supremacy in religious affairs or in the formal church hierarchy. The patriarch of Jerusalem also performed, within the dioceses under his jurisdiction, the functions accorded in civil administrative matters to the patriarch of Constantinople as head of the Ottoman Armenian millet. He was invested with great power in the local administration of the community, collected community taxes in the name of the government, and had sole responsibility for birth, marriage and death registration, as well as for matters of divorce and inheritance. He was even provided with his own means of coercion in the form of local guards, police, penal institutions and religious courts, whose jurisdiction extended to all civil affairs of the community and could imprison or exile any of its members.

The subordination of the patriarchate of Jerusalem to that of Constantinople worked in general because the patriarchate of Jerusalem was in constant need of the financial assistance provided by its Constantinople counterpart. Excessive official and other illicit taxes not sanctioned by imperial authority, bribes, which had to be paid to corrupt government officials on all levels, especially to retain at all costs the Armenian share of the holy places and other privately owned ecclesiastical establishments, as well as forced loans, with exorbitant rates of interest, drained all the resources of the Jerusalem see throughout the four centuries of Ottoman domination in Palestine. Hence, the expenditures of the patriarchate could not be predicted, and it was often constrained to spend considerably more than its actual revenues warranted, and had to incur heavy debts. Pilgrimage, which under the Ottomans assumed an organized character, formed the patriarchate's main source of income, and pilgrims made significant donations for the upkeep of rooms in the monastery. By the middle of the seventeenth century, following this important construction activity during the reign of Patriarch Grigor Paronter (1613-45), enough space had been created within the monastery to accommodate about 2,000 pilgrims. In the nineteenth century, with the improvement in all forms of transport, the number of pilgrims reached record heights of 8,000–10,000 a year. Moreover, following the Crimean War (1853–6), the patriarchate also began to invest in income-bearing real estate outside the city walls. In times of need, however, the Armenian millet as a whole, and particularly wealthy Armenians of Constantinople, had to step in and provide the necessary financial support. The good will and assistance of the patriarchate of Constantinople was also desired to protect Armenian rights and privileges in the holy places before the Sublime Porte, especially in cases of conflict with the other Christian communities. A special representative of the Jerusalem see resided in special quarters in Constantinople known as Yerusaghematun (Jerusalem House), serving as liaison between the two patriarchates and representing the see of Jerusalem in front of the Sublime Porte. He also oversaw the activities of the emissaries, who organized pilgrimages and went on fund-raising missions to most towns of the Ottoman Empire and to far-flung places like India, Crimea, Poland, the Balkans and Russia.

However, this dependence was also often marred by controversies over the extent of control of the patriarchate of Constantinople over Jerusalem's financial affairs, internal administration and the election of new patriarchs. Until about the end of the seventeenth century, the patriarchs of Jerusalem were elected by the bishops and priests of the monastic brotherhood from among its own members. This election was subject, however, to confirmation by the head of state reigning over the Holy Land. In the second half of the seventeenth century, however, certain irregularities began to occur in the way patriarchs were elected. Most ecclesiastics who occupied and reoccupied the patriarchal throne at this juncture achieved their appointments with gifts and bribes, and in order to meet their large monetary commitments they often mortgaged the see's properties and sacred vessels. The Ottoman authorities were obviously less interested in the stability of a subject minority than in political expediency and, perhaps more importantly, in financial remuneration. From 1657 to 1659, and later for a decade beginning in 1704, the Jerusalem patriarchate was abolished and the see was administered through special representatives sent from Constantinople. Although such steps may have been intended to prevent financial chaos in Jerusalem, they actually accentuated the problem. The see's debt reached tremendous sums, and the brotherhood could not meet the demands of the creditors, who then felt free to enter the monastery at will and carry away anything of value that came to their notice. Finally, the Armenian patriarchate of Jerusalem was re-established in 1714 as a separate administrative and financial entity. Through the joint efforts of the newly elected patriarch of Constantinople, Hovhannes Kolot Baghishetsi, and his appointee as patriarch of Jerusalem, Grigor 'the

Chain-Bearer' Shirvantsi (1715–49), considered today as one of the greatest of the patriarchs of Jerusalem, the debt was eventually repaid and steps were taken to restore the Armenian churches to their past brilliance and make the monastery self-supporting. Properties were purchased in Jaffa, Ramallah, Damascus and Aleppo, all major stops on the sea and overland pilgrims' routes to Jerusalem, to support the Armenian monasteries and pilgrim accommodations there.[12]

Patriarchs Hovhannes and Grigor also played a pivotal role in formulating in 1726 the first of a long series of attempts to reform the internal organization of the patriarchate of Jerusalem, limiting the previously uncontested authority of the patriarch within the Armenian community of Jerusalem and granting a share of power to other members of the brotherhood. On the other hand, they reversed the trend set by Patriarch Grigor Paronter, who had entrusted important administrative responsibilities within the patriarchate to capable laymen, even dispatching some of them to distant countries on fund-raising missions.[13] A peculiar situation began to emerge, in which the Armenian laymen of Jerusalem were under the jurisdiction of the religious authorities in civil and religious matters, but could not participate in the administration of the community. Indeed, Jerusalem remains to date the only Armenian community where laymen have no formal say in the selection of top church officials and the government of their community.

The Armenian millet authorities at Constantinople did not, however, abandon their right to supervise the affairs of the patriarchate of Jerusalem. Especially in the second half of the nineteenth century, centralization of authority became their primary objective. The Armenian National Assembly sitting in Constantinople assumed the right to elect the patriarch of Jerusalem from an initial list of seven candidates presented by the brotherhood, as well as the right to supervise and control the patriarchate's finances, the negotiation of loans, and the sale and purchase of properties. The brotherhood rejected these attempts, and this corresponded perfectly to the views of Sultan Abdülhamid II and his government. His edict confirming the election of Patriarch Haroutioun Vehabedian in 1888 restored patriarchal authority in its traditional absolutist form, and rule by the National Assembly never came into effect in Jerusalem. The patriarchs of this period were indeed elected in Constantinople, but they managed the affairs of the patriarchate on their own, and their responsibility to Constantinople remained purely formal.[14]

Besides repeated attempts at reform, the nineteenth century was also characterized by advances in the cultural sphere, financed largely by wealthy Armenians from Constantinople, Egypt and Syria. The first printing press in Jerusalem was an Armenian one, set up in 1833, which published, during the next eighty-two years, some 400 Armenian titles.[15] In 1843, a seminary was established to replace the age-old tradition of providing education for boys dedicated to the priesthood through priests already living in the convent. The seminary functioned, with brief interludes, until the years of the First World

War, with an annual student intake varying between twenty and forty. Students from Egypt, Syria and Lebanon were given living quarters in rooms originally intended for pilgrims. The seminary failed, however, to achieve high academic standards or produce good theologians and scholars. Yet, in the main, its graduate monks attained a relatively higher level of educational training than had been the case prior to its establishment. Wealthy Armenians also sponsored the publication from 1866 to 1877 of the patriarchate's monthly periodical, *Sion*. There also existed a large photography workshop founded in 1855 by the future Patriarch Yessayi Garabedian.[16]

By the time of the Ottoman conquest of the Holy Land in 1517, the Greeks, Latins and Armenians had emerged as the principal custodians of the holy places, with the Copts, Syrians and Ethiopians possessing some minor privileges in the sites owned exclusively by the Armenians. Sultan Selim I confirmed the ancient rights and privileges of the Armenian patriarchate. Yet the four centuries of Ottoman rule were to witness major struggles between the rival Christian churches for control of the holy places. This struggle was conducted with an almost fanatical zeal and was frequently attended by violence. The local and central authorities were invariably called upon to adjudicate between contending Christians, and the role which they played in these cases was sometimes motivated by considerations of justice, law and order. More often than not, however, they played one community against the other and were frequently influenced by the possibility of financial gain and the requirements of international diplomacy. Although, at times, the Ottoman government supported the Armenian patriarchate in this struggle, in the long run, the Armenians lost some of their historic prerogatives to Latin and Greek incursions. They lost some privileges in the Holy Sepulchre as well as control of some other sites, though less than did other oriental churches. In three separate instances (1616–59, 1734–9 and 1808–13) they even came close to losing the St James monastery to the Greeks, and indeed lost control of it for eighteen months in 1658–9. In the eighteenth and nineteenth centuries particularly, with the decline of Ottoman power, the lack of support from foreign powers became a serious liability for the Armenians. Heavy bribes to local Ottoman officials and the influence of Armenian bankers in Constantinople were the only leverage they could use to offset adverse foreign influences.

Finally, in February 1852, Sultan Abdülmecid, after a thorough inquiry into the question, issued the famous firman of Status Quo, which rejected any further demands for changes in the different churches' control over the holy places and declared that all matters relating to the latter were to be referred in the future to the Sublime Porte itself. This firman was the result of long historical evolution and established a most complicated network of rights and privileges, becoming the centrepiece regulating relations between different churches and communities in Jerusalem, and bringing them a measure of harmony. It has been confirmed by various instruments of international law and has on the whole been observed since, both during the remaining years of Ottoman rule and by the succeeding British, Jordanian and Israeli authorities in Jerusalem.

The status quo took only the three major rites – Greeks, Armenians and Latins – into consideration in all matters of principle relating to the holy places, and accorded the last of these the sole right to repair these sanctuaries, which also implied exclusive possession. In terms of overall control of Christian holy places the Armenian church now ranks third, after the Greeks and Latins, and ahead of many larger Christian churches, such as the Russian Orthodox and the various Protestant denominations. Armenians now own – in addition to their rights, with Greeks and Latins, in the church of the Holy Sepulchre, the church of the Nativity in Bethlehem, and the church of the Holy Ascension of Christ on the Mount of Olives and, with the Greeks, in the church of St Mary in the Garden of Gethsemane – about a dozen convents and churches in the Holy Land, like the Aceldama (Potter's Field) and the Charnier, the monasteries of St Nicholas in Jaffa and of St George in Ramallah. They also have sole jurisdiction over the cathedral of St James and the houses of Annas and Caiaphas.[17]

Nevertheless, great tension still persists between the rival Christian churches, especially in the sites under joint control. In recent years, for example, the repair of one section of the great rotunda of the Holy Sepulchre remained under scaffolding for over thirty years because of disputes between the Armenian and Syrian Orthodox clergy. Disputes also often erupt on the use of lamps, decorations and pictures, on cleaning parts of the sanctuaries, and on prompt and unfailing performance of religious services, since all of these are taken as symbols of control, and laxity in these matters is thought to lead to a weakening of rights by default. Such tension is most apparent on those occasions, such as Easter, when large numbers of pilgrims arrive at Jerusalem and several denominations hold services simultaneously in the Holy Sepulchre. Each church tries to surpass the others in pomp and is very sensitive to the rights conferred on it by the Status Quo agreement as to its territory and the precise order and procedure of the services.

The Armenian lay population of Jerusalem, which had probably decreased after the Ottoman conquest, began to grow again from about 500 in 1800 to 640 in 1870. Following the massacres of Armenians in Anatolia and Cilicia in 1895–6 and in 1909, their numbers in Jerusalem rose again to reach about 1,300 in 1910.[18] These resident Armenians lived in the Armenian quarter in houses provided to them by the patriarchate. Families that had to live outside the quarter owing to the lack of housing or for convenience got cash to cover their rent. The lay residents as a rule were not allowed to enrol in the seminary or join the brotherhood. Pilgrims could stay within the monastery for years, but when they decided to settle down in Jerusalem, they had to move to the streets clustered around it. With the passage of time, these lay Armenians were integrated with and accepted by the local population, becoming known over the years as *kaghakatsis* (locals). They adopted for daily use the Arabic language, which they spoke fluently but with a slight accent. Many of them served the church, primarily in menial jobs like guards or cleaners. Others became jewellers, gold- and silversmiths, tailors, shoe-makers and carpenters. They also pioneered the introduction of photography into Palestine. They were trusted by the Ottoman regime and given positions in government departments, such as the customs and the post office, had seats on government councils and in the municipality. Some of them, due to their western education and business acumen, also occupied important economic positions, serving as representatives of foreign companies, and a few even served as honorary consuls for certain western powers. The patriar-chate, which had, in the meantime, assumed responsibility for establishing and maintaining parochial schools for the Armenian secular communities at Bethlehem, Jaffa, Damascus, Beirut and Latakia, covered, in Jerusalem as well, all the expenses not only of the coeducational Armenian kindergarten, but also of the primary Mesropian (founded 1846) and Gayaniants (founded 1862) schools for boys and girls respectively. The kindergarten had around 100 students in 1915, but enrolment at Mesropian and Gayaniants stood at only thirty and twenty respectively, as the 'locals' preferred to send their chil-dren to foreign schools.

During the massacres of Armenians in 1915, the Armenians of Palestine were not deported, allegedly because of the friendly ties of Cemal Pasha with the former patriarch of Constantinople, Maghakia Ormanian, and the catholicos of Cilicia, Sahak Khabayan, both of whom resided in Jerusalem during the war. However, young Armenians from Jerusalem, including semi-narians, were taken to the army, some never to return, and 'locals' working in government departments were relieved of their posts. In 1915 the govern-ment closed down the monastery press, and, a year later, completely cut off the relations of the Ottoman Armenian millet with the catholicosate of All Armenians at Etchmiadzin, creating a single Armenian ecclesiastical hierar-chy within the Ottoman Empire under Catholicos Sahak of Cilicia, with headquarters in Jerusalem. In the summer of 1917 the seminary was also shut down, and all bishops and leading ecclesiastics were exiled to Damascus because of the impending occupation of Jerusalem by the British army.

Upon the termination of Ottoman rule in the Levant, the exiled clergy returned, and the separate sees of Cilicia, Constantinople and Jerusalem were restored. The patriarchate of Jerusalem now emerged as an institution completely independent of Constantinople, but still within the general frame-work of the catholicosate of Etchmiadzin. With the approval of the latter, the patriarchate of Jerusalem generously transferred in 1929 to the see of Cilicia – now based in Antelias, north of Beirut – all of its churches, schools and diocesan offices in Syria, Lebanon and Cyprus. This transfer strengthened the monastic image of the Jerusalem see and freed it from administrative functions as head of a millet covering a large area. Only the small Armenian communities of Palestine and Transjordan were left under its jurisdiction, for earlier, in 1839, its jurisdiction over the Egyptian dioceses had also passed to Etchmiadzin.

The Armenian Church and Community under the British Mandate

Under the British mandate in Palestine (1917–48), a large measure of democratization was introduced into the government of the brotherhood, and a new constitution empowered it to govern its own affairs fully. Police functions, prisons and far-reaching secular powers of the court were abolished. The monastery guards (*kavas*), who in their ceremonial dress and the swords they continued to carry symbolized those police functions of the past, now served simply as doorkeepers.

After the British capture of Jerusalem, there was an influx of Armenian survivors of the genocide of 1915. By 1920 about 10,000 Armenian refugees had arrived in Palestine. Some established their new homes in Haifa and Amman. Most, however, settled around the patriarchate of Jerusalem. Of these, 4,000 were housed in the very primitive pilgrim accommodation within the convent itself, which had to be altered to make it more suitable for family use.

Most refugees remained within the monastery for only a short time. They were sent to, or left for, other countries. Of those who remained in Palestine, some moved to other towns or to the new neighbourhoods in Jerusalem. A considerable number, however, continued to live within the monastery walls, forcing the clergy to make great adjustments to accommodate itself to living so close to a large lay population. Because the Ottoman millet system was maintained by the British, local administrative matters concerning the new lay population were still the patriarchate's responsibility, and these laymen had to be fed, given shelter and facilities for education, entertainment and cultural activities, and, finally, helped to find jobs. They spoke no Arabic, only Armenian and Turkish. They had brought with them different traditions and customs, distinguishing them from the 'locals'. In the thirty years of the British mandate, however, they displayed a great ability to recover and improve their economic position through aggressive entrepreneurship, business flair and educational and professional skills. Even the 'locals', by coming into contact with these refugees, readopted Armenian as their vernacular.

Although the Armenian genocide of 1915 and the Bolshevik revolution of 1917 had considerably dampened traditional popular pilgrimage, and hence the patriarchate's main source of revenue, the 1920s and 1930s are now considered as years during which the St James monastery emerged as a leading Armenian cultural centre. The newly elected patriarch, Yeghishe Tourian, reopened the seminary, which now emerged as an important centre of

Armenian religious learning. Tourian resumed in 1927 the publication of *Sion*, which immediately turned into a leading periodical on religion, philosophy, literature and history. The monastery press published important Armenian literary works and supplied most of the liturgical books used in Armenian churches around the world. In 1929, Tourian founded the now famous library sponsored by the Armenian oil magnate and philanthropist Calouste Gulbenkian. Finally, he combined, again in 1929, the existing Armenian primary schools of Jerusalem into one institution, the Surb Tarkmanchats (the Holy Translators of the Scriptures into Armenian) School, with a kindergarten and elementary classes on the site of the old girls' school. By 1948, this school had 850 students. The patriarchate also supervised three other schools and two kindergartens in Jaffa, Haifa and Amman, with a total enrolment in 1948 of around 750.

The Armenian Church and Community under Israeli and Jordanian Rule

The Armenian community of Palestine was shattered again by the Arab-Israeli war in 1948. With the outbreak of the war, stray shells and bullets fell on the monastery, killing about thirty people. Still, between 3,000 and 4,000 Armenians, who lived in the coastal towns and Jerusalem's new neighbourhoods, took shelter there, in response to Patriarch Guregh Israelian's call. Refuge was also given to some Muslims from the Nabi Dawud area, who for centuries had been on good neighbourly terms with the Armenians. Every room was filled and tents were put up in many of the courtyards. After the cessation of hostilities, those refugees who had fled from areas that remained on the Israeli side could not return. They were unable to reclaim their property and, within a few years, most emigrated to Lebanon, Soviet Armenia, western Europe or America. Those who remained in Jerusalem found new homes and jobs. The church of the Holy Saviour on Mount Zion, the burial place for the Armenian community for nearly 350 years, fell into an area of no man's land, and was partly occupied by the Israeli army, mined and made inaccessible. Armenians living in east Jerusalem, therefore, had to bury their dead within the monastery compound. The number of Armenians left inside Israel was small, around 800 to 1,000 people, living in Jaffa, Haifa and west Jerusalem. Although the patriarchate kept a resident priest on the Israeli side and leading clergymen frequently crossed from Jordan to visit their kinsmen living in Israel, these laymen were largely cut off from the centre of Armenian community life. They were allowed to visit the patriarchate and their relatives living under Jordanian rule only for twenty-four hours every Christmas.

Following the division of Jerusalem, the patriarchate faced renewed financial difficulties, for the greater part of its property in the western (Jewish) sector of the New City remained under Israeli control. However, since the Israeli government was anxious not to antagonize prospective Christian support, it soon allowed Armenian and other Christian clergy based in east Jerusalem to coordinate activities with their co-religionists in Israel by obtaining special passes to cross the armistice line. In 1949, it also released the assets of religious institutions from the custodian of abandoned property and allowed part of their income to be transferred to Jordan while the balance remained in Israeli banks. The Armenians proved willing to lease large areas they owned in Israel to the Jewish National Fund, and in the mid-1950s their religious head in Israel was permitted by the Israeli foreign exchange authorities to transfer £500 of the income from the property to the patriarchate every month.[19] This amount did not, of course, prove sufficient in view of the steep rise in the cost of living in Jordan; the patriarchate's budget deficit reached 60 per cent and had to be financed by donations from abroad.

Crisis in Church–State Relations: Cold War and Ecclesiastical Politics in Jerusalem

The division of Jerusalem also led to Israeli and Jordanian interference in the internal affairs of the Christian communities in the Holy City, with each side aiming to secure the installation at the head of those communities of clerics amenable to its political point of view. The Armenian community of Jerusalem, too, was rocked in the second half of the 1950s by a conflict related to the election of a new patriarch. This issue exploded within the monastic brotherhood, but soon involved the lay community living in the Armenian quarter, who offered support to rival factions of clergymen. Finally the intervention of the Jordanian government ensured the election of Archbishop Yeghishe Derderian as patriarch.[20]

The election of a new patriarch to succeed Guregh Israelian (d. 19 October 1949) had been delayed to attend first to the pressing problems created as a consequence of the 1948 war. The second-highest office-holder in the monastery, the grand sacristan, that is, the cleric responsible for allocating priests to conduct religious services, the upkeep of the churches, and matters related to conversion or eligibility for marriage, 39-year-old Father Yeghishe Derderian, who had been elected *locum tenens* on 7 November 1949, deferred the pending patriarchal election, arguing that as long as negotiations for the internationalization of Jerusalem were going on, the patriarchate should avoid applying for recognition to either the Jordanian or Israeli governments. During his long tenure as *locum tenens*, however, he made numerous enemies within the monastic brotherhood and the lay community, who accused him of misusing funds collected for refugees and making a personal fortune. In 1951 his name was put to the Communist Party leadership in Armenia by the Council on Armenian Church Affairs as a possible candidate to become an aide to the then ailing catholicos of All Armenians, Gevork VI (1945–54),[21] but Derderian himself discouraged the proposition.

At the end of 1955, however, Archbishop Tiran Nersoyan and a few other fellow members of the St James Brotherhood returned to Jerusalem, and soon asked for an investigation of the patriarchate's finances during the past six years, as well as for a reform in its overall financial administration. They also took action to secure the election of a new patriarch, rejecting Derderian's argument and pointing out that the newly elected Greek patriarch had soon been recognized by both Israel and Jordan. On 28 July 1956 this dissident group achieved a significant victory, when a General Assembly meeting of the brotherhood, held at their insistence, refused to approve the fiscal report presented by Derderian, and established a three-man commission to study the issue of the patriarchal election and report back to the assembly in early September.

Derderian concluded that Nersoyan himself coveted the office of patriarch and had found numerous supporters within both the secular community and the monastic brotherhood. The laity was critical of the way the monastery was administered by the upper clergy and supported Nersoyan to indicate its desire for a share in the management of the patriarchate. An American citizen, Nersoyan was certainly better educated than Derderian, and had undertaken pastoral work in London (1940–4) and New York (1944–55). Derderian, however, enjoyed the support of the Jordanian government. The British Embassy in Amman reported that Derderian's pastimes were reported to include playing poker with Sa'd Jum'ah, an influential official in the ministry of the interior.[22] Following Jum'ah's appointment as ambassador in Tehran, Bahjat al-Talhuni, the head of the royal *diwan*, became Derderian's most ardent backer.

The dispute between Derderian and Nersoyan was primarily of a personal nature, but was soon affected by political turmoil both in Jordan and within the Armenian church in the Middle East. The Jordanian monarchy was under pressure at the time from radical pan-Arab nationalist and left-wing forces, and was hence very sensitive to even the slightest of leftist manifestations. It reportedly feared that all Christians in Israel were very much under the influence of communism. And since it regarded Israel as a centre of communist influence, it believed that having the head of any church in Jerusalem under any sort of suspicion of pro-Soviet association involved serious security risks. It was also believed that a strict mail censorship existed in Jordan, and hence all matters relating in any way to the relationship between the USSR and Soviet Armenia (or the churches there) and churches in Jordan should be rigorously avoided in any open correspondence.[23] On the other hand, elections for the office of the Armenian catholicos of Cilicia, based in Antelias, had recently become an arena of intense rivalry between the anti-Soviet Dashnak Party and its Armenian opponents, who preferred to retain links with the Holy See at Etchmiadzin.[24] Although both Nersoyan and Derderian were considered to be fully loyal to Etchmiadzin, the latter – believed to be the less principled of the two – manipulated the rivalry between the two catholicosates, seeking Dashnak support with promises of eventually transferring Jerusalem's allegiance to Antelias, and threatening Etchmiadzin that he would do the same if it went against his wishes.

But for the moment, and in a desperate attempt to cling to his privileges, Derderian obstructed, as *locum tenens*, the convening of the established commission and was widely believed to have arranged – through denunciation, and probably bribery – the order which Nersoyan received from the Jordanian government on 28 July to leave the country. He was accused of being a communist, having written in 1942 a book titled *A Christian Approach to Communism*.[25] Nersoyan argued that the book had originally been a paper delivered to a group in London, mostly Anglicans, who had been considering then what might be done to help the Russian Orthodox church after the Second World War. There had initially been no thought of publication, until the archbishop of Canterbury, William Temple (1942–4), had become interested and pressed him to have the essay published. It was indeed published, almost as it stood, and had an unexpected circulation in the Near East. Nersoyan said that his book was 'quite blatantly anti-Communist to anyone who took the trouble to read it', but its trenchant attacks on some forms of anti-communism and its wide admissions about the vitality of the USSR, however, had already made trouble in Armenian circles, perhaps in conjunction with his absolute loyalty to Etchmiadzin.[26] One British Foreign Office civil servant noted, for example,

> that the Archbishop's claim that his book is 'blatantly anti-Communist' is scarcely true. Although the present atheism of the USSR is deplored, the Communist State is praised and equated with Christian teachings and the book consists of suggestions on how Christianity should adapt itself to make more appeal to those already living according to the provisions of the dialectic.[27]

Later, and probably to keep the charges of pro-communist bias on the front burner, Nersoyan was accused of having communicated with a Soviet agent called Yanchenko who had visited Jordan in February 1957 disguised as a journalist. Derderian also produced a letter addressed to the Soviet ambassador in Beirut, Sergei Kiktiev, and supposedly written by Nersoyan on 2 November 1956, in which he asked the ambassador to approach and influence the catholicos of All Armenians, Vazgen I (1955–94). He promised that his election as patriarch of Jerusalem and his taking charge of the campaign in the name of Etchmiadzin against the Dashnaks and the newly elected pro-Dashnak catholicos of Cilicia would result in driving away Derderian. Nersoyan, in turn, produced seven pages of argument to prove that the letter was a forgery, and was able to sway the British and US embassies to his point of view.

Nersoyan and his supporters managed to have the execution of the deportation order postponed. On 19 August 1956, however, the minister of the interior issued another such order on the grounds that Nersoyan was interfering in Jordanian politics and was in contact with a foreign state. Nersoyan reacted vigorously this time and filed a case before the Jordanian Supreme Court. He also saw both the king and Prime Minister Ibrahim Hashim. Moreover, some members of the Armenian community submitted a petition to the king in Nersoyan's favour, and the expulsion order was suspended until the Supreme Court revoked, on 17 September, all accusations against Nersoyan and annulled the deportation order.

With Nersoyan appearing to have weathered the storm and Derderian himself facing mounting local pressure, Derderian left Jerusalem on 19 September without giving any official notice to the brotherhood and after having appointed Archbishop Hairig Arslanian as his vicar. While he was still in Amman, fourteen brothers asked him not to leave Jordan, so that patriarchal elections could be held as soon as possible. Derderian, however, did not return, and eventually turned up with his confidant, Father Shahe Ajamian, in Etchmiadzin to raise support. Catholicos Vazgen I, however, urged Derderian, in view of the accusations of misconduct raised against him, to resign and not to return to Jerusalem. Derderian, indeed, did not appear in Jerusalem after returning to Jordan on 19 November.

Meanwhile, another deportation order had been served on Nersoyan on 27 September. The latter appealed again to the Supreme Court, but was deported to Beirut by the police on 9 October even though his case was still being heard. The expulsion caused consternation in the Armenian community. Shops were closed in the Old City, and a procession headed by members of the brotherhood made its way from the patriarchate to the governor's office, demanding Nersoyan's return. Soon afterwards, the General Assembly of the brotherhood deposed Derderian from his offices of *locum tenens* and grand sacristan, and appointed the 72-year-old Bishop Suren Kemhajian as chief administrator of the patriarchate until Nersoyan, who was nominated to replace Derderian as *locum tenens*, could take over his new office. These decisions were communicated to Hasan al-Katib, the governor of Jerusalem. The Jordanian government, however, did not formally accept Derderian's dismissal.

Soon, the political climate in Jordan changed drastically. During the general election of 21 October 1956 – the freest that Jordan had ever experienced – the opposition pan-Arab nationalist National Socialist Party won the single largest number of seats in Parliament. Its chairman, Sulayman al-Nabulsi, was appointed prime minister. On 24 October the deportation order was revoked by the Supreme Court, and the new government agreed to Nersoyan's return on 15 November. He was given a hero's welcome and immediately elected as *locum tenens*. Behind the scenes, the new government reportedly even attempted to mediate in the dispute, but Derderian refused to resign. It was probably after this futile mediation attempt that the government formally recognized Nersoyan as *locum tenens* on 16 December.

On 19 December, the General Assembly of the brotherhood proceeded

with the election process by nominating five candidates for the office of patriarch. Derderian received only one vote out of twenty-three and could not
enter the final list of candidates. The election itself was scheduled for 20
December, but Derderian managed to have it postponed by contesting in the
courts the legality of his dismissal and disputing Nersoyan's election as *locum
tenens*. This plea began to be heard only on 13 February 1957 and was
dismissed on 17 March. Meanwhile Derderian had been expelled from the
brotherhood, reduced to the rank of a simple bishop and suspended from all
religious and ecclesiastical functions by a decree of Catholicos Vazgen I.

After the rejection of Derderian's plea by the courts, the patriarchate felt
free to proceed on 20 March with the election, and Nersoyan was lawfully
elected patriarch. However, Derderian had filed, very early that morning, a
further suit in the Jerusalem Court of First Instance. The notification from the
court asking the governor of Jerusalem to forbid the election *pendente lite*
reached the latter's office at 10.45 a.m. He dispatched an urgent written
order to the patriarchate asking them to hold up proceedings, but Nersoyan
reportedly opened the letter only a quarter of an hour after the election had
taken place and therefore considered himself to have been duly elected as
patriarch. Five days later, Bishop Shenork Kaloustian, another American citizen and a Nersoyan supporter, was elected grand sacristan.

Soon after these developments, however, the king and Prime Minister al-
Nabulsi sharply disagreed on the future course of Jordan's foreign policy. The
king suspected that his opponents were preparing a coup against the monarchy. He therefore forced al-Nabulsi to resign, put him under house arrest and
imposed martial law. Many pro-western officials, dismissed by the al-Nabulsi
cabinet, including Jum'ah, al-Katib, and 'Abd al-Mun'im al-Rifa'i (see
below), were returned to their posts, and the fortunes of Nersoyan, which
had sharply improved during al-Nabulsi's brief tenure, were again reversed.

In July 1957 the Jerusalem Court of First Instance heard Derderian's case
and ruled on 1 August that the Ottoman statute law dealing with the
Armenian patriarchal elections must be treated as a self-contained code and
interpreted without reference to the canon law and previous practice of the
Armenian church. Since the said code had made no provision for the possibility of a *locum tenens* having to be deposed either because he refused to carry
out the election of a patriarch or for other scandalous reasons, the court ruled
that Derderian should still be recognized as *locum tenens*, and everything else
done by the patriarchate since his dismissal was illegal. No administrative
action was taken by the authorities, however, to withdraw their *de facto*
recognition of Nersoyan, who continued to administer the patriarchate as
'Armenian patriarch-elect'.

The brotherhood, now headed by Nersoyan, went to the Court of Appeal
to reverse this judgment, arguing that civil courts and administrative bodies
had no jurisdiction in the exclusively ecclesiastical acts of expelling and
suspending Derderian. The Appeal Court, indeed, quashed the previous

judgement on 22 October and declared that the courts had no jurisdiction over the patriarchal election. Derderian appealed as a last resort to the Court of Cassation, which, however, upheld, on 4 December, the decision of the Court of Appeal.

Meanwhile, Nersoyan had asked the US ambassador to intervene on his behalf. Although American consular officers in Jerusalem appeared to be satisfied that Nersoyan was not a communist agent and had been informed that New York had nothing against him from his sojourn in the USA, he was told that the USA had no *locus standi* to intervene. The same response came from Charles Johnston, the British ambassador in Jordan. The British government wanted to avoid any row in the Armenian church, which, they believed, would then be exploited by the Soviets. In a tacit endorsement of Nersoyan's position, a Foreign Office official wrote: 'It is certainly not desirable from the purely ecclesiastical point of view that all the Armenians of the diaspora should give up their centuries-old allegiance to Etchmiadzin'.[28] This was not seen, however, as a sufficient motive 'to get mixed up in local politics in Jerusalem'.[29] Johnston told Nersoyan that:

> it was our fixed policy not to intervene in matters where no direct British interest was involved, or to do anything which might suggest that we were still trying to run the country. In fact it might do more harm than good if I were to say a word on the Archbishop's behalf, since the present Jordanian regime, however friendly, were jealous of their independence, and might react strongly against anything which seemed to them like unjustified interference.[30]

Nersoyan's attempts to use his contacts in the Anglican church hierarchy in Jerusalem to push the British and the Americans to adopt a more favourable attitude towards his cause also proved unsuccessful.

Indeed, not only was the king's endorsement (*berat*) of Nersoyan's election delayed, but on 30 January 1958 another order for his deportation as an 'undesirable' was prepared for the king's signature. This understandably caused renewed agitation among the Armenian community: shops were closed again in protest and a group of youngsters entered the patriarchate courtyard in an attempt to resist execution of the order. The monks advised Nersoyan not to leave the convent, so that the government would have to send in the police to fetch him, and this would provide them with an excellent opportunity to demonstrate their loyalty. On the other hand, a series of appeals to the king and his ministers succeeded in getting the order's execution suspended pending further consideration. Finally, the governor of Jerusalem informed the Armenian patriarchate 'that the deportation order was being held in abeyance, that Archbishop Tiran Nersoyan's election as Patriarch would not be approved, and that the election of a new Patriarch should be held soon under the supervision of the Jordanian Government'.[31] The government further gave its assurance that Derderian would be prevented from returning to Jerusalem and would not be allowed to stand in the forthcoming fresh elections.

The Anglican church was in sympathy with Nersoyan's cause, believing that the duly elected head of the Armenian community in Jerusalem should not be set aside by government action on the basis of accusations made by an evidently aggrieved party. Nersoyan was highly regarded at Lambeth Palace as an outstanding member of his church as far as intelligence and integrity were concerned. Church of England officials believed that he enjoyed the full support of the Armenian monks and laity in Jerusalem and had almost certainly no communist sympathies – being interested only in preserving religious links with Armenians in the USSR. Furthermore, they disliked Derderian's manner and believed that Nersoyan's accusers were 'men of a very venal character'.[32] The secretary-general of the Church of England Council for Foreign Relations urged the British Foreign Office on 1 February to take every opportunity to have the deportation order reversed. The most that the latter agreed to, however, was that the archbishop of Canterbury, Geoffrey Fisher (1945–61), should invite Jordan's new ambassador in London, 'Abd al-Mun'im al-Rifa'i, to Lambeth Palace and discuss with him the issue of Nersoyan's deportation. On 28 February the ambassador denied that there had been any deportation order and told Fisher that his government did not believe any of the accusations of pro-communism against Nersoyan, but had not recognized him as patriarch, for it did not wish to get mixed up in internal Armenian quarrels in light of the accusations of irregularity in the election brought by Derderian. Indeed, on 29 March, the military governor of Jerusalem said that Nersoyan would be permitted to reside in Jerusalem, but that the authorities would continue to deal with Chief Administrator Kemhajian in matters concerning the Armenian church.

On the afternoon of Saturday 30 August, however, Nersoyan was stopped by a strong military and police force on his way to a service at the tomb of the Virgin Mary. He was taken to the airport without luggage or passport and ordered to board the Middle East Airlines plane making the normal flight to Beirut. A request for a twenty-four hour delay in the execution of the deportation was refused. In the meantime, the police also went to the Armenian convent in order to search three rooms, where they believed arms and subversive literature were kept. People barricaded themselves behind the monastery gates to prevent the entry of government troops, who had to force their way in. There was some fighting, and around twenty persons were arrested. The convent was put under heavy police guard, and the three rooms were searched. However, nothing was found.

The British consul-general, Charles Stewart, deplored the manner of deportation, but the Foreign Office wanted to keep out of the issue. Archbishop Fisher, however, protested to Ambassador al-Rifa'i that Nersoyan's deportation was without any justification. The US consulate-general in Jerusalem had no prior knowledge of the deportation, and the vice-consul, who was at the airport at the time on other business, was unable to render Nersoyan any assistance. Later, the US ambassador in Amman was instructed to express Washington's concern to the Jordanian government at the deportation. The governor of Jerusalem explained that the order for the immediate deportation had come from Amman, which had received new information that Nersoyan had been engaging 'again' in communist activities.[33]

Nersoyan described his deportation 'as being partly due to the machinations of Bishop Derderian and partly to motives of revenge on the part of certain Jordanian officials whose requests for money [he] had refused'.[34] The dissension in the Armenian patriarchate in Jerusalem had grown worse and become unduly complicated, he said, because of the ill will, corruption and cynicism of the Jordanian government, since 'all the decent people in Jordan were in prison or in exile; that there was not a single individual in the present Administration who was not corrupt, and that his troubles were solely due to his refusal to pay bribes'.[35] The Dashnaks also received a fair share of the blame. Nersoyan wrote that:

> since May 1957 the hostile attitude of the Jordan Government towards the Armenian Patriarchate of Jerusalem is due to the underground activities of Dashnaks. They fabricated forged papers, sent in false reports, bribed corrupt officials, enlisted the help of certain Lebanese and American high officials and in the end, after a sustained effort of sixteen months, they succeeded in inducing the Jordan Government to deport [Nersoyan].

'There is no doubt', continued Nersoyan, that if he 'had denounced openly the Catholicos of Etchmiadzin and had recognized the jurisdiction of the Antelias catholicate in Beirut, [he] would not be in his present predicament'. He agreed that Soviet efforts to win the sympathy of Christian minorities of the region should be counteracted, but the western powers should not go as far as subsidizing specific political factions within separate Christian communities (like the Dashnaks among the Armenians) to help them take control of the church and turn it into an agency for political action and propaganda. He opposed the Dashnak attempt to sever all relations of the Armenian churches in the Diaspora with Etchmiadzin, for he believed that good Christians in the Soviet Union should not be abandoned. When the State Department openly helped the Dashnaks and sponsored the newly elected catholicos at Antelias, argued Nersoyan, it brought upon itself the opposition of the main bulk of the conservative Armenian church people and put a welcome weapon into the hands of Soviet propagandists.[36] He alleged that Derderian had entered into an agreement with the Dashnaks and the catholicos at Antelias that, in exchange for their full support in his attempt to secure his own restoration, he would – after recovering control of the Jerusalem see – break with Etchmiadzin and declare his allegiance to Antelias.[37]

Even after Nersoyan's deportation, his supporters still had some hope that he might eventually be allowed to return and perhaps even assume the patriarchal throne. Indeed, the king indicated to Bishop Kaloustian that, if the Armenians could convince Prime Minister Samir al-Rifaʿi that Nersoyan had no communist leanings, he might be allowed back in Jordan. Al-Rifaʿi, in turn, said that it would be of assistance to his government if the Armenians could obtain a letter from the Americans or the British clearing Nersoyan of suspicions of communist sympathies.[38]

At the end of 1958, however, renewal of the residence permits of Bishop Kaloustian and two other non-Jordanian priests was refused because of their behaviour at the time of Nersoyan's deportation. The governor of Jerusalem alleged that when the soldiers had been trying to enter a room in the convent these three clerics had slammed the door against them, breaking the ankle of a soldier. The military authorities had wished to arrest and try them under martial law, but the governor had suggested the alternative of non-renewal of residence permits at the end of the year, which would ultimately force them to leave the country. The governor reported that the three persons concerned appealed against this refusal on the grounds that their presence was necessary to attend to the problems of the election of a new patriarch, and he recommended therefore to the Ministry of the Interior that their permits be renewed for 1959. His recommendation was accepted, but not before the news of the initial refusal had leaked to the foreign press, resulting in an American inquiry about the reasons behind the deportation, and a telegram from Archbishop Fisher to King Husayn urging the immediate suspension of the deportation until further inquiry into the matter.

Despite this worrying incident, the Church of England Council on Foreign Relations still believed, on the basis of Kaloustian's interviews with the king and prime minister, that things were going better from Nersoyan's point of view. On 16 January 1959, Archbishop Fisher sent a letter to Chief Administrator Kemhajian, knowing well that the latter would show it to the Jordanian government. In that letter, Fisher stated specifically that 'in my opinion, and according to all the information in my possession, Archbishop Tiran Nersoyan has never been a Communist nor even had any Communist sympathies' and that his wish to remain under the spiritual jurisdiction of the catholicos at Etchmiadzin 'should not be regarded as having any political implication whatsoever, since the Patriarchate of Jerusalem has always recognised the Catholicos of Etchmiadzin as being Supreme Catholicos of all Armenians'. Pro-Nersoyan Armenians indeed distributed copies of the archbishop's letter to the king, the prime minister and other appropriate authorities, and when a delegation from the patriarchate called on the king and prime minister in late February, they were told that their case would be considered and a decision whether to allow Nersoyan to return to Jordan, and, if so, in what capacity, would be given soon.[39] In April 1959, the British Foreign Office received a visit from a representative of the World Council of Churches to try out the ground and investigate the possibilities of an approach to King Husayn on Nersoyan's behalf during his forthcoming visit to Britain and the USA. Now that the American government was seen to have taken matters up with the Jordanian authorities, even some Foreign Office officials thought it would be useful if they could, in turn, tell the Jordanians that the British government, too, had no evidence of communist leanings on Nersoyan's part and did not seriously think that his book, written in 1942, could be taken as evidence of such convictions. Ultimately the Americans decided to take no further part in the affair, however, and King Husayn was told by State Department officials 'that the Americans no longer wished to suggest that in considering the case of Nersoyan he should take account of the views they had previously expressed on the subject'.[40]

The Jordanian government began to show clear signs that it wanted to see new patriarchal elections. Twice in December 1959, the governor of Jerusalem asked Armenian bishops whether, if the government would not accept a candidate chosen as patriarch, the candidate receiving the second-largest number of votes would be elected in his place. The bishops replied, however, that custom demanded that, under such circumstances, an entirely new election would have to be arranged. Then, in an apparent attempt to force the brotherhood to organize a new election, three brothers, Bishop Kaloustian, Father Torgom Manoogian, the head of the seminary (both US citizens) and Father Vazgen Kibrislian, a Lebanese national, whose residence permits had been briefly withheld the year before, were bundled into a jeep on 2 January 1960 and escorted by the police first to the airport at Jerusalem and then, since no plane was available to take them to Beirut, from there to the airport in Amman, whence they were forcibly deported. The governor explained that they had been expelled because they were known to be intransigently pro-Nersoyan, so that while they were present there was no hope of any compromise on a third candidate. Kaloustian later alleged that the brotherhood had at that stage been on the verge of agreeing in principle to the election of Kemhajian, despite his age, as patriarch, and blamed Derderian for engineering the deportations by paying considerable sums of money to Jordanian officials.

Following the expulsion of the three clerics, Nersoyan submitted to the brotherhood his resignation both as *locum tenens* and as patriarch-elect. He retired to the eastern United States, where he would become – until his death on 1 September 1989 at the age of eighty-five – the guiding spirit of the St Nerses Shnorhali Armenian seminary, established in 1962. Kemhajian sent a copy of Nersoyan's letter of resignation to the governor and said that the brotherhood would proceed with new elections.

Derderian had meanwhile attempted to collect signatures for a petition asking for his reinstallation as *locum tenens*, but only six or seven brothers had reportedly agreed to sign. On the morning of 26 March, however, he was escorted by the police to the Armenian convent and installed there just as elections for a new *locum tenens* were about to start. Derderian claimed that he was still *locum tenens* and that elections were, therefore, unnecessary, or that he should preside over them. After a heated discussion, the governor post-poned the elections until 4 April, before which date he promised to inquire into Derderian's status. He meanwhile insisted that Derderian should be allowed to remain in the convent and made it known that fifty leading Armenians would be held responsible for the future good conduct of the community. Consequently, when a crowd of 200 women barracked Derderian, accusing him of immorality and demanding his expulsion, around eighty young laymen were arrested as instigators of the incident. The timing of this move, on the eve of the Muslim feast of 'Id al-Fitr, was designed to prevent Armenian represen-tations to the government during the next few days.

Reaction among other Christian churches was sympathetic to the Armenians, but various forms of self-interest dictated caution. According to the British consul-general, for example:

> the Greek Patriarch regards himself as Derderian's intellectual superior and is also supposed to share some of his less spiritual proclivities. Nersoyan, on the other hand, he regarded as a dangerous opponent, who might easily have caused him considerable trouble over the restoration of the Church of the Holy Sepulchre.[41]

On 2 April an Armenian delegation presented arguments to the minister of the interior that the governor's letter of 1956 recognizing Nersoyan as *locum tenens* made it impossible for the government to say that Derderian had not been legally deposed. Another delegation was told by Prime Minister Hazza' al-Majali that Derderian had simply been sent to the convent at his own desire and could be regarded either as a member of the brotherhood or as a 'guest'. He would not be a candidate for the patriarchal elections, and his legal claim to be *locum tenens* had been left undecided.

The Armenian community in Jerusalem believed that Derderian had made as much as £30,000 selling jewels from the crucifixes and other relics of the Armenian church, and was now spending the sum oiling the wheels in Amman. As Derderian's opponents had feared, the next move was the gover-nor's decision on 5 April to terminate forthwith Kemhajian's appointment as chief administrator and replace him with Derderian's former deputy, Bishop Hairig Arslanian. This decision was correctly interpreted as an implicit recog-nition by the government that Derderian was still *locum tenens*. The archbishop of Canterbury cabled King Husayn expressing grave concern at the appointment of a new chief administrator without consultation with the brotherhood, and at the enforced reinsertion of Derderian into the convent, while a representative of the World Council of Churches called at the US State Department to discuss the possibility of raising the matter before the United Nations Commissioner on Human Rights. Even the Jordanian foreign minister, Musa Nasir, a Christian, privately asked Charles Johnston to use British influence to stop the palace's intervention in the Armenian affair.

While Derderian was keeping strictly to his rooms in the convent and refusing to enter the cathedral or perform any religious function, Arslanian rapidly dismissed pro-Nersoyan officials in the convent. High-handed tactics were used against members of the brotherhood until fifteen of them (out of twenty-five residing in Jordan at the time) agreed to sign a letter to the governor asking for the restoration of Derderian as *locum tenens*. The governor also received a letter from Bishop Norayr Bogharian stating that in the considered opinion of the brotherhood, Derderian's dismissal and expulsion in 1956 had been invalid under the ecclesiastical law of the patriarchate. Meanwhile, in mid-April, Arslanian also sent a telegram to Catholicos Vazgen I asking on behalf of 'a majority' of the brotherhood of Jerusalem for the cancellation of Derderian's suspension. Derderian said he wished to remain under the jurisdiction of Etchmiadzin but made no secret of the fact that he would be ready to switch over to Antelias if there were no response from the former. Vazgen I named a three-man commission to inquire into the situation, but the Jordanian government refused visas for two of its members, who were Soviet citizens, and only Bishop Serovpé Manoogian, the Armenian bishop in Paris, arrived in Jerusalem in mid-May and went ahead with his inquiries alone, showing an unconcealed inclination towards Derderian.

On 2 June, just before another Muslim feast, 'Id al-Adha, the governor again called at the convent, with the vice-mayor, and announced that, in response to the wishes of a majority of the brotherhood, he had agreed to the restoration of Derderian as *locum tenens*. Failure to recognize him as such would be construed henceforth as disobedience to the government's wishes, and arrangements for the election of a new patriarch should be put in train. Any non-Jordanians who did not like this decision could leave the country, while the Jordanians, who did not agree, could give up their nationality.

On 6 June, Derderian, as *locum tenens*, called a General Assembly meeting of the brotherhood and, by thirteen votes to eleven, expelled eleven brothers, who lived abroad. The list included Nersoyan, Kaloustian, Manoogian and Kibrislian. Their dismissal was carried out to reduce the number of members of the brotherhood, and hence the necessary quorum for the patriarchal election. That same day, Derderian also asked the governor and immediately received permission to hold elections, despite the fact that the offices were closed because of the feast. He was elected patriarch on 8 June receiving eighteen votes out of twenty-three. He immediately assumed full administrative duties, but was still not permitted to officiate in the church. He therefore cabled Vazgen I for confirmation of his election and for the removal of the ban on his officiating.

With the law courts closed during the feast, it was impossible for Derderian's opponents to appeal for any postponement of the elections. It was believed that the governor himself had advised Derderian on such a timing of events. Moreover, on 9 June, a telegram from Vazgen I cancelled the suspension he had imposed on Derderian and restored him to the rank of archbishop. On that afternoon, Derderian finally proceeded to the cathedral for the first time in three years and officiated at a service there.

Nevertheless, on June 11 Kemhajian appealed to the Supreme Court to annul the forced reintroduction of Derderian into the brotherhood and his appointment as *locum tenens*. The hearing began in July. The government refused, however, on the grounds of 'public policy', to allow the governor's file on the Armenian patriarchate to be produced. The court, therefore, had to rely on contradictory oral testimony. It seemed to prefer the testimony of the police officer in charge of status quo affairs over that of the vice-mayor, and ruled on 3 August that in the absence of any evidence of written orders it was not convinced that the words of the governor had at any time constituted an administrative order. The opponents of Derderian, therefore, had not shown cause why the governor's actions and Derderian's election should be annulled. Kemhajian's counsel were quick to seize on this finding, and cabled members of the cabinet that if, in fact, there had been no administrative order from the governor, then Derderian's whole position and every action since his return to the convent rested on no authority whatsoever. On 5 August, Kemhajian belatedly discovered an exchange of letters dated 6 June between the governor and Derderian, published in *Sion*. His counsel immediately made them the basis for a further petition to the court, which agreed to hear the case after 13 August. However, on 10 August, the king handed over to Derderian the royal *berat* approving his election, and Kemhajian had to drop the new proceedings.

Derderian was enthroned on 21 August at a ceremony held in St James's cathedral. The Jordanian authorities, the consular corps, and the other churches were well represented, with the notable exception of the Church of England. The archbishop of Canterbury, however, later sent him a message of congratulation. After the enthronement, twenty-eight brothers, including Kemhajian, filed past Derderian to kiss his cross and ring, and so accept his authority.

This climax seemed not to please the Dashnaks. Derderian had outmanœuvred them and used the threat to transfer Jerusalem's allegiance to Antelias only to get a pardon from Catholicos Vazgen. In early August, Nersoyan alleged that he had been approached by the Dashnaks in the USA, who had promised to support him if only he would break with Etchmiadzin. Nersoyan said that he had refused the suggestion absolutely.

Derderian had thus used his advantages as a Jordanian citizen well acquainted with the Jordanian political and administrative system and of having influential friends very close to King Husayn. Nersoyan, on the other hand, was an outsider, somewhat stubborn by character, and had opted for and gained the support of the secular community. His attempts to secure British and American backing, were, on the whole, fruitless. The Jordanian government may have been suspicious of the internal reform that he intended to introduce, lest it arouse similar demands and agitation among the other Christian communities. The events of the 1950s left some deep scars in the

Armenian community of Jerusalem, as seen by the great reluctance of its members to talk about this subject even some thirty years later.[42]

The Armenian Community and Church in Jerusalem after 1967

Derderian's subsequent thirty-year tenure is seen today as a grey page in Armenian church history. Derderian was still patriarch when the 1967 Arab–Israeli war practically removed the frontier across Jerusalem. The resumption of unrestricted contact between all Armenians and the monastery, and the re-establishment of the patriarchate's full control over its assets in the Israeli sector, made life much easier for Armenians. They also resumed burying their dead in their old cemetery on Mount Zion, just outside the monastery walls. On the other hand, pilgrimage from neighbouring Arab lands stopped, and some areas of the Armenian quarter inhabited by Arabs were expropriated and added to the renovated Jewish quarter. The Armenians of the newly occupied territories preserved their Jordanian citizenship, which enabled them to travel freely to other Middle Eastern countries. As patriarch, Derderian also presided over the long-delayed restoration of the church of the Holy Sepulchre in 1963, and, after the establishment of diplomatic relations between Jordan and the USSR, hosted a reconciliation in Jerusalem between the catholici of Etchmiadzin and Antelias. In 1975, the new Alex and Mary Manoogian Theological Seminary, which can house 100 seminarians, was inaugurated, aiming to make Jerusalem the principal supplier of priests to Armenian diasporan communities. Its inauguration was the occasion for one of the most important gatherings in many years, with the visit to Jerusalem of the catholicos of Etchmiadzin, the donor Manoogian himself, and many other church dignitaries and lay leaders of different communities in the Diaspora, including the once deported Archbishop Shenork Kaloustian, who had been elected Armenian patriarch of Istanbul in 1961. Another Armenian benefactor from the USA, Edward Mardigian, sponsored the construction in the monastery of a new museum.

Derderian's reign will be long remembered, however, for the numerous controversies that hit the Jerusalem see. In March 1967, for example, it was discovered that twenty-eight manuscripts had been stolen from the St James collection, probably because of their covers, inlaid with precious stones, and that twenty-three of them, ranging in date from AD 1262 to the eighteenth century and valued at $500,000, were being auctioned in London. Prompt action by Catholicos Vazgen I and Armenian communities throughout the world forced the vendor to withdraw them, the auction was called off, and the manuscripts were returned to Jerusalem. Although the synod of the patri-archate and the Jordanian government officially accused Bishops Kaloustian and Kemhajian of organizing the theft in 1959, they did not press charges, alleging that the crime was covered by the royal amnesty of 1965. Most people seem to be in agreement, however, with Kaloustian, who, in turn, accused Derderian and his close associates, Arslanian and Ajamian, of being behind the burglary. Kaloustian suggests that one reason why Vazgen I did not seek Derderian's punishment again was his age-old fear that the latter might yet transfer his allegiance to Antelias.[43]

In the early seventies, the alleged willingness of the Armenian patriarchate to sell land and property to the Israel Lands Administration prompted disquiet in the Armenian lay community and ultimately led to a public rupture with the Israeli government. Ajamian, whom Derderian had made a member of the brotherhood in 1960, had been responsible for those sales. As chancellor, he was the second most powerful person in the patriarchate. Following a dispute with the patriarch, however, he was relieved in 1982 of all his functions in the brotherhood. It has been suggested that the breach between the two concerned the management of property, and that Derderian had become apprehensive of Ajamian's growing power.

However, this time it was Israel's turn to intervene in the patriarchate's internal administrative matters. Teddy Kollek, the Israeli mayor of Jerusalem, wanted to keep Ajamian in the monastery at all costs. The scion of an immensely rich family, charming and multilingual, the latter had extremely good relations with Kollek and was a frequent host to his foreign guests. He spoke frequently at Israeli-sponsored conferences on genocide on the similarity of the fates of Jews and Armenians, and used to extol the virtues of an Israeli administration over a unified Jerusalem. He had also voted against World Council of Churches conference resolutions critical of Israel. Kollek and three high officials, therefore, reportedly visited the convent on the eve of the deposition meeting of the synod in order to prevent the action, but failed. Later, and in order to put pressure on the patriarch, the Israeli authorities withheld tax exemption and permits for repair projects. When Derderian attempted to replace Ajamian with Archbishop Karekin Kazanjian, who had arrived from Australia, Kollek and the minister of the interior attempted to get the latter deported, explaining that his deportation would prevent the disintegration of the patriarchate and the strengthening there of pro-Jordanian and anti-Israeli elements. The Greek, Latin and Armenian patriarchs appealed to the Israeli president for an explanation and threatened to protest by closing the holy places to the many pilgrims expected to come at Christmas time. This public furore obliged the government to desist from deporting Kazanjian, but his visitor's visa was not renewed, and he remained in Jerusalem without a residency permit, laying him open to further government and municipality pressures. Ajamian continued to appear at Israeli receptions and was granted passage by the Israelis to Jordan without customs checks. He sought the intervention of Catholicos Vazgen I, remaining in his office in the patriarchate and continuing to use all his former privileges. The dispute again divided the patriarchate and also involved the secular community. Violence broke out between the supporters of Derderian and Ajamian, and twelve people were injured during the Easter procession in 1984. In May 1985 arsonists set fire to Ajamian's house, and two years later a supporter of his was stabbed to death. In both cases police intervention was required to restore order. Subsequent developments revealed that Ajamian and Raphael Levy, the Israeli district commissioner of the ministry of the interior in Jerusalem, were involved in bribe-taking, smuggling and currency offences. In November 1986, Levy and Ajamian were arrested. The former was charged with misuse of public office, bribe-taking and various currency offences. Ajamian, however, was released on heavy bail after having been held in police detention for over a month. He too was reportedly suspected of bribery, smuggling and the unauthorized possession of firearms. It was not denied that Kollek had again tried to secure Ajamian's release.[44] Finally, when Derderian died on 1 February 1990, aged eighty, a private account belonging to him was discovered in a Swiss bank, with only a few dollars remaining, although thousands had allegedly been siphoned off from patriarchate funds.

Shortly after Derderian's death, Archbishop Torgom Manoogian returned to Jerusalem from the USA and was immediately elected as *locum tenens*. He succeeded in securing wide-ranging support, and, on 22 March, was elected patriarch, receiving forty votes out of a possible fifty-five, and was conse-crated on 27 October, inheriting, as one periodical said, 'not only . . . the rich history of Jerusalem Patriarchate, but also its tarnished image'.[45] One of the earliest symbolic acts, which he presided over, was to reinter on 14 September 1993 the remains of Nersoyan, as the latter had wished, in the special tomb of the Armenian patriarchs at the church of St Saviour. Ajamian, who had reportedly made an unsuccessful attempt to persuade the Israeli ministry of religious affairs to interfere in the elections on his behalf, soon left for newly independent Armenia, where he is, at the time of writing, the Dean of the newly established faculty of theology at Yerevan State University. Kazanjian, in turn, was elected Armenian patriarch of Istanbul on 5 September 1990, succeeding Kaloustian, but died in 1998.

There were approximately fifty members of the brotherhood in 1992, more than half of whom were scattered worldwide, serving various Armenian communities. The number of seminarians has recently declined to about twenty, as, since 1979, the Turkish authorities no longer allow young Armenians expressing a desire to study in Jerusalem to leave Istanbul, claim-ing that the Armenian Secret Army for the Liberation of Armenia (ASALA), a terrorist Armenian organization active against Turkish targets in the late 1970s and early 1980s, has a strong influence in Jerusalem.[46] Under Manoogian, the patriarchate has ceased to make headlines with its scandals, but as long as there is no fair and comprehensive peace between Israel and her Arab neighbours, and as long as the future status of Jerusalem is in dispute, further interference by political authorities in the internal affairs of the Armenian patriarchate cannot be ruled out.

Meanwhile, the growing political and economic instability in and around Jerusalem has caused a continuous Armenian emigration. The Armenian community has shrunk to less than 3,000, but the great majority of laymen who inhabit the Old City continue to live within the monastery. Less than one-fourth, including all the 'locals', live in the structures surrounding the monastery walls, and a few of the wealthiest families entirely outside the Armenian quarter, in the high-status northern suburbs of Jerusalem and in Ramallah. While some of the laymen, who live within the monastery, work for the church as clerks or teachers in the church-run school, most are independent shopkeepers and businessmen, whose workplaces are outside the monastery in the central business streets of the Old City. They specialize in jewellery, souvenir shops and photography. Indeed, certain crafts and trades, like ceramics, goldsmithing, photography and pharmacy, are considered Armenian specialities. Most Armenians run truly family businesses and employ very few non-Armenians. They usually shun public office or salaried jobs, and only a very few have entered the liberal professions.

Finally, mention should be made that there has been a distinct Armenian Catholic community in Jerusalem for at least two centuries, currently numbering just over 150 people. Catholic Armenians, too, engage in no proselytism among non-Armenians, with the result that no arabization has occurred among them either. The even smaller body of Armenian Protestants, however, do not have a separate religious organization or a communal identity of their own, but belong to various Protestant denominations that are open to non-Armenians as well.[47]

Notes

[1] For some general studies on the history and identity of the Armenian church see M. Ormanian, *The Church of Armenia* (London, 1912; 2nd rev. edn, 1955); Karekin Sarkissian, *The Council of Chalcedon and the Armenian Church* (London, 1965); Papken Catholicos Gulesserian, *The Armenian Church* (New York, 1970); Claire Seda Mouradian, 'The Armenian Apostolic church', in Pedro Ramet (ed.), *Eastern Christianity and Politics in the Twentieth Century*, vol. I: *Christianity under Stress* (Durham, NC and London, 1988), 353–74; Felix Corley, *Armenia and Karabakh: Ancient Faith, Modern War* (London, 1992); Hratch Tchilingirian, *A Brief Historical and Theological Introduction to the Armenian Church* (Montreal, 1995).

[2] Kevork Hintlian, *History of the Armenians in the Holy Land* (Jerusalem, 1976), 13; Avedis K. Sanjian, 'Anastas Vardapet's list of Armenian monasteries in seventh-century Jerusalem: a critical examination', *Le Muséon*, 82, 3–4 (1969), 290; Arthur Hagopian, 'The mosaic affair: Jerusalem's Armenian community and the Antiquities Department aren't talking – again', *Armenian International Magazine (AIM)* (July 1993), 14–15.

[3] Sylva Natalie Manoogian and Taline Satamian, 'A slice of Eden: Armenian Jerusalem at a crossroads', *AIM* (December 1992), 27.

[4] Hintlian, *History*, 4.

[5] Sanjian, 'Anastas', 282.

[6] Victor Azarya, *The Armenian Quarter of Jerusalem* (London, Los Angeles and Berkeley, 1984), 59–60.

[7] On relations between the Armenian church and the Latin East in the Cilician period see Charles A. Frazee, 'The Christian church in Cilician Armenia: its relations with Rome and Constantinople to 1198', *Church History* 45 (1976), 166–84; idem, 'Church and state in the kingdom of Cilician Armenia 1198–1375', *Byzantine Studies*, 3, 2 (1976), 30–58.

[8] Hintlian, *History*, 4, 19–21, 23.

[9] Azarya, *Quarter*, 60.

[10] Avedis K. Sanjian, *The Armenian Communities in Syria under Ottoman Dominion* (Cambridge, Mass., 1965), 97–99.

[11] Ibid., 98, 102.

[12] Roberta Ervine, 'Grigor the Chainbearer (1715–1749): the rebirth of the Armenian patriarchate', in Anthony O'Mahony, Göran Gunner and Kevork Hintlian (eds), *The Christian Heritage in the Holy Land* (London, 1995), 108–11.

[13] See details of successive reforms and reform proposals in Sanjian, *Communities*, 112–16.

[14] Sanjian, *Communities*, 125; Bishop Shahe Ajamian, 'Sultan Abdul Hamid and the Armenian patriarchate of Jerusalem', in Moshe Ma'oz (ed.), *Studies on Palestine during the Ottoman Period* (Jerusalem, 1975), 344–7.

[15] See details in Sanjian, *Communities*, 86.

[16] George A. Bournoutian, *A History of the Armenian People*, vol. II (Costa Mesa, Calif., 1994), 57-9; Sanjian, *Communities*, 81–2, 86; Azarya, *Quarter*, 68–70. For the contribution of Patriarch Garabedian, in particular, to the development of photography in Palestine, see Ruth Victor-Hummel, 'Culture and image: Christians and the beginning of local photography in 19th century Ottoman Palestine', in O'Mahony et al. (eds), *Christian Heritage*, 181–96.

[17] Hintlian, *History*, 16, 40–5; Azarya, *Quarter*, 3.

[18] Bournoutian, *History*, II, 57; Azarya, *Quarter*, 74.

[19] FO371/133892/V1782/17, HM consulate-general, Jerusalem to Levant Dept, FO, 12 March 1958.

[20] Azarya, *Quarter*, 114–17 and Daphne Tsimhoni, *Christian Communities in Jerusalem and the West Bank since 1948* (Westport, 1993), 67–9, have already referred briefly to this crisis in their respective monographs. The latter, in particular, has made use of Jordanian government files, held since 1967 in the Israeli state archives. This article attempts to shed further light on this crisis through the thorough use of British Foreign Office general correspondence (FO371) files kept at the Public Record Office in London.

[21] Stepan Stepaniants, *Hay Arakelakan Ekeghetsin Stalinian Brnapetutian Orok* (The Armenian Apostolic church under the Stalinist dictatorship) (Yerevan, 1994), 227.

[22] FO371/127803/V1781/9, Chancery, Amman to Levant Dept, FO, 2 September 1957; FO371/150887/ V1781/15, Johnston to Beith, 20 May 1960.

[23] FO371/127805/V1783/6, Every to Satterthwaite, 15 September 1957. Israel, in contrast with Jordan, had not banned the Communist Party.

[24] The Dashnak Party (full name in Armenian: Hai Heghapokhakan Dashnaktsutiun, or Armenian Revolutionary Federation) was established in 1890 to improve the social and political conditions of Armenians in both the Ottoman Empire and Imperial Russia. After the Russian Revolutions of 1917, the Dashnaks headed the short-lived independent Republic of Armenia. Long opposed to Bolshevik ideology and practices, the Dashnaks held the Russian communists responsible for the collapse of that independent Armenian state in 1920 and thereafter opposed communist rule in Soviet Armenia. In the 1950s, the Dashnaks were the staunch allies of the anti-communist forces in the Middle East and succeeded in 1956 in having their nominee elected as catholicos in Antelias. The latter's election disrupted relations between Antelias and Etchmiadzin. For the early history of the Dashnak Party see Louise Nalbandian, *The Armenian Revolutionary Movement: The Development of Armenian Political Parties through the Nineteenth Century* (Berkeley and Los Angeles, 1963), 151–78; Hratch Dasnabedian, *History of the Armenian Revolutionary Federation Dashnaktsutiun 1890–1924* (Milan, 1989). Unfortunately, no scholarly study is yet available on the later history of the party.

[25] Tiran Nersoyan, *A Christian Approach to Communism: Ideological Similarities between Dialectical Materialism and Christian Philosophy* (London, 1942).

[26] FO371/133892/V1782/26, Chancery, Beirut to Levant Dept, FO, 12 September 1958; FO371/127805/ V1783/6, Every to Satterthwaite, 15 September 1957.

[27] FO371/133892/V1782/27, FO minute by Riley, 30 September 1958.
[28] FO371/127803/V1781/15, FO minute by Miller, 9 December 1957.
[29] FO371/133892/V1782/8, FO minute by Hadow, 5 February 1958.
[30] FO371/133892/V1782/2, Johnston to Hadow, 15 January 1958.
[31] FO371/133892/V1782/12, HM consulate-general, Jerusalem to Levant Dept, FO, 10 February 1958.
[32] FO371/133892/V1782/1, HM consulate-general, Jerusalem to Levant Dept, FO, 31 December 1957; FO371/133892/V1782/5, Waddams to Rose, 1 February 1958.
[33] FO371/133892/V1782/23, Stewart to Lloyd, 2 September 1958.
[34] FO371/133892/V1782/26, Chancery, Beirut to Levant Dept, FO, 12 September 1958.
[35] FO371/133892/V1782/27, Hadow to Mason, 6 October 1958.
[36] See memorandum by Nersoyan in FO371/133892/V1782/28.
[37] FO371/127803/V1781/15, HM consulate-general, Jerusalem to Levant Dept, FO, 13 November 1957. On the other hand, a lay supporter of Derderian alleged that Nersoyan was sending to the USA those monks in the convent who supported Derderian and replacing them by Lebanese monks who were opposed to Antelias. He claimed that before Nersoyan had resorted to this manœuvre about 50 per cent of the convent had been supporters of Derderian; see FO371/133892/V1782/20(A), HM consulate-general, Jerusalem to Levant Dept, FO, 26 July 1958.
[38] FO371/141876/V1781/3, Stewart to Hadow, 2 January 1959.
[39] FO371/141876/V1781/6, Stewart to Hadow, 6 March 1959.
[40] FO371/141876/V1781/8, Weir to Tesh, 2 May 1959.
[41] FO371/150887/V1781/11, Walsh to Beith, 8 April 1960.
[42] See also Tsimhoni, *Christian Communities*, 68–9; Azarya, *Quarter*, 117.
[43] See details in Patriarch Shenork Kaloustian (comp.), *Dseragreru Goghutean Gaitakghutiune* (The Fiasco of the Theft of the Manuscripts) (Istanbul, 1969); David Marshall Lang, *Armenia: Cradle of Civilization* (London, 1970), 243–4; and Vrej Nerses Nersessian (ed.), *Armenia*, World Bibliographical Series, 163 (Oxford, 1993), 220.
[44] See details in Azarya, *Quarter*, 125, 218n.; Naomi Shepherd, *The Mayor and the Citadel* (London, 1987), 75–6, 160–2; Tsimhoni, *Christian Communities*, 71; Michael Dumper, 'Church–State relations in Jerusalem since 1948', in O'Mahony et al. (eds), *Christian Heritage*, 279–80.
[45] Manoogian and Satamian, 'A slice of Eden', 28.
[46] For some general studies on the history of ASALA see Anat Kurz and Ariel Merari, *ASALA: Irrational Terror or Political Tool* (Boulder, Colo., 1985); Michael M. Gunter, *'Pursuing the Just Cause of Their People': A Study of Contemporary Armenian Terrorism* (New York, 1986); idem, *Transnational Armenian Terrorism* (London, 1990); and Francis P. Hyland, *Armenian Terrorism: The Past, the Present, the Prospects* (Boulder, Colo., 1991).
[47] For general studies on the history of the Armenian Catholic and Protestant communities see Charles A. Frazee, 'The formation of the Armenian Catholic community in the Ottoman Empire', *Eastern Churches Review*, 7 (1975), 149–69; Vartan H. Artinian, 'The formation of Catholic and Protestant millets in the Ottoman Empire', *Armenian Review* 28, 1 (1975), 3–15; Mesrob J. Terzian, *Le patriarcat de Cilicie et les Arméniens catholiques, 1740–1812* (Beirut, 1955); idem, *L'Institut patriarcal de Bzommar* (Beirut, 1983); Vartan Tékéyan, *Le patriarcat arménien catholique de Cilicie au temps de Grégoire Pierre II, 1812–1840* (Beirut, 1954); Leon Arpee, *A Century of Armenian Protestantism, 1846–1946* (New York, 1946); Hagop A. Chakmakjian, *The Armenian Evangelical Church and the Armenian People* (Yettem, Calif., 1961); Giragos H. Chopourian, *The Armenian Evangelical Reformation: Causes and Effects* (New York, 1972); Vahan H. Tootikian, *The Armenian Evangelical Church* (Southfield, Mich., 1981).

4

THE LATINS OF THE EAST: THE VATICAN, JERUSALEM AND THE PALESTINIAN CHRISTIANS

Anthony O'Mahony

Rome and Jerusalem

The years 1945–9 were a time of profound political and social transformation for Palestine. Few other periods in its history match these changes, which left no community unaffected. The Palestinian-Arab Christian and Muslim community were reduced from a majority to a minority in the west and north sections of mandate Palestine, subject to the rule of a staunchly nationalistic Jewish and Zionist state.[1] The events of 1948–9 were particularly devastating: a large number of Palestinians became refugees, including approximately 50–70 per cent of the Palestinian Christian population.[2] Nearly half of the Christian community of Jerusalem had lived and had their businesses in the more modern and developed western sector of the city, now under Israeli occupation; their property was sequestered after they fled or were compelled to leave. Most of them were forced to seek refuge in the Old City, in monasteries and other church buildings. Many others were forced to flee elsewhere, some leaving the former mandate territory altogether. Hence the division of Jerusalem into Jordanian and Israeli sectors was of considerable importance to the Christian communities in Jerusalem. The Arab quarters of west Jerusalem which had been taken by the Israelis were almost entirely Christian Arab quarters, and much of the centre of west Jerusalem was Christian church property on which the holy places and other shrines, monasteries and religious institutions of eastern Jerusalem depended for their maintenance. In addition, the heads of various communities lived and worked, almost without exception, in places which fell under Jordanian control. The lot of the Christian communities could not escape notice in the Vatican, which had always paid tremendous attention to Jerusalem as the birthplace of Christianity and a place of sacramental significance.[3]

The Holy See during this period tried to steer a neutral course, but in the latter half of 1948 the situation of the Palestinian Arab refugees and the question of Jerusalem's future status made for a modification in the Vatican's position. The Holy See was immediately galvanized into a massive relief effort on behalf of all Palestinian Arab refugees, without distinction between Christian and Muslim. It also set about the search for a viable long-term political solution to the problem of the refugees, and sought in particular the return of Palestinian Christians to Jerusalem.[4] From this date, the Vatican maintained several distinct policies: a permanent interest in the fate of all Palestinian Arab refugees;[5] a commitment to help find a long-term solution to the Middle East and to the Israeli–Arab conflict in particular;[6] and a concern with the question of Jerusalem and the Holy Places.[7]

Thus Papal policy towards Jerusalem can be divided into three periods.

1. From 1897 to 1947, when the popes spoke of the Holy Land in general and of Jerusalem, insisting primarily on the need to protect the physical integrity of the holy places and on the needs of the local Catholic community and its institutions.
2. From 1947 to 1964 (Pope Paul VI's pilgrimage to the Holy Land); here the stress is on safeguarding the holy places, on freedom of access for all faithful of the three monotheistic faiths, and the right of each of the three religions to have control of its own holy places.
3. From 1964 to the present day; a period during which the emphasis moves to Jerusalem in a global context and to the preservation of its identity and vocation: the holy places; the areas surrounding them; guarantees for everybody of their own cultural and religious identity; freedom of religion and conscience for inhabitants and pilgrims; the cultural dimension.

The Development of Vatican Policy towards Jerusalem

The fate of Jerusalem and the other holy places in Palestine, so strongly linked with the origins of Christianity, has always commanded the Holy See's interest and has led it on a number of occasions to undertake political initiatives designed to guarantee a Christian presence in the Holy Land.[8] As early as 1922, Cardinal Gasparri, the Vatican secretary of state, had publicly expressed the fear that the terms of the British mandate for Palestine, which at the time was being approved by the League of Nations, might give the Jewish population a privileged position which might compromise the rights of the Catholic church regarding the protection of the holy places. These fears gradually faded away in the following years; but the problem of the fate of Palestine was reawakened by the Second World War. Persecution throughout Europe, increasingly urgent and determined requests to allow Jews to emigrate en masse to Palestine and the British government's decision to relinquish its mandate created a new political and religious climate within which papal policy had to operate. In the aftermath of the Second World War, the Holy See avoided taking a stance either in favour of or against the creation of a Jewish state in Palestine, although it continued to follow attentively the evolution of the political situation in the Middle East. [9] In an uncertain and changeable political climate, the Holy See decided after some hesitation that the best solution to protect the Catholic church's rights and the Christian communities in the Holy Land in Palestine would be the internationalization of Jerusalem.[10] The Holy See set about concentrating its own forces in an attempt to obtain international legal status for Jerusalem, as it was foreseen in the plan for the division of Palestine approved on 29 November 1947 by the General Assembly of the United Nations. To this end the Vatican encouraged several political and diplomatic alternatives and sought to mobilize the Catholic hierarchy and faithful throughout the world in support of such a move.[11] The attitude taken by the Vatican on the Palestine issue at the end of the Second World War was unequivocally and succinctly stated in the summer of 1949 by the British plenipotentiary minister at the Holy See:

> The Vatican would have preferred, from the point of view of the fate of the Holy Places and of Catholic interests in Palestine generally, that neither Jews nor Arabs, but a Third Power, should have control in the Holy Land. Such a solution it well knew, however, was unattainable, and in the actual circumstances it preferred the Arabs to the Jews.[12]

There is considerable evidence proving this diagnosis to be true. Once the Holy See had overcome its suspicion of the Balfour Declaration, it was generally satisfied with the British management of the Palestine mandate, and particularly with the rigorous respect for the status quo that Britain assured, which had prevented the Orthodox church from gaining new positions in the possession and administration of the holy places, and which had permitted the Vatican to distance itself from France, whose traditional function as the protector of Catholic interests in the Holy Land had by now lost most of its meaning.[13] Thus, in respect of the arrangements made for Palestine following the First World War, the Vatican and the Catholic powers acquiesced in a situation not consonant with their desires but at least not unsatisfactory to them. Control of Jerusalem and the holy places went with control of Palestine, and British control in their view was better than Turkish control.[14] If they had been unable to improve the position of the Latins in the holy places, they had at least prevented it from deteriorating further. The Orthodox were satisfied with British control of Jerusalem and Bethlehem as long as the Status Quo of 1852 was adhered to. Since Jerusalem was in the hands of a Protestant power, Protestants found little of a religious nature to complain about. Against this background it was understandable that the British decision to relinquish the Palestine mandate, announced in spring 1947, was greeted with dismay by the Holy See, which could see no satisfactory alternative way of protecting Catholic interests in the Holy Land.[15] As there was now no chance of Britain's mandate in the Holy Land being extended, and because doubts were growing regarding the wisdom of entrusting Palestine to UN administration for fear of allowing Soviet penetration in the Middle East, the Vatican was faced with an alternative: a divided Holy Land as the result of the creation of a Jewish state and an Arab state, or the creation of a single state in Palestine representing both sides but with an Arab majority, considered to be the lesser evil than the creation of a Jewish state.[16]

The creation of a single Arab-controlled state in Palestine was openly supported by the Middle Eastern Catholic community and by influential Catholic elements in Jerusalem and Palestine. In Rome these positions were greeted favourably in some ecclesiastical circles close to the Sacred Oriental Congregation, highly aware of the implications of the Palestine question for the future of Catholic activities throughout the Middle East. However, the Vatican did not pronounce itself in favour of an Arab state in Palestine although it knew perfectly well that, generally, Catholic communities and most ecclesiastical authorities preferred this solution to the division of the Holy Land. This reticence is explained by the Vatican's hopes for the internationalization of Jerusalem, which was an important feature of the plan to divide Palestine approved in the summer of 1947 by the majority of the United Nations Special Committee on Palestine (UNSCOP). The creation of a Jewish state in Palestine was viewed even less favourably. The fears and worries of leading exponents of the Curia in Rome and the Holy See's concern over growing Jewish immigration into the Holy Land are well known. There is nothing to suggest that this attitude changed after the end of the Second World War. As well as coming up against the incomprehension and suspicion of those sections of Catholicism inclined to interpret the dispersion of the Jewish people in theological terms,[17] the return of the Jews to Palestine was something of an unknown quantity in relation to the protection of the holy places and the safeguarding of Christian interests. The Holy See preferred not to choose between these unsatisfactory alternatives. Despite pressures from Arab countries and particularly intense pressure from the Christian Arab community in the Middle East, the Vatican managed to avoid making any statement about the territorial aspects of the Palestine issue.

Meanwhile, the Vatican continued to oppose any plan for making permanent the division of Jerusalem between Jordan and Israel, since under such an arrangement there would be little prospect for concentrating a Christian population in Jerusalem in sufficient numbers to have much say in the conduct of the affairs of the city or to provide a base for the promotion of Vatican interests in the Near East. Proposals for functional internationalization of the shrines were also not very appealing. The introduction of the authority of the UN into the already complicated picture of the holy places might only serve to erode Latin rights, especially since it would be difficult to control the composition of the proposed UN commission for the holy places. Consequently Pope Pius XII issued an encyclical on Palestine, *Redemptoris nostri*, on 15 April, restating his support for full territorial internationalization. He urged all the faithful to exert every effort to see that their governments supported this course of action.[18]

The idea of establishing Jerusalem as a separate entity, directly controlled by the United Nations, was developed during the summer of 1947 in a subcommittee of UNSCOP, which was responsible for studying the problem of the holy places in Palestine. It was then included among the proposals put forward by the majority of this body and became an essential aspect of the plan to divide Palestine. For this reason, it obtained the support (albeit reluctant) of the Jewish Agency and of the countries which supported the creation of a Jewish state in the Holy Land. Thus it was again proposed in the report made by the first subcommittee set up in October 1947 by the ad hoc committee of the United Nations, approved by the United Nations on 25 November 1947 (as part, however, of a much wider plan for the division of Palestine) and finally accepted by the General Assembly under Resolution 181 (II) on 29 November 1947. During this period the Holy See made no request, either publicly or confidentially, for the internationalization of Jerusalem.[19]

It would seem, then, that initially the Holy See came to favour a system of guarantees which did not necessarily imply the creation of Jerusalem as a *corpus separatum*. But it is equally obvious that the Vatican was extremely pleased when this solution received the support of the majority of UNSCOP. The Vatican felt it gave the best protection possible to the holy places and the Catholic community in Palestine and, in addition, satisfied a number of spiritual ideals (a legal and institutional framework embodying the universal meaning of the holy places) and political ideals (preventing Jerusalem from becoming part of a Jewish or Arab state) that were deeply rooted in the Catholic world. The origin of the internationalization plan cannot therefore be directly attributed to requests put forward by Christian religious confessions, even though the desire to remove the holy places from Jewish and Arab control undoubtedly contributed to encouraging this solution. Rather, the plan must be attributed to the international policies of those countries, especially France,[20] which were interested in obtaining a sphere of influence throughout the Middle East by virtue of the UN presence in the Holy City.

The question of Jerusalem now moved to the UN. The debate on this occasion centred on three different proposals. The first was the Palestine Conciliation Commission's proposal suggesting that Israel and Jordan should each govern the two zones into which Jerusalem was divided as a result of the fighting in 1948 and that a UN commissioner should be appointed, with the task, among other things, of protecting the holy places. The second was put forward by Sweden and Holland and proposed to limit UN activity to the protection of the holy places, not far removed from the 'functional' internationalization of Jerusalem that the Israel government had stated it was willing to implement on several occasions. The third proposal was supported by Australia, which suggested a return to the principle of Jerusalem's territorial internationalization favoured in Resolution 181 (II) of 29 November 1947. The Australian draft resolution, fiercely contested by Israel and opposed by the US and the UK, was supported by the Arab bloc (save Jordan), the communist bloc (which saw the internationalization of Jerusalem as a chance to enter Middle East politics) and the majority of Catholic countries, no doubt heavily influenced by the Vatican. In Australia, the Labour government, facing national elections in 1949, was particularly mindful that some 40 per cent of the Australian electorate was Catholic. At the end of a heated debate this heterogeneous coalition managed to obtain sufficient votes for the Australian resolution to be approved, and with it the reaffirmation of the principle of territorial internationalization for Jerusalem.

There can be no doubt, that the Vatican did everything in its power to support Jerusalem's territorial internationalization. Had the Australian resolution been rejected, the General Assembly would probably have approved the project for the 'functional' internationalization proposed by Sweden and Holland. It would have been a very serious blow to the Vatican, which would have been forced, by the will of the UN, to accept a solution that it had refused on every occasion it was proposed by the Israelis in the course of direct negotiations.

The vote taken on 9 December 1949, reaffirming the General Assembly's will to internationalize Jerusalem territorially, further stiffened the position of Israel and Jordan. They intensified their negotiations to find an agreement based on Jerusalem's division, and accelerated the process of integrating the sections of Jerusalem they controlled into their respective states. The Israeli parliament proclaimed Jerusalem its capital and transferred its headquarters and main government offices there. The king of Jordan, worried by the rise of dangerous rivalry with Amman, merely appointed a supreme custodian of the holy places in Jerusalem.

The Thoughts of Paul VI and John Paul II on Jerusalem

The Holy See was firm in its request for the territorial internationalization of Jerusalem up until 1967. After the 1967 war, however, the new situation that had been created with the unification of the city in Israeli hands pushed the Vatican to reconsider its strategy.[21]

In the first place it must be kept in mind that, after the Second Vatican Council, many theological objections to the reconstitution of a Jewish state had been removed: the declaration *Nostra aetate*, in affirming that the death of Christ 'cannot be either indirectly attributed to those Jews living at the time, or to the Jews living in our day', dismissed the traditional theological justification of the Jewish Diaspora, relegating the existence of the state of Israel to an exclusively political dimension.

From this perspective the reconstitution of a Jewish nation, while still continuing to be the object of debate from a theological standpoint, ceased to be a problem on the political landscape, as demonstrated by the frequent references of John Paul II to the state of Israel and the right of the Jewish people to live in security and tranquillity.[22] The Vatican's withholding of diplomatic recognition of Israel can be explained by prevalently political motives, among which figure the unresolved problem of Jerusalem,[23] the enduring tensions among the states of the Middle Eastern region, the absence of internationally recognized borders and the lack of justice for the Palestinian people, for whom the Holy See continues to champion the right to their homeland.

Pope Paul VI[24] totally redefined the position of the Holy See with his speech on 22 December 1967, in which he indicated the elements that the Holy See judged 'essential and indispensable' in any solution to the problem of Jerusalem and the holy places: the first, according to the pope, regarded the holy places as justly so called by the three great monotheistic faiths – the Jewish, the Christian and the Muslim – in order to protect freedom of worship, respect for, conservation of and access to these very holy places, guarded by special immunities by means of their special status, whose observance was to be guaranteed by an institution of international character, with particular attention paid to the historic and religious physiognomy of Jerusalem. The second aspect of the question referred to the free enjoyment of religious and civil rights, legitimately due to all persons and activities of all the communities present in the territory of Palestine.

With this speech, the pope did not revive – nor did he explicitly exclude – the request for the territorial internationalization of Jerusalem, but indicated the specifics which in the Holy See's judgement would have to qualify any alternative formula. These were three: first, the safeguarding of the holy places and of the historic and religious character of the city; second, the international nature of their status as applicable to any and all parties; and third, the protection of the civil and religious rights of the Palestinian communities.

In order to understand the position of the Holy See, particular attention should be directed to the reference to the necessity of protecting (in addition to the holy places) the 'historic and religious physiognomy' of Jerusalem, inserted into Paul VI's speech and constantly repeated afterwards: implicit in this, in fact, was the refusal of a solution founded solely on the extraterritoriality of the holy places, which, while it would have adequately protected them, would not have been able to provide any guarantee whatsoever against transformations, demographic, urban, architectural, that would irreparably alter the sacred character of the entire city.

Of equal importance appeared to be the reference to the 'religious and civil rights' due to 'all the communities present in the territory of Palestine'. Understood in this appeal was the obvious intention of Paul VI to guarantee the indispensable conditions for the survival of the Christian community in Palestine, with the aim of stopping a flow of emigration that threatened to transform the holy places into 'museums void of life'.[25] From this preoccupation came an acute sensitivity to the demands of the Arab community (to which the greater majority of Christians in the Holy Land belong) and to the lot of the Palestinian people, whose destiny appeared in a certain way connected with that of Christianity itself in the Holy Land. Here is the source of the close relationship interwoven in papal documents between the question of the holy places and the Palestinian question. It is certainly no coincidence that it was Paul VI himself – the pope who most appreciated the opportunity to enlarge the focus from the holy places to include the Christian community in the Holy Land – who recognized in 1972 that the Palestinians were something more than simple refugees, but indeed a 'people' which had the right to 'equal recognition of its aspirations' and, as John Paul II would add later, a homeland.

Confronted by these worrying developments, the Holy See, guided by John Paul II, clarified its position in three documents, of which the most important was the apostolic letter *Redemptionis Anno* of 20 April 1984.

John Paul II described the importance of Jerusalem:

> Jews ardently love [Jerusalem] and in every age venerate her memory, abundant as she is in many remains and monuments from the time of David, who chose her as the capital, and Solomon, who built the Temple there. Therefore they turn their minds to her daily, one may say, and point to her as the sign of their nation. Christians honour her with a religious and intent concern because there the words of Christ so often resounded, there the great events of Redemption were accomplished: the Passion, Death and Resurrection of the Lord. In the city of Jerusalem the first Christian community sprang up and remained throughout the centuries a continual ecclesial presence despite difficulties. Muslims also call Jerusalem 'Holy', with a profound attachment that goes back to the origins of Islam and springs from the fact that there have been many special places of pilgrimage, and for more than a thousand years have dwelt there, almost without interruption.

Further, he says: 'I am convinced that the failure to find an adequate solution to the question of Jerusalem, and the resigned postponement of the problem, only compromise further the longed-for peaceful and just settlement of the crisis of the whole Middle East.'

In this letter the pope took care to identify two principles which he judged unacceptable: first of all, methodologically, the unilateral search for a solution to the question of Jerusalem (as Israel had done in proclaiming the city capital of the state), or even by way of 'bilateral understandings between one and other states' (as was the case at Camp David); and secondly, substantially, the reduction of the problem to the simple 'free access for all to the holy places' (which was the text sustained by the government of Israel).

Thus, clearing the field of all possible ambiguities, the Holy See was able to outline the framework of its own project for Jerusalem. This plan departs from the establishment of the predominant religious significance of the Holy City, 'crossroads between earth and heaven', a significance that today translates into the vocation of Jerusalem to become the place of encounter and recognition among the believers of the three great monotheistic religions, existing on 'a level of equality, without any one having to feel subordinate, and with respect for the others'.[26]

The political problem of Jerusalem could find its resolution, therefore, in the recognition of a legal status that allowed the city to realize its historical function. From this comes the necessity of legal guarantees that protect on the one hand 'the existence of the religious communities, their conditions, their future', and on the other, the habitat in which they find themselves, and thus the historic, urban and architectural configuration that the city has assumed.

These legal guarantees in addition must have, in the Holy See's judgement, an international nature, first of all in order to provide them with a stable character; and secondly because the involvement of the entire international community in the protection of the city would express the universal significance of Jerusalem. Yet it does not seem necessary that these guarantees cover the entire city, nor that they be incompatible with the sovereignty exercised over it by one or more states.[27]

Considered in its entirety, in the thoughts of Pope John Paul II on the Jerusalem question we can delineate an 'organic' development of themes earlier affirmed by Paul VI, although reformulated in light of the theological and political currents that inspire John Paul II. The accent put on the religious meaning of the Holy City – already present in the statements of Paul VI – is coherent with all the thoughts and actions of John Paul II, and above all with the idea (a newer one) that the resolution of the question of Jerusalem is a preliminary condition for a consequent Middle Eastern peace settlement.

It would be simplistic to read this affirmation as merely a report on the attempts to relegate the problem of Jerusalem to the margins of international diplomatic negotiations: in reality, it explains the Pope's conviction that the reconstruction of peace in the Middle East can only be based on the rediscovery of a common faith in God on the part of Christians, Jews and Muslims,[28] just as – indicating another field of application for this very same principle of the priority of the 'religious' over the 'political' – the reconstruction of the unity of the European peoples can be based only on the rediscovery of the Christian soul of Europe, according to the Pontiff.[29]

The Re-establishment of the Latin Patriarchate of Jerusalem

Whether they are Catholic or non-Catholic, eleven of the twelve Christian churches in the Arab world have in common the fact that they belong to the world of the Christian orient. Unique in its kind, the twelfth church is Latin in rite and Roman in discipline: 95 per cent of its faithful are Arabs, and its current patriarch is a Palestinian.[30]

The reasons for this particularity are historical. After seeking for a long time to re-establish the unity of the Church by negotiations between ecclesiastical hierarchies, from the sixteenth century onwards the papacy attempted to reconstitute Catholic unity at grass-roots level,[31] benefiting from the development of European influence in the Ottoman Empire.[32]

In the whole of the Middle East it has not more than 75,000 faithful, the majority of whom come under the jurisdiction of the Latin patriarchate of Jerusalem, which largely corresponds to the territories of Jordan, Palestine and Israel. Other small Latin communities exist also in Syria (3,000 people), Lebanon (5,000), Turkey (5,000), Iraq (3,500) and Cyprus (1,000). The influence of this church is, however, not limited to the meagre number of its flock. It is strongly supported by the Roman institutions and partakes more than any other part of the Catholic church of the orient of the power and authority of the Vatican, which can express itself through the patriarchate on issues relating to the acutely important regional and geopolitical problems. Moreover, the presence of foreign missions in the Middle East, complemented by a dense network of schools and medical and social establishments, gives Latin Catholicism an influence which goes far beyond the modest appearance of its structures at diocese and parish level.[33]

The idea of establishing a Latin-rite church in the Middle East took shape during the crusades. When the Franks entered Jerusalem in 1099 the patriarchal see was vacant because the titular had fled.[34] In addition, the victors, of their own authority, decided to replace him with a Latin patriarch, of Catholic faith, Latin in rite and Roman in discipline. Its jurisdiction was subsequently to extend to the bishoprics of Lebanon (excluding Tripoli and Jubeil). In 1100, a second Latin patriarchate was created in Antioch. For almost a century the new church was closely dependent on the crusader principalities, and the devolution of patriarchal and episcopal charges was decided locally depending on the political balance of power. However, with the fall of Jerusalem and the withdrawal of the patriarchate to Saint-Jean-d'Acre at the end of the twelth century, the weakening of the Latin states enabled the papacy to take matters back into its own hands by imposing its right to nominate the patriarch. In 1291, the last Latin patriarch died, drowned in the ditches of Saint-Jean-d'Acre when the last crusader citadel was taken. The patriarchal title, which was deprived of real jurisdiction, was, however, to survive until 1847 in favour of the Latin titular prelates established in Europe.

The disappearance of the resident patriarch in Jerusalem, however, did not put an end to all Latin presence. It was maintained thanks to the Franciscan order, which from 1219 onwards established a province and then a 'custody' of the Holy Land despite the hostility of the Greek church (which had been re-established in Palestine after the departure of the crusaders). The Franciscans persuaded the Mamelukes to accept their presence in Jerusalem as well as the existence of 'Catholic rights' over the holy places (the church of the Holy Sepulchre in Jerusalem and the church of the Nativity in Bethlehem), which were exercised by the Franciscans. The legal basis of these rights was constituted by an agreement concluded in 1333 between the king of Naples, Robert d'Anjou, and the Mameluke sultan of Egypt, and was ratified by the pope in 1342.[35] This recognition was, however, not enough to protect the friars efficiently, as they were very isolated in a hostile environment, and experienced several difficult moments. In the mid-sixteenth century they were even expelled from their custodial see (on Mount Zion) by the Ottomans and obliged to withdraw to the convent of the Holy Saviour where they are still based today.

In 1847, the Latin patriarchate was re-established in Jerusalem; up to that point the Greek Catholic patriarchate of Antioch had considered itself to be the representative of the oriental Catholics in Palestine. The choice of Palestine is paradoxical, as the largest Latin parishes were rather to be found in Lebanon. It is explained by the fact that the Holy See was determined to ensure the safeguarding of Catholic rights over the holy places which were threatened by the aggressive machinations of the Greek Orthodox clergy, which had only accepted the presence of the Latins in Jerusalem unwillingly. The protection offered by French diplomacy had for a long time been sufficient to preserve the position of the Franciscans.[36] In the mid-eighteenth century the situation changed with the appearance of Russia, which after the treaty of Kuchuk Kainardja (1774) presented itself as protector of the Orthodox in the Ottoman Empire. This change in the balance of power led to a first retreat by the Latins after 1757 from their position in the holy places. The Latins had exclusive rights over the Holy Sepulchre from 1690, with the support of French diplomacy, but were partly turned out following an attack by the Greeks, which the Ottoman government ratified.[37].

In the mid-nineteenth century this balance of power evolved even more unfavourably for the Catholics. Jerusalem was the object of rivalry between the European powers, which was exercised through the churches.[38] Whereas Britain and Prussia acted in unison to reinforce their political and religious influence by establishing an (Anglican) Anglo-Prussian bishopric in Jerusalem, Russia dispatched an ecclesiastical high dignitary to the Levant in the following year, in order to mark its interest and concern for the local Orthodox churches. As far as France was concerned, its retreat during the Syrian–Egyptian crisis in 1840 did not allow it to make any reply. In this unfavourable context for the Catholics, the Greek church of Jerusalem multiplied its pressure in order to undermine Latin rights over the holy places. In 1847, the silver star of the church of the Nativity, symbol of these rights, was taken down. This incident convinced the papacy (which was strongly supported by the Catholic powers) that the time had come to put a stop to the process of trying to eliminate Catholic rights. Rejecting the concerns of the Franciscans, who wanted to maintain their monopoly over the protection of Catholic rights as well as of the other oriental Catholic churches, Pius IX in his bull Nulla celebrior decided to re-establish a Latin patriarchate residing in Jerusalem, five and a half centuries after the disappearance of that which had existed during the crusades. Giuseppe Valerga was appointed the first Latin patriarch of Jerusalem.[39]

The creation of a new see, which had to be ratified by the Ottoman government, was the opportunity to open negotiations with a view to determining its prerogatives; these were in fact to extend to the protection of Catholic rights in the Holy City. This task was performed by French diplomacy. The patriarch was not formally recognized but was able to exercise his jurisdiction and authority in practice and was, on a diplomatic level, treated like the other patriarchs in the city. The division of rights over the Christian holy places between Greeks, Armenians and Latins was the subject of a firman in 1852 which settled the dispute concerning the church in Bethlehem and perpetuated the situation which existed in 1757, following the first trespass by the Greeks. This is the famous Status Quo which is given international recognition by the treaty of Berlin (1878) and which is still *in situ* today.[40]

The Latin patriarchate of Jerusalem was established without the necessity or the ambition to create a Latin Catholic community in the Holy Land. However, in fact a community did come into being as the result of the creation of the patriarchate. In only a few decades, the 4,000 Latin Catholics in the Holy Land multiplied by ten (not counting those who were settled outside the patriarchal jurisdiction in Lebanon, Syria, Mesopotamia and Constantinople). Many Christians in the Holy Land rallied to the new patriarchate, particularly those who felt culturally close to Europe, those taken by the modernity of the institution, and those just wishing for a more demanding spirituality and discipline. Others were simply aware that by being part of Latin Catholicism they would enjoy better protection in Ottoman Palestine and would be able to benefit from the services of efficient social and educational establishments.

However, the creation of the Latin patriarchate of Jerusalem was questioned by all the existing oriental Catholic hierarchies, who understandably felt nervous about the creation of this new and challenging *Ecclesia*. It became particularly clear during the First Vatican Council, when the work of the preparatory commission on the oriental churches, which was undertaken in the absence of the oriental prelates, led to a 'Latinist' programme, which was not adopted due to the Council's premature suspension. The dispute lessened during the pontificate of Leo XIII, who put an end to most of the Latinizing tendencies amongst the growing Catholic communities in the Christian Orient, and the Congrès Eucharistique International in Jerusalem called by the Pope in 1893 confirmed this policy. The new pope was at pains to renew dialogue between eastern and western Christendom and was aware of the key role which the oriental Catholic churches might play in disarming the distrust generated between these two parts of the Christian church.[41] Moreover, among other initiatives he published the encyclical *Orientalium dignitas*, which recognized the value of the oriental rites and prohibited oriental Christians from converting to the Latin rite, under threat of punishment. The document provoked the discontent of the Latin authorities in Jerusalem. Under Benedict XV, the founder of the Congregation for the Oriental Church and the Oriental Pontifical Institute, 'Latinism' was again prohibited. The need for Catholicism to be diffused using the oriental rites was soon realized with such great clarity that Pius XI at one point considered abolishing the Latin patriarchate of Jerusalem and leaving the field for the Franciscan custody of the holy places and the Greek Catholic Melkite church. Odo Russell of the British mission to the Vatican wrote:

> The whole question of the Oriental Church is being closely studied by the Holy See, and the tendency is rather to 'delatinise' than to Latinise the Catholics of the East. It may therefore come about that the Patriarchate at Jerusalem will be handed over to the Greek Uniates.[42]

The pope eventually refrained from doing so, for reasons more to do with diplomacy than with religion. Forceful political intervention and determined resistance from the Latin patriarch Barlassina,[43] who had support in the Curia and among influential members of the French hierarchy, led the Pope eventually to abandon the idea.[44]

After the First World War, it appeared that the departure of the Ottomans and the establishment of the British mandate would open great opportunities for Christianity in Jerusalem and Palestine. However, the project of a Jewish national home, to which Britain had agreed in the Balfour Declaration of 1917, would compete with Christian ambitions. In the 1920s, fears of Catholic rights over the holy places being questioned led the Latin patriarch of Jerusalem, Mgr Barlassina, to adopt an openly anti-Zionist stance which he also tried to convey to Europe (without great success). It also provided the belated partisans of Latinization with ammunition, presenting the Latin patriarchate as a bulwark for the protection of Catholics in the Middle East. Although the future remained heavily threatened, the British mandate period was nevertheless favourable to the Christian communities in the Holy Land, including the Latins, who were able to develop their institutions and gained in number through converts.

Following the Second World War the dreaded upheavals occurred. Whereas the UN division plan of 1947 provided for the establishment of Jerusalem as a *corpus separatum*, the Holy City became the subject of combat between Jews and Arabs, which led to it being split in two in 1949 (with the Latin patriarchate and the holy places on the Arab side). More seriously, however, the clashes led to a massive exodus of the Palestinian population. For the Latin church in the Holy Land, whose flock was already small, the result was catastrophic: large parishes were emptied; others, like those in Haifa and Jaffa, were almost ruined. The new state of Israel was not very welcoming to the Christian Arabs, and the economic situation in Jordan was hardly flourishing.

This time the exodus was not restricted to the neighbouring countries: many faithful were aware of how easily they would be able to integrate elsewhere due to their belonging to a global Catholic church, and therefore left to settle in Europe and America. Of the 10,000 Latins who were found in Jerusalem and the neighbouring towns after the 1948 war, only 3,000 remained in the early 1970s. Yet although the patriarchate was faced with declining numbers and a weakening of its institutions, it became more firmly rooted in the Palestinian Arab experience. It had found its vocation in representing Palestinian Christianity in Jerusalem, which neither the Greek nor the Armenian patriarchate could incarnate. The fact that an Italian patriarch was at its head (which had been the case since the beginning) constituted an anachronism. The last Italian patriarch, Beltritti,[45] was replaced by Michel Sabbah,[46] a Palestinian Arab (1987), from which moment the Latin patriarchate in Jerusalem has been able to present itself as representative of the church of the Palestinians in the Holy Land.

The Contemporary Situation of the Latin Patriarchate

Unlike the other oriental Catholic patriarchates the Latin patriarchate of Jerusalem is not responsible for all Latin Arabs in the Middle East, but exercises its jurisdiction in a limited area (Israel, Jordan, the occupied territories, including Jerusalem, and Cyprus).[47] Apart from this area (where two-thirds of the Latins in the region are to be found) there are other Latin communities which fall under the authority of either apostolic vicars (Lebanon, Syria, Turkey, Egypt, Kuwait, United Arab Emirates), or bishops (two in Sudan, one in Iraq), or of apostolic administrators (Djibouti, Somalia). The apostolic vicariate of Lebanon (which was created in 1938 and has been exercised by an archbishop resident in Beirut) is the most notable Latin structure apart from the patriarchate of Jerusalem, given the importance of this country for oriental Christianity (despite the small number of Latin faithful – hardly 5,000). The apostolic vicariate of Turkey has direct authority over the Latins in Istanbul and indirect authority over those in Izmir who fall under the authority of an archbishop. The Latin archbishopric of Baghdad, which was established in 1638, had only 3,500 indigenous faithful, although until the outbreak of the Gulf War in 1991 it provided ecclesiastical services to the 25,000 foreign Catholics resident there.

Within the area of jurisdiction of the Latin Patriarchate there are approximately 72,000 faithful,[48] which means that the Latins are the second largest Christian community in this area, after the Greek Orthodox (slightly less than 100,000) but before the Greek Catholics (40,000). Of these, about 25,000 live in Jordan, 17,000 in Israel (mainly in the Nazareth area where the Arabs are in the majority) and 8,000 in the West Bank (of whom 4,000 are in Jerusalem and the remainder around Bethlehem and Ramallah). Although the Latin community grew until 1973 owing to its high birth rate, it has since declined in number through the high level of emigration; this tendency has gained momentum during the Palestinian uprisings (Intifada).[49]

The guardianship of these Latin communities was for a long time ensured by the Sacred Congregation for the Propagation of the Faith; since the papacy of Pius XI it has been exercised by the Sacred Congregation for the Oriental

Churches, which is a more flexible structure. From 1984 it has been represented locally by an Apostolic Delegation based in Jerusalem which
co-ordinates all Catholic institutions and activities in Israel, Jordan, the
Occupied Territories and Cyprus. Since the Second Vatican Council (1967)[50]
there is also a Conference of the Latin Bishops in the Arab Regions
(Conférence des Évêques Latins dans les Régions Arabes, CELRA) which
meets every year under the presidency of the patriarch of Jerusalem and the
vice-presidency of the apostolic vicar of Lebanon; all patriarchal vicars, apostolic vicars and Latin bishops in the Middle East are members (archbishopric
of Baghdad; apostolic vicariates of Beirut, Alexandria, Aleppo, Kuwait and
Arabia; patriarchal auxiliaries of Israel, Jordan and Cyprus; apostolic administrators of Djibouti and Somalia).

The Latin church in the Holy Land has a patriarchal structure only in
appearance: it does not have true autonomy, and the legal status of its head is
very restricted compared with what the appointment as patriarch means in
the Arab world. Unlike other oriental Catholic patriarchs (whose appointment is the task of the local synod although the Holy See plays a role in the
process), the pope directly appoints the Latin patriarch. Falling under the
authority of the Sacred Congregation for the Oriental Churches through the
apostolic delegate, to whom he is subordinated, he therefore ranks only
number two in the Catholic hierarchy in the Holy Land. However, he
presides over CELRA and the Order of Knighthood of the Holy Sepulchre,
an institution that dates back to the Middle Ages and is today dedicated to
supporting the development of the patriarchate's educational and social activities. Auxiliary bishops, called patriarchal vicars, represent the patriarch in
the three districts of his area of jurisdiction (Israel, Jordan and Cyprus), plus
an episcopal vicar for the Hebrew-speaking community. Under his authority,
patriarchal tribunals (inherited from the Ottoman system) rule on matters of
personal status affecting Latin Christians (three courts of first instance in
Israel, Jordan, the Occupied Territories and Cyprus, two appeal courts in
Jerusalem and Amman).

Although legally speaking he is hardly more than a bishop, the Latin patriarch enjoys a prestige and exerts an influence far beyond his legal powers. In
fact, since 1987 the see of Jerusalem has been occupied by a Palestinian who,
taking into account the particularities of the Greek and Armenian churches,
is the only Arab patriarch of the Holy City. Sabbah is aware of his responsibilities as the figurehead of Palestinian Christianity and of the effects which
his nomination has had in the Christian Arab milieu; he plays a very active
role both at local level and abroad, in the context of CELRA, as well as
among the oriental Catholic patriarchs.

The organizational structure of the patriarchate is Roman. The patriarch
has a Curia with ten members; a presbytery council consisting of elected and
appointed members, which represents the three districts in the patriarchal
area of jurisdiction; and a chapter consisting of three canons. Eleven diocesan

commissions consisting of priests and religious deal with questions regarding doctrine, pastoral theology, liturgy, catechism, ecumenism and relations with Islam. A patriarchal seminary exists in Bayt Jala: it currently has about sixty seminarians. The number of parishes totals more than sixty, of which half are in Jordan, a quarter in Israel, a quarter in the West Bank and Cyprus. A secular clergy of about eighty priests serves them, although some are held by religious orders (mainly Franciscans). These priests are almost exclusively Arabs and have generally gone through the patriarchal seminary of Bayt Jala where they are trained in the Latin discipline; this gives them a homogeneity and superior training in many respects compared with the other churches in the Holy Land.

Despite its limited human resources and its modest financial means the Latin patriarchate in the Holy Land shows a dynamism which is unmatched by the other Christian churches. Its greatest success is in education: about twenty patriarchal secondary schools, thirty-five primary schools and thirty kindergartens have a total number of 15,000 pupils, 11,000 of whom are in Jordan and 4,000 in the West Bank. Some of the religious congregations organize education for 28,000 pupils in the same area, which supplements the efforts of the patriarchate. Thus the majority of pupils from the Christian community in Jordan – a country where the educational public sector is strongly influenced by Islam – can receive a Catholic education.[51] The patriarchal schools recruit pupils far beyond the Latin community (one-third of their pupils are Greek Orthodox or Greek Catholics, and one-quarter are Muslim), which largely explains why the influence of the Latin church stretches far beyond into Palestinian Arab society.

This generous contribution to keeping the Palestinian population in Palestine and to promoting it would not be complete without higher educational structures, as it is when the young people think of going to university that the temptation to leave is greatest. During his visit to the Holy Land, Pope Paul VI convinced himself of the need for a Catholic university within the patriarchal area of jurisdiction: it was finally set up in Bethlehem in 1973.

A Hebrew Catholic Ecclesia

Within the jurisdiction of the Latin Patriarchate there also exists a body which attempts to express and take care of the Hebrew Catholic community, the Œuvre de Saint-Jacques l'Apôtre. Its creation was approved by the former patriarch, Alberto Gori, in 1955, after several years of discussion and preparation, and it received warm encouragement from Cardinal Tisserant, then prefect of the Sacred Congregation for the Oriental Churches. The decision to found the Œuvre was prompted principally by the patriarch's pastoral solicitude for the Catholics, apparently some several thousand of them, who arrived in Israel as refugees or immigrants in the years following the Second

World War and the creation of the state of Israel (1948), and who continued to arrive throughout the 1950s. They came almost invariably from the countries of eastern Europe and were either converted Jews or descendants of such converts, or Catholic spouses in mixed marriages and their (often) baptized children – though in a few cases they had no connection at all with Jews and Judaism, and were simply anxious to emigrate from their countries, now communist or in the process of becoming so. The patriarchate, especially in the person of the then vicar in Israel, Mgr Vergani, was conscious of its duty to those immigrants and, fearing that because of differences of mentality and language, as well as of the complexity of the socio-political situation, the immigrants might not easily find their place within the normal parochial organization, favoured the creation of a distinct framework within its jurisdiction specially designed to meet their needs. It was accepted that the pastoral centres envisaged would adopt Hebrew, as being the lingua franca for immigrants originating from a number of different countries.[52] The statutes of the Œuvre approved on 11 February 1956 exhort its members to

> acquire an understanding of the mystery of Israel. We insist upon a biblical formation; we try to promote a Jewish Christian culture and a spirituality in conformity with that culture ... [We aim] to combat all forms of anti-Semitism, attempting to develop mutual understanding, sympathy and friendly relations between the Catholic world and Israel.

The majority of those who supported the creation of the Œuvre seemed to have felt that, even though an open missionary drive among Israeli Jews would in the circumstances be unthinkable, their task was to make the Christian faith accessible to those Hebrew-speaking Israelis whom God might prompt to seek membership of the Church. A smaller number of the 'founding fathers' were (and still are) motivated by a much larger vision, which could be summed up as a desire to implant the Church within the Jewish people in such a way that Jews who become Christians should be able to preserve their national character, in much the same way that members of any other people or nation are able or invited to so do.[53] The best-known protagonist of this view is the convert Carmelite priest Daniel Rufeisen, whose unsuccessful legal battle to get it stated in the civil registry that he is 'nationally' a Jew, although religiously a Christian, supporting his stand with the *halachic* (rabbinical) ruling that 'a Jew, although he has [converted to another religion] remains a Jew', resulted in one of the most famous decisions of the Israeli High Court of Justice, which denied that the rabbinical maxim could have any practical application at the present time. Thus the Law of Return, being a secular law, should be interpreted according to secular criteria. Rufeisen was thus not recognized as a Jew, and therefore could not benefit from the Law of Return.[54] Extensive autonomy was granted to the Œuvre, which is officially supervised, on behalf of the patriarch, by his episcopal vicar,[55] with four *foyers* (or communities) in Tel Aviv, Haifa, Jerusalem and Beersheva which together amount to between several hundred and two thousand.

The Latin Catholic Church of Jerusalem: What Identity?

The Latin church has long experienced an identity problem, and it took a long time for its vocation to gain a clear outline. At any rate, its vocation was never clearly outlined by Rome. The defence of the Catholic rights over the holy places had been invoked to explain the re-establishment of a patriarchate residing in Palestine, but it could not by itself justify the creation of specific structures at the level of the Middle East as a whole; yet apostolic and diocesan vicariates exist beyond the patriarchal area of jurisdiction of Jerusalem. Thinking logically, the end of proselytism and the recognition of the oriental rites by the Holy See should therefore have resulted in the disappearance of the Latin church in the orient. In spite of this, it had become by then an established reality. What vocation should it be assigned, given the conditions? There were considerable obstacles. However, this church, behind which the shadow of the Vatican and the powerful institutions of the Catholic church are clearly aligned, is attractive: the solidity of its structures, its discipline, the quality of its clergy, the dynamism of its social, educational and pastoral action are all the more seductive as the other oriental churches are deprived of external support and far from showing the same degree of vitality. Moreover, the Latin church in the orient has to try to steer a middle course. Whereas all religious references link it with the West, it has to legitimize its presence by giving itself an indisputably Arab image.[56]

In order to be accepted, the Latin church in the orient has had to remove many prejudices existing even within the other Catholic churches established in the region. The most reluctant was the Greek Catholic church, which also was strongly established in Palestine and therefore was in competition with the Latins. Although the establishment of a Latin patriarchate in Jerusalem was beneficial to all Catholic churches (to which it brought greater protection and a wave of conversions) the Melkite church has repeatedly claimed that, owing to the fact that it was itself a synthesis of local religious tradition and in union with Rome, it was the Melkite church which should represent Catholicism in the orient and defend Catholic rights over the holy places. The quarrel lasted until the Second Vatican Council, when the Melkite patriarch Maximos IV reiterated his claim for the Latin patriarchate to be abolished (nearly 120 years after its re-establishment).[57]

Local political circumstances have since emptied this controversy of much of its substance: since for many decades east Jerusalem and the West Bank have been occupied by Israel it would in any case be impossible for the Melkite patriarch (whose residence is at Damascus) to ensure efficiently the protection of Catholics in the Holy Land, or even to make pastoral visits. The Melkites and Latins are moreover aware of the fact that any change in the current situation might upset the fragile balance of the Status Quo in the holy places. The Greek Orthodox church, which already finds it difficult to respect the Catholic rights represented by the Latin patriarch, could not in any case accept their transfer to the Melkites, whom it still sees as dissidents who wrongly claim Byzantine religious 'legitimacy'. In Jerusalem where the Orthodox hierarchy has remained Hellenistic in culture, whereas the Melkites insist on being rooted in 'Arabness', the divide between the two Greek churches is even wider than in the rest of the Middle East.

By contrast, the presence of the Israeli occupier, the rise of Islamic radicalism and the threat of a complete disappearance of Christianity in the Holy Land have made possible a certain rapprochement between Latins and Greek Catholics, which has been facilitated by both sides renouncing proselytism as well as by the increased arabization of the Latin church. Moreover the two communities tend to become 'bi-ritual' – they use the services of one or the other church, depending on circumstances, and practise the two liturgies – and there are outlines of pastoral co-operation, the first result of which is the St Cyril Centre in Jerusalem created by the Latin patriarchate, the Greek Catholic patriarchal vicariate and the Franciscan custody in 1981 for the religious training of adults and the pedagogical preparation of catechists. Even so, it is not yet true that all mistrust has been overcome, and the relationship between the two religious hierarchies is not yet as close as required by the situation. The hierarchy is in fact constrained in more than one way: its Church is spread between the West Bank, Jordan and Israel and cannot ignore the feelings of its Palestinian faithful, although neither can it get involved in an open conflict with the authorities of the occupier which would not be without consequences for the situation of the Latin Catholics in Israel and the foreign religious communities. Moreover, it cannot freely take a position, as it is placed under the supervision of the Apostolic Delegation, which represents the Vatican in the Holy Land and takes an approach to the Arab-Israeli problem which does not only take the interests of Palestinian Christianity into account.

The appointment of a Palestinian priest as Latin patriarch in Jerusalem in 1987 was highly symbolic. This event did not fail to have an effect on the political attitude of the patriarchate. Soon after his nomination Mgr Sabbah adopted a very firm line on the Palestinian question: he limited his formal contacts with the Israeli authorities to a minimum, abolished all ceremonies associated with religious feast days (other than the offices of the liturgy) because of the Intifada, and associated himself with the joint reply of the churches of Jerusalem when their rights were infringed (this reply went as far as the closure of Christian holy places).[58] At the head of the conference of the Latin bishops of the Arab regions, Mgr Sabbah has inspired more vigorous viewpoints on the Arab–Israeli conflict; he considers the PLO to be the only representative of the Palestinian people.[59]

This evolution in the political stance of the Latin church is the logical complement of its arabization and should finally provide it with the specific vocation which it has sought since the project of Latinizing the oriental churches was abandoned. Whereas the Greek Orthodox and Armenian patriarchates of Jerusalem continue to represent religious milieux and traditions which are not Arab, and the Greek Catholic Church is handicapped by the lack of resident see in the Holy Land (as well as by its links with Syria, where its patriarch is to be found), the Latin Church finally seems to be in the best position to incarnate Palestinian Christianity. History has made the Latin church in the orient a reality. It is probably in the interests of global Catholicism finally to provide it with what it needs to express to the full the potentialities of its existence in the process of 'inculturation' as advocated by John Paul II: an *Ecclesia* for and within Jerusalem which will give the pilgrim and the stranger a home.

Notes

[1]   For a general survey see Ian Lustick, *Arabs in the Jewish State: Israel's Control of a National Minority* (Austin, 1980). For the position of the Christian communities within the state of Israel see Ammon Kapeliouk 'Les Arabes chrétiens en Israël (1948–1957)' (thèse de doctorat, Sorbonne, 1968); and *idem*, 'L'état social, économique, culturel et juridique des Arabes chrétiens en Israël', *Asian and African Studies*, 5 (1969), 51–95.
[2]   The number of Christian refugees is a difficult and controversial question. Robert Brenton Betts, *Christians in the Arab East: A Political Study* (Atlanta, 1978), 212, estimated the figure at 55,000 refugees, or 50 per cent of the Christians living in what was to become the state of Israel after the 1949 armistice. However, according to Edward Duff, 'Honor in Israel' in the American Jesuit review, *America*, 26 March 1949, 677, there were 150,000 Christian refugees, of whom 55,000 were Catholic. Bernard Sabella, 'Palestinian Christian emigration from the Holy Land', *Proche-Orient Chrétien*, 41 (1991), 74, suggests that the war of 1948 witnessed the forced migration of 714,000 Palestinians, of whom 50,000 were Christians, or 7 per cent of all refugees and 35 per cent of all Christians who lived in Palestine prior to 15 May 1948. However, their travails did not end here. For an attempt to remove Arab Christians from the Galilee after 1948, see Nur Masalha, 'An Israeli plan to transfer Galilee's Christians to South America: Yosef Weitz and 'Operation Yohanan', 1949–1953', in Anthony O'Mahony (ed.) *Palestinian Christians: Religion, Politics and Society in the Holy Land* (London, 1999), 190–222.
[3]   Anthony O'Mahony, 'The Vatican, Palestinian Christians, Israel and Jerusalem: religion, politics, diplomacy and holy places, 1945–1950', *Studies in Church History: The Holy Land, Holy Lands and Christian History*, 36 (2000), 358–74.
[4]   Catholic institutions and agencies were swift to respond to the crisis, providing humanitarian support for the Palestinian Arab refugees in advance of parallel Protestant institutions and the UN, and far exceeding all other Christian and other institutions in their efforts. From summer 1948 to February 1950, the American National Catholic Welfare Conference sent $1.3 million, much more than the American Protestant Church World Service, which contributed $331,000. Catholics outside North America gave some $5 million, while various Red Cross organizations contributed just $2 million. This multinational and well-organized Catholic relief effort was provided for all Palestinian refugees, Muslim and Christian, and was formulated by the foundation of the Pontifical Mission to Palestine on 4 June 1949. The Vatican, moreover, did not intend to limit itself to emergency aid, as its avowed goal was to create a viable and long-term political solution to the Christian refugee problem at least, in order to preserve a stable social base for

the Church and to prevent future upheavals in the region. See Andrej Kreutz, *Vatican Policy on the Palestinian–Israeli Conflict: The Struggle for the Holy Land* (Westport, Conn., 1990), 87–111.

[5] M.-A. Boisard, 'Le Saint-Siège et la Palestine', *Relations Internationales*, 28 (1981), 443–55, and the studies by A. Kreutz, 'The Vatican and the Palestinians: a historical overview', *Islamochristiana*, 18 (1992), 109–25; 'The Vatican and the Palestinian question', *Social Compass*, 37 (1990), 239–54; and 'The Vatican and the Palestinians', in Peter C. Kent and John F. Pollard (eds), *Papal Diplomacy in the Modern Age* (Westport, Conn., 1994), 167–79.

[6] For a general appreciation of Vatican policy to the Middle East see Gerald Arboit, *Le Saint-Siège et le nouvel ordre au moyen orient, de la guerre du Golfe à la reconnaissance diplomatique d'Israël* (Paris, 1996); and George E. Irani, *The Papacy and the Middle East: The Role of the Holy See in the Arab–Israeli conflict, 1962–1984* (Notre Dame, Ind., 1986).

[7] Jean-Dominique Montoisy, *Le Vatican et le problème des Lieux-Saints* (Jerusalem, 1984) and Edmond Farhat (ed.), *Gerusalemme nei documenti pontifici* (Rome, 1987).

[8] For a general view of these endeavours see S. I. Minerbi, *The Vatican and Zionism: Conflict in the Holy Land, 1895–1925* (Oxford, 1990), 15–95; H. F. Kock, *Der Vatikan und Palästina* (Vienna–Munich, 1973); G. Pierazzi, 'Der Vatikan and die Heiligen Statten in Palästina, 1919–1922 und 1947–1950', *Jahrbuch der Diplomatischen Akademie Wien* (1973), 99–110; Daniella Fabrizio, *La questione dei Luoghi Santi e l'assetto della Palestina, 1914–1922* (Milan, 2000). For an attempt by Belgian Catholics to get the mandate for Palestine and hence to protect the holy places of Christianity see Roger Aubert, 'Les démarches du cardinal Mercier en vue de l'octroi à la Belgique d'un mandaté sur la Palestine', *Académie Royale de Belgique. Bulletin de la Classe des lettres et des sciences, morales et politque*, 65 (1979), 145–228.

[9] On the background to the Vatican opposition to the Zionist plan for Palestine see Meir Mendes, *Le Vatican et Israel* (Paris, 1990), 69–96; André Chouraqui, *La reconnaissance, le Saint-Siège, les Juifs et Israël* (Paris, 1992), 101–68; and for a history of Vatican–Zionist relations, Michael Perko, 'Toward a 'sound and lasting basis': relations between the Holy See, the Zionist movement and Israel, 1896–1996', *Israel Studies*, 2, 1 (1998), 1–26.

[10] Pietro Pastorelli, 'La Santa Sede e il problema di Gerusalemme', *Storia e Politica*, 21 (1982), 57–98.

[11] See the fundamental work by Silvio Ferrari on Vatican policy towards the Jerusalem question, 'The Vatican, Israel and the question of Jerusalem (1943–1984)', *Middle East Journal*, 39 (1985), 316–31; 'The struggle for Jerusalem', *European Journal of International Affairs*, 1 (1991), 22–39; 'Il Vaticano e la questione di Gerusalemme nel carteggio Spellman–Truman', *Storia Contemporanea*, 13, 2 (1982), 285–320; 'La Santa Sede e il problema della Palestina nel secondo dopoguerra', *Communitá* (1985), 400–46; 'Per Gerusalemme una e indivible', *Limes*, 2 (1994), 149–62.

[12] London, Public Record Office (PRO), fo. 371/WV 1011, Perowne to Attlee, 9 August 1949; see also FO 371/E6425, Perowne to Bevin, 4 May 1948.

[13] On the Vatican and the ending of the French protectorate in Palestine see Sergio I. Minerbi, *L'Italie et la Palestine, 1914–1920* (Paris, 1970); idem, 'L'Italie contre le Protectorat religieux français en Palestine (1914–1920)', *Asian and African Studies*, 4 (1968), 23–56; Daniela Fabrizio, 'Il protettorato religioso sui Cattolici in oriente: la questione delle relazioni diplomatiche dirette tra Santa Sede e Impero Ottomano, 1901–1918', *Nuova Rivista Storica*, 82 (1998), 583–626, and Catherine Nicault, 'La fin du protectorat religieux de la France à Jérusalem (1918–1924)', *Bulletin du Centre de recherche française de Jérusalem*, 4 (1999), 7–24.

[14] Maria Grazia Enardu, 'Palestine in Anglo-Vatican relations, 1936–1939' (Università degli studi di Firenze, Facoltà di Scienze Politiche 'Cesare Alfari', 1980).

[15] Paolo Pieraccini, *Gerusalemme, luoghi santi e communitá religiose nella politica internazionale* (Bologna, 1997), 47–78.

[16] S. Ferrari, *Vaticano e Israele dal secondo conflitto mondiale alla guerra del Golfo* (Florence, 1991), 29–54.

[17] See the following studies on the positions taken by some leading Catholic thinkers regarding the theological and political status of the state of Israel: for the leading French philosopher Jacques Maritain see Esther Starobinski-Safran, 'Judaïsme, peuple juif et état d'Israël', in *Jacques Maritain face à la modernité. Enjeux d'une approche philosophique. Colloque de Cerisy*. Textes réunis par Michael Bressolette et René Mougel (Paris, 1995), 219–43; and Sylvain Guéna, 'La passion d'Israël. Réflexions de Jacques Maritain sur la Shoah', *Istina*, 45 (2000), 16–36; the Swiss Cardinal Journet, founder of the influential periodical *Nova et Vetera*: Esther Starobinski-Safran, 'Les destinées d'Israël, son mystère et la foi mosaïque selon Charles Journet', in *Charles Journet (1891–1975). Un théologien en son siècle*, Actes du colloque de Genève, 1991, sous la direction de Philippe Chenaux (Fribourg, 1992), 72–88; and Louis Massignon the French Islamicist, mystic and political activist: Anthony O'Mahony, 'Le pèlerin de Jérusalem: Louis Massignon, Palestinian Christians, Islam and the state of Israel', in O'Mahony (ed.), *Palestinian Christians: Religion, Politics and Society in the Holy Land* (London, 1999), 166–89, and Dominique Bourel, 'Massignon face à face Israël', *Louis Massignon: mystique en dialogue*, Collection 'Question de' 90 (Paris, 1992), 67–75.

[18] H. Eugene Bovis, *Jerusalem Question, 1917–1968* (Stanford, 1971), 71. The original text is in *Oriente Moderno*, 29 (1949), 52–3; translated text in the *New York Times*, 16 April 1949.

[19] S. Ferrari, 'The Holy See and the postwar Palestine issue: the internationalization of Jerusalem and the protection of the holy places', *International Affairs*, 60, 2 (1984), 261–83.

[20] On French Catholic opinion see D. Lazar, *L'opinion française et la naissance de l'état d'Israël, 1945–1949* (Paris, 1972), 177–219; and for the development of that thought, Y. Rash, *Déminer un champ fertile: les catholiques français et l'état d'Israël* (Paris, 1982); and *idem*, *Catholiques de France, un Israëlien vous parle* (Paris, 1981).

[21] S. Ferrari, 'Le Saint-Siège, l'état d'Israël et les Lieux-Saints de Jérusalem', in J.-B. d'Onorio (ed.), *Le Saint-Siège dans les relations internationales* (Paris, 1989), 301–21.

[22] Phillippe Levillain, 'Israël et le Saint-Siège. L'accord fondamental entre le Saint-Siège et Israël', in P. Levillain (ed.), *Dictionnaire historique de la papauté* (Paris, 1994), 915–17; F. Yerly, 'Le Saint-Siège, l'état d'Israël et la paix au Moyen-Orient', *Vingtième Siècle*, 51 (1996), 3–14; and for an Israeli perspective see Sergio I. Minerbi, 'The Vatican and Israel', in *Papal Diplomacy in the Modern Age*, 189–201; *idem*, 'The Catholic church, Judaism and the state of Israel', *Christian–Jewish Relations*, 21, 2 (1988), 26–35; and for an alternative Catholic perpective, George E. Irani, The Holy See and the Israeli–Palestinian conflict', in Kail C. Ellis (ed.), *The Vatican, Islam and the Middle East* (Syracuse, 1987), 125–42. The entire religious and diplomatic environment was subsequently changed by the visit to the Holy Land in March, 2000 by Pope John Paul II; see 'Jean-Paul II en Terre Sainte', *Istina*, 41 (2000), 113–95.

[23] The Vatican established diplomatic relations between the Holy See and Jordan on 3 March 1994. For the background to the relationship see Joseph L. Ryan, 'The Holy See and Jordan', in *The Vatican, Islam and the Middle East*, 163–88. For relations between the Holy See and Israel, established on 14 June 1994, see 'Accord fondamental entre le Saint-Siège et l'état d'Israël', *Istina*, 41 (1996), 401–28.

[24] For the background and the impact upon Paul VI of his pilgrimage to Jerusalem and the Holy Land see Claude Soetens, 'Entre concile et initiative pontificale: Paul VI en Terre Sainte', *Cristianesimo nella Storia*, 19 (1998), 333–65.

[25] On the whole question of Christian emigration from the Holy Land see Bernard Sabella, 'Socio-economic characteristics and challenges to Palestinian Christians in the Holy Land', in *Palestinian Christians. Religion, Politics and Society in the Holy Land*, 82–95; and 'Palestinian Christians: realities and hopes', in *The Holy Land, Holy Lands, and Christian History: Studies in Church History*, 373–97.

[26] S. Ferrari, 'Coabitazioni tra religioni a Gerusalemme', in A. Riccardi (ed.), *Il Mediterraneo nel Novecento* (Cinisello Balsamo, 1994), 316–36.

[27] For the development of Vatican and Catholic thinking on the Jerusalem question see the ensemble of works by the French Franciscan, Bernardin Collin: *Les Lieux-Saints* (Paris, 1948); *Le problème juridique des Lieux-Saints* (Paris, 1956); *Les Lieux-Saints* (Paris, 1968); *Pour une solution au problème des Lieux-Saints* (Paris, 1974); *Rome, Jérusalem et les Lieux-Saints* (Paris, 1981); and *Recueil de documents concernant Jérusalem et les Lieux-Saints* (Jerusalem, 1982).

[28] S. Ferrari, 'The religious significance of Jerusalem in the Middle East peace process: some legal implications', *Catholic University Law Review*, 45, 3 (1996), 733–43.

[29] Michael Sutton, 'John Paul II's idea of Europe', *Religion, State and Society*, 25, 1 (1997), 17–30.

[30] Frans Bouwen, 'The churches in the Middle East' and 'The churches in Jerusalem', in Lawrence S. Cunningham (ed.), *Ecumenism: Present Realities and Future Prospects* (Notre Dame, IN, 1998), 25–36 and 37–49.

[31] Bernard Heyberger, *Les Chrétiens du Proche-Orient au temps de la Réforme catholique* (Rome, 1994).

[32] Joseph Hajjar, 'La question religieuse en orient au déclin de l'empire Ottoman (1683–1814)', *Istina*, 13 (1968), 153–260.

[33] Anton Issa, 'Il patriarcato latino di Gerusalemme', in Giovanni Bissoli (ed.), *Gerusalemme. Realtà, sogni e speranze* (Jerusalem, 1996), 142–60.

[34] Bernard Hamilton, 'The Latin church in the crusader states', in K. Ciggar, A. Davids and H. Teule (eds), *East and West in the Crusader States* (Louvain, 1996), 1–20.

[35] M. Roncaglia, 'The Sons of St Francis in the Holy Land: official entrance of the Franciscans as custodians of the basilica of the Nativity in Bethlehem', *Franciscan Studies*, 10 (1950), 257–85.

[36] On the modern history of the Franciscan custody see A. Giovannelli, *La Santa Sede e la Palestina. La custodia di Terra Santa tra la fine dell'impero ottomano e la guerra dei sei giorni* (Rome, 2000).

[37] M. Roncaglia, 'La questione dei Luoghi Santi Nuovi documenti (1757)', *Studia Orientalia Christiana Collectanea*, 1 (1956), 135–8 and 2 (1957), 65–9.

[38] Thomas Stransky, 'Origins of western Christian missions in Jerusalem and the Holy Land', in Y. Ben-Arieh and M. Davis (eds), *Jerusalem in the Mind of the Western World, 1800–1948* (Westport, Conn., 1997), 1–19; Catherine Mayeur-Jaouen, 'Les Chrétiens d'orient au XIXe siècle: un renouveau lourd de menaces', in *Histoire du christianisme des origines à nos jours*, XI: *Libéralisme, industrialisation, expansion européenne (1830–1914)* (Paris, 1996), 793–849.

[39] S. Manna, *Chiesa latina e chiese orientali all'epoca del patriarca Giuseppe Valerga (1813–1872)* (Naples–Rome, 1972); Pierre Duvignau, *Une vie au service de l'Église. S. B. Mgr Joseph Valerga, Patriarche Latin de Jérusalem, 1813–1872* (Jerusalem, 1972).

[40] Selim Sayegh, *Le status quo des Lieux-Saints. Nature juridique et portée internationale* (Rome, 1971).

[41] Claude Soetens, *Le congrès eucharistique international de Jérusalem (1893) dans le cadre de la politique orientale du Pape Léon XIII* (Louvain, 1977), 245–89.

[42] FO141–667, file no. 6023, Russell to Curzon (13 November 1923).

[43] P. Pierracini, 'Il patriarcato Latino di Gerusalemme (1918–1938): ritratto di un patriarca scomodo. Luigi Barlassina', in G. Meynier and M. Russo (eds), *L'Europe et la méditerranée* (Paris, 1999), 243–58.

[44] S. Ferrari, 'Pio XI, la Palestina e i Luoghi Santi', in *Achille Ratti Pape Pie XI* (Rome, 1996), 909–24.

[45] The list of patriarchs since the re-establishment of the Latin patriarch in 1847: Giuseppe Valerga, 1847–72; Vincenzo Bracco, 1873–89; Luigi Piavi, 1889–1905; Filippo Camassei, 1907–19; Luigi Barlassina, 1920–47; Alberto Gori, 1949–70; Giacomo Beltritti, 1970–87.

[46] Michel Sabbah, who was born in Nazareth in 1933, was ordained priest in 1955.

Most of his ecclesiastical career has been in Palestine where he was parochial vicar in Madaba, Arabic teacher at the patriarchal seminary, student chaplain, general chaplain of the youth movement and then director-general of the schools of the patriarchate. From 1968 to 1970 he served in Djibouti, after which he was curate in the parish of Christ the King in Amman. He holds a doctorate in Arab philology from the Sorbonne, became president of the Pontifical University of Bethlehem in 1981, was elected Latin Patriarch of Jerusalem in 1987, and consecrated in Rome in January 1988.

[47] The term 'Holy Land,' as regards the hierarchy of the Catholic church, embraces Cyprus, the West Bank, Jordan and Israel. Until 1929, the Holy Land was under the jurisdiction of the apostolic delegate in Syria who resided in Beirut. In March of that year Pius XI decided that Palestine (which was then under British mandate) should become the responsibility of the pontifical representative in Cairo, who had a residence in Jerusalem. On 11 February 1948 Pius XII established the Apostolic Delegation in Jerusalem and Palestine, which covered Israel, Jordan and Cyprus. Following the establishment of diplomatic relations between the Holy See and Jordan on 3 March 1994, and between the Holy See and Israel on 14 June 1994, the Apostolic Delegation covers only Jerusalem and the Palestinian Autonomous Territories. At the present time there is an apostolic nunciature in Amman and another in Tel Aviv.

[48] This figure is given by the *Annuaire de l'Église catholique en Terre Sainte* (Jerusalem, 1999), 29, although other sources suggest a lower figure: 50,000 according to Jean-Pierre Valognes, *Vie et mort des Chrétiens d'orient. Des origines à nos jours* (Paris, 1996), 507.

[49] B. Sabella, 'Palestinian Christian emigration from the Holy Land', *Proche-Orient Chrétien*, 41 (1991), 74–85. On the general question of Christian migration from the region: B. Sabella, 'L'émigration des Arabes chrétiens: dimensions et causes de l'exode', *Proche-Orient Chrétien*, 47 (1997), 141–169; and Élie Austin, 'L'immigration massive des Chrétiens d'orient', *Études*, 373 (1990), 101–6.

[50] J. Hajjar, 'Les églises du Proche-Orient au Concile Vatican II. Aperçu historique (1958–1978)', *Istina*, 41 (1996), 253–308; and Emmanuel Lanne, 'Un christianisme contesté. L'orient catholique entre mythe et réalité', in *The Christian East. Its Institutions and its Thought: A Critical Reflection* (Rome, 1996), 85–106.

[51] Jean-Pierre Valognes, 'Les Chrétiens de Jordanie', in *Vie et mort des Chrétiens d'orient*, 614–35; G. Chatelard, 'Jordanie: entre appartenance communautaire et identité nationale', *Les Cahiers de l'Orient: Édition Chrétiens de l'Orient*, 48 (1997), 117–22; and M. Haddad: '"Detribalizing" and "Retribalizing": the double role of the Church among the Christian Arabs in Jordan: a study in the anthropology of religion', *The Muslim World*, 82 (1992).

[52] In fact the Œuvre was granted permission by the patriarchate and the Vatican to have the liturgy in Hebrew as early as 1957. For the pioneering work of the French Jewish convert priest Jean-Roger Henné in creating a Hebrew Catholic culture see Dominique Trimbur, 'Les Assomptionistes de Jérusalem, les Juifs et le sionisme', *Tsafon: Revue d'Études Juives du Nord*, 48 (1999–2000), 71–111.

[53] David-Maria Hunter (D.-M. A. Jaeger), 'Holy Land Christians: Hebrew-speaking communities', *The Tablet*, 7 January 1978, 5–7; S. Ferrari, 'La liberté religieuse en Israël', in Joël-Benoît d'Onorio (ed.), *La liberté religieuse dans le monde* (Paris, 1991), 243–54.

[54] Bernard Dupuy, 'Le père Daniel-Oswald Rufeisen (1922–1998)', *Istina*, 44 (1999), 159–67.

[55] The Benedictine abbot, Jean-Bapiste Gourion, at Abou-Gosh, Église de la Résurrection.

[56] Apart from the important pastoral letters of the patriarch, Michel Sabbah, in particular 'Reading the Bible today in the land of the Bible' (November 1993), there is a growing body of theological-political reflection from within the Latin Palestinian Catholic community: Rafiq Khoury, *La catéchèse dans l'église locale de Jérusalem: histoire, situation actuelle et perspectives d'avenir* (Rome, 1978); 'Chrétiens arabes de la

Terre Sainte', *Études*, 369 (1988), 395–408; and Anton Odeh Issa, *Les minorités chrétiennes de Palestine à travers les siècles. Étude historico-juridique et développement
moderne international* (Jerusalem, 1976).

[57] On the sometimes difficult relations between the Melkites and Latins over who
should represent Catholic rights and interests in Jerusalem and the Holy Land see
Catholicisme ou Latinisme? A propos du patriarcat latin de Jérusalem (Harissa, 1961);
and *The Custody of the Holy Land: Status Quo and the Oriental Rites* (Jerusalem,
1961).

[58] Andrea Pacini, 'Socio-political and community dynamics of Arab Christians in Jordan,
Israel, and the autonomous Palestinian territories', in A. Pacini (ed.), *Christian
Communities in the Arab Middle East: The Challenge of the Future* (Oxford, 1998),
259–85; and Thomas Stransky, *A Catholic Views Political Zionism and the State of
Israel* (South Orange, NJ, 2000), 21–54.

[59] For the accord between the Vatican and the Palestinian authorities see Paolo Ferrari
da Passano, 'L'accordo tra la Santa Sede e l'Organizzazione per la Liberazione della
Palestina', *La Civiltà Cattolica*, 1 (2000), 364–71.

5

EGYPT AND THE HOLY LAND: THE COPTIC CHURCH AND COMMUNITY IN JERUSALEM

John Watson

The Copts are more visible in Jerusalem today than they have ever been. They are a living expression of the thoroughly documented Coptic renaissance of the last four decades.[1] The Coptic presence has distinction. It is also a captive presence, unable to escape from the centuries of denominational conflict within the oriental Orthodox communities in Jerusalem, or from a certain endemic servility to Egyptian political life.

The *qalansuwa* is the visible expression of the Coptic revival: the black monastic cowl which covers the head and the back of the neck. It is divided into halves by a sewn line in the middle, and has six crosses on each panel with a lone cross at the base of the neck. The crosses signify Christ and the apostles. This apparently innocent piece of ecclesiastical garb is in reality an eloquent statement of allegiance to the Coptic patriarch in Cairo and an expression of commitment to the religious and political renaissance he has directed.[2] The *qalansuwa* has only been seen in Jerusalem in recent years. The garment was introduced into the Coptic Orthodox church by Pope Shenouda III, by tradition the 117th successor of the evangelist St Mark, who in 1996 celebrated his twenty-fifth anniversary as patriarch. The *qalansuwa* is a monastic uniform, an outward sign of the kind which has become essential to the benevolent autocracy in the Coptic church at present. Regimentation is the order of the day. Shenouda's rationale for imposing the *qalansuwa* is that it resembles the skullcap of St Antony the Great.[3] In reality the clothing signifies a process of clericalization and professionalism which may have been Shenouda's most important contribution to the Coptic church.[4]

For centuries the desert fathers were indistinguishable from Egyptian peasants, except when they entered the sanctuary for the liturgy. Today the cowl is worn like a papal livery, though in some independent monasteries it is rejected because it is said to be of Syrian-Antiochene origin. Theologically, critics are concerned that the autonomous, prophetic and eschatological role of the desert monks has been lost in the new habit. The Coptic monks in Jerusalem now follow the example of their new metropolitan in wearing the *qalansuwa*. Contemporary photographs show that the previous patriarch and metropolitan did not wear the cowl.[5] The adoption of the headdress is as significant as the changes in Coptic Orthodox leadership.

Archbishop Basilius IV was installed as metropolitan of Jerusalem and the Middle East in 1959 by the saintly Pope Kyrillos VI.[6] Tradition dictated that the metropolitan should be chosen from among the monks of the monastery of St Antony the Great by the Red Sea, so it was that the monk, Abouna (Father) Kyrillos El Antuni became the leader of Jerusalem's Copts. He held a doctorate in patristics and maintained his scholarly interests throughout his life. He was rarely drawn into public controversy and had little sympathy with the unhappy abeyance of theological thought in favour of the flexing of Coptic political muscle in Egypt. When Archbishop Basil died in 1991, Pope Shenouda turned to the Western Desert for a representative of the more politically conscious and assertive style which he preferred. On 17 November 1991 (7 Hatur, 1708 of the Coptic Calendar, which calculates from the era of Diocletian's persecutions of the Copts, beginning in AD 284) the *qummus* (archpriest) Sidraq El Amba Bishoi was consecrated as *amba* (bishop) and *mutran* (metropolitan and archbishop) of Jerusalem and the Middle East by Pope Shenouda III. The ceremony took place in Cairo. The metropolitan took the name Abra'am (Abraham).

Amba Abra'am the First of Jerusalem arrived in the Holy City on 3 January 1992. He was wearing the *qalansuwa*, and over it the *'imma*, the circular bishop's head-cover, once a sign of ignominy enforced by the Ottoman imperial power, now a sign of episcopal dignity. The archbishop is a man of great personal charm with a delightful sense of humour. He is representative of the new breed of well-educated Coptic monks, many of whom come from the medical profession. He is a scientist by training, and has a sharpened mind. Metropolitan Abra'am has a secure record as spiritual adviser, including to expatriates in Cairo who sought him out when he was *qummus* at the monastery of St Bishoi. His pastoral work was singled out for special and favourable mention by at least one astute western commentator.[7] Like most of the monks of the Coptic renaissance who come from professions where they have received a thorough specialist education, incorporating all that is best in modern study, the archbishop has felt no need for a comparable theological training. His ready smile and sparkling eyes attract even the world-weary and cynical. It is Amba Abra'am who enlivens the front cover and some of the inside pages of the popular French work on Coptic monasticism by Alain and Evelyne Chevillat.[8] In francophone circles at least, the archbishop is the icon of the modern Egyptian monk.

In his reformation of the Coptic archbishopric in Jerusalem, Amba Abra'am focused upon the scandal of the disunity of Christians in the Holy City, which was often expressed not merely by the indifference which characterizes so much ecumenical work, but by open hostility, even physical violence. Within a year of his arrival, the new Coptic prelate organized a special service for the week of prayer for Christian unity in January 1993. Clergy and laity of the various Christian communities represented in Jerusalem were invited to a celebration of the Coptic Orthodox liturgy. On this occasion, Amba Matthewos, the Ethiopian archbishop of Jerusalem, concelebrated the eucharist with Amba Abra'am. The location for this ecumenical exercise was the church of St Antony the Great, an important modern Coptic site.[9]

The church of St Antony lies within the Dair Mar Antunius, the monastery of St Antony which is owned by the Copts. In earlier times St Antony's was considered to be a part of the Dair al-Sultan, the monastery of the Sultan.[10] In 1875 the monastery of St Antony was restored as a result of donations from wealthy Copts in Egypt,[11] and rebuilding continued into the twentieth century.[12]

The monastery of St Antony has three churches. At ground level is the church of St Helena with a narthex that leads to the large cistern, which is normally filled with water. The main church of St Antony was built during the primacy of Amba Basilius II (1856–99) and dedicated by his successor Amba Timutheus (1899–1925). The church is decorated with frescos portraying incidents in the life of Christ, including the institution of the eucharist. A third church is dedicated to the *Theotokos*, commemorating her apparition to Coptic students in 1954. Amba Yaqubus (1946–56) conse-crated the room of the apparitions into a church where Coptic monks celebrate the divine liturgy once a week on the same morning as the Blessed Virgin's appearances. Amba Abra'am chose the main church for the ecumeni-cal events of 1993 because the site was free from the controversy which affects so many sites in Jerusalem and because of its associations with recent Coptic archbishops. The ecumenical impact of the occasion was consider-able. Ecumenism is not an optional extra in the Holy Land. It alone lends authenticity and credibility to Christian claims of universality. No more than 2.5 per cent of the population is Christian.

In the year after his first major ecumenical venture at St Antony's monastery, Amba Abra'am examined the Coptic Orthodox educational system in Jerusalem. He found that the Coptic School, the College of St Antony and the school of St Dimiana had a total of only 400 students. In 1994 the students were served by a faculty of twenty-eight members, the majority of whom were graduates of universities in Egypt, Europe or the USA; the student body was 70 per cent Muslim. In the same year there were fewer than 1,000 Copts living in Jerusalem and about 2,000 in the state of Israel and the West Bank combined.[13] The position of the Christian minori-ties in the Middle East is precarious.

His Holiness Pope Shenouda III (born 1923, enthroned 1971) has often expressed his dislike for the term 'Diaspora' when applied to the Copts in North America, Australia and Europe. His natural, patriotic loyalty suppresses his sense of political reality. The persecution of Egypt's Christian minority is occasionally violent and public, but more often it is a petty, daily discrimina-tion, much worse for being so underhand. In Egypt the serious incidence of emigration amongst highly educated Copts is a direct consequence of Islamic and governmental attitudes and actions. In Jerusalem and Israel there are feelings of impasse and despair which drive Copts and other Christians to seek their future elsewhere. In 1995 Amba Abra'am looked at some plain questions: Does the Coptic metropolitan in Jerusalem preside over an important Christian museum of holy places? Does the archbishop merely attempt to assist Coptic pilgrims in gaining access to sacred spots? Is he pastor of a static Coptic community? Or does the *mutran* minister to a dynamic holy people who can be fulfilled in their social and devotional life in the Holy City?

Archbishop George Khodr of Hadeth, Beirut, made a pointed comment in 1971:

> According to our knowledge . . . no Christians will be left in Jerusalem. The result will be that the Holy Places will remain without the presence of the people. It will be an assemblage of churches . . . viewed in that land as a pre-Israeli relic . . . it will be like visiting Baalbec when you see the Temples of Bacchus and Zeus and then without emotion expect the aesthetic emotion. Some religious influences will be left, some nuns . . . and highly qualified professors of theology, and archaeologists from the Protestant world who will serve as natural guides for tourists.[14]

The bitterness which underlies this statement is a measure of the profound anxiety which affects the minorities in the Holy Land and throughout the region. There is a 'steady attrition of a living Christian presence in the land of Christian beginnings', and the Copts know with everyone else that 'the governance of Jerusalem can never be fulfilled in antiquities'.[15]

The major restoration of old buildings, the renovation of the large subterranean cistern close to the church of St Helena, and the explosion of social and educational projects, like the new College of St Antony at Bet Hanina which was opened in late 1993, are tangible evidences of the Coptic intention to be an effective presence in Jerusalem and its environs, not simply a historical relic. Retrospection is inevitable in such an ancient community, but for Amba Abra'am examining the past was only of real value if it confirmed the present rights of the Copts and anticipated the future: renaissance must renew legitimate pride without arrogance.

Pope Shenouda's new Copts know that there is a long Coptic history in Jerusalem, which may be briefly surveyed.

There are few significant references to the Copts in Jerusalem before the eleventh century, and the gaps in our knowledge, amounting to centuries, are the norm. No secure conclusion can be deduced from the presence of Egyptians during the apostolic preaching on Pentecost in Acts 2:1–41. By the end of the fourth century, following the discovery of the Cross by Helena, the mother of Constantine, in AD 328, the church of the Resurrection, the Anastasis, known significantly in the West as the church of the Holy Sepulchre, was a centre of pilgrimage where many 'joined in adoration of the Resurrection of our Lord Jesus Christ'.[16] By the sixth century stories of the pilgrimage to Jerusalem of St Mary the Egyptian, once an actress and courtesan, now a model of repentance, were circulating in the East. This famous Coptic saint died in about AD 431.[17] The Palestine Pilgrims' Texts Society has also shown that Coptic monks were in Jerusalem during the pilgrimages of AD 386, and that a Spanish abbess saw Egyptian monastics in the city later in the same century.[18]

The Copts are also mentioned as pilgrims in the 'Letter of Guarantee' attributed to the second of the Rightly-Guided Caliphs, *Al-Khulafa ar-Rashidun*, 'Umar b. al-Khattab, in the fifteenth year of the *Hijra*, AD 637, but the authenticity of this document is often questioned by scholars.[19] The period of Islamic expansion *c.*632–750 was important for the Copts. Islam became the context in which Coptic theology now had to operate, and there can be little doubt that the fifth pillar of Islam – the *Haj* to Mecca at least once in the believer's lifetime – strengthened the notion of pilgrimage amongst Christians. At the same time, travel became more difficult. In the era of conquests the Copts were often reduced to urban communities enclosed in their own districts or to rural centres surviving in insecurity and imperma-nence.[20] There is, however, a record in the patriarchate of Amba Yaqub (810–30) which shows that the Copts had their own church in Jerusalem during his reign.[21] A Coptic papyrus of the ninth century refers to a Coptic lady traveller in Jerusalem;[22] and the *History of the Coptic Patriarchs* records a similar visit at the end of the eleventh century.[23] During this period (*c.*1089) a Copt called Mansur al-Tilbani became an assistant to the Muslim governor of Jerusalem. Mansur al-Tilbani reconstructed an old church and requested the Coptic patriarch to send a bishop to the Holy City to consecrate the altar. This took place in the Coptic month of Barmahat in the 'Year of the Coptic Martyrs', AM 808 (AD 1092).[24] Such sparse references as these give, at the very least, an impression of some Christian movement between Alexandria and Jerusalem.

From the time of the crusades the Coptic picture is clearer and the records more numerous and precise. The turn of the eleventh and twelfth centuries saw the establishment of the European crusaders in Jerusalem. Godfrey of Bouillon captured the city in 1099. The Catholics of the West were generally opposed to the eastern churches but good relations existed between the Latins and the oriental Christians. [25] The arrival of the Latin armies and the establishment of a Latin kingdom anticipated the inevitable decline of the Fatimid dynasty (909–1171), but did not bring political or religious continu-ity to the Holy Land, least of all to the Christian churches. Instability throughout the region was aggravated by the crusaders' advance into Egypt and their brief tenure of Damietta in the Nile delta. Here they established the Latin-Catholic patriarchate of Alexandria.[26] The Fatimid era was finally concluded by the rise to power of the great Kurdish chieftain Salah al-Din, who, from his mastery of Egypt and Syria, outmatched and outfought the

Latins and decisively defeated their kingdom at the Horns of Hattin in 1187. Jerusalem surrendered three months later.[27] Salah al-Din seems to have had a special relationship with the Copts for, though it is true that there are records of many conversions to Islam in his time and of some forms of persecution by exile or the imposition of special dress,[28] the great Ayyubid made special concessions for the Copts and raised them to important positions in his administration. Few visitors gazing upon the magnificence of Saladin's most enduring monument realize that the Cairo citadel was built for him on the Muqattam hills by two Coptic architects, Abu Mansur and Abu Mashkur,[29] but it has been remarked of this period that 'subjection and stolidity defined each other in the Coptic psyche'.[30]

Salah al-Din witnessed a dramatic increase in Christian pilgrimages to Jerusalem and was petitioned by various groups who wished to establish themselves on a permanent basis in the Holy City. In 1187 he granted exemptions from taxes for Copts who visited Jerusalem as pilgrims, and by the same ordinance the sultan confirmed the privilege of the Copts and the Ethiopians to own certain sites in the church of the Resurrection.[31]

Otto Meinardus has surveyed the pilgrim documents of several centuries, and these are important testimonies to the constant Coptic presence in Jerusalem, and especially in the church of the Resurrection. Documents of the fourteenth century reveal that nine pilgrims in the period between 1336 and 1384 saw Copts worshipping in the Holy Sepulchre.[32] Eighteen testimonies, ranging from that of Henry Porner in 1419 to that of the Duke of Saxony in 1498, show that the Copts remained active in the Resurrection church.[33] Meinardus studied twenty-four sources from the period 1500–92. These too showed that there was a Coptic presence in Jerusalem in the sixteenth century. In 1537 the Copts had a small chapel directly adjoining the *Kouvouklion*: called the Aedicule in the West, it is a marble construction built directly over the Holy Sepulchre and the chapel of the Angel. The Copts still possess this chapel, usually regarded as the holiest Coptic site because the head of Christ rested here at his burial.[34] In his examination of twenty-three seventeenth-century documents, varying from the Iberian pilgrim Castella in 1600 to the German visitor Maundrell in 1697, Meinardus again found confirmation of Coptic worship in the church. In the eighteenth century five out of six sources consulted revealed Coptic worship from 1704 to 1760.[35] The Coptic chapel adjoining the *Kouvouklion* was restored by Amba Timutheus in 1901 and continues in daily use by the monks assigned to the church: the Coptic Orthodox Church has no records comparable to the pilgrim documents studied by Meinardus, but, as Amba Abra'am remarked in 1994, 'We are here, we have always been here and we shall be here until the Lord comes again.'

The Coptic *mutran* at the end of the twentieth century can look back to the middle of the thirteenth century as a time when the Coptic archbishopric was firmly, and apparently permanently, established in Jerusalem. Tension and misunderstanding between the Copts and Syrians, usually involving property, led the patriarch of Alexandria, Kyrillos III (1235–43), to appoint an Egyptian archbishop in 1238. He succeeded in regaining the Coptic chapel in the Holy Sepulchre–Resurrection church and recovered the church of Mansur al-Tilbani. The first Coptic archbishop of Jerusalem was Amba Basilius I (1238–60).[36] The seventy-eighth successor of St Mark on the Alexandrian throne (Ghobrial III, 1268–71) was 'blessed in the holy places' as a pilgrim and was actually ordained as a Coptic priest in the church of the Resurrection.[37] Such happy events in the history of Jerusalem have to be weighed against some that have been dispiriting. The least happy period was in the eighteenth century. Ecumenism is constantly undermined by the discovery that the real intention in interdenominational relations is to weaken the partner in dialogue. Coptic–Catholic attempts at conciliation go back to the Council of Ferrara–Florence in 1438,[38] but by the end of the seventeenth century two Catholic missions[39] to the Copts had been established in Egypt: the Franciscans in Upper Egypt and the Jesuits in Cairo.[40] It is a characteristic of Catholic and Protestant European missions in Muslim lands that they concentrate upon the conversion of local Christians away from their own traditional churches whilst studiously avoiding any serious attempt to convert Muslims to Christianity. The Franciscan and Jesuit missions to the Copts had no response until 1741, when the Coptic archbishop in Jerusalem, Amba Athanasius, became a Roman Catholic. The Catholic Pope Benedict XIV immediately consecrated Athanasius as Coptic-Catholic Metropolitan with jurisdiction over all of Egypt. Athanasius remained in Jerusalem, working vigorously at proselytism amongst the eastern Christians. He appointed a distinguished Coptic priest, Fr Yustus Maraglic, as Catholic vicar-general in Egypt. Much later three Coptic monks became Roman Catholic priests in 1862 and remained to work in the Holy City: a small movement of Copts from the Orthodox to the Catholic tradition continues to the present day. The regular succession of Coptic archbishops from the thirteenth century until the present was briefly broken for a period of four years after the death of Archbishop Athanasius but was renewed in 1770 under Metropolitan Yusab (Joseph).

The present archiepiscopal residence is on the Via Dolorosa, but some Coptic metropolitans have on occasion lived outside Jerusalem. There are hints that some holders of the office returned for extended periods to the desert monastery of St Antony, near the Red Sea, from which most of them have come. According to A. Goodrich-Freer in 1904, the Coptic archbishop in the Holy Land resided in Jaffa.[41] At the beginning of the twentieth century the Copts had a large monastery at Jaffa which provided pilgrim accommodation for tens of thousands of Coptic pilgrims. Oriental Orthodox pilgrimages to the holy places were common until the late 1940s. Certainly, the role of the archbishop has been bound to the business of Coptic pilgrimage, and it has often been his primary duty to preside at some major pilgrim events whilst leaving the daily business of the church to others. This enabled Basilius IV (1959–91) to carry out his scholarly work in seclusion.

One annual event of importance is associated with the Coptic metropolitan. On Easter Eve the ceremony of the Holy Fire (*Hagios Phos*) takes place. It is clear that the Copts have taken part in this ceremony for centuries. The Chevalier d'Arvieux saw the Copts at the ceremony in 1660, as did Hasselquist in 1751.[42] Though the Copts do not have the right to celebrate the divine liturgy in the Holy Sepulchre itself, a right reserved for the Greek Orthodox as representatives of the Byzantine churches, the Latin Catholics representing the West and the Armenians from the oriental Orthodox tradition, the Copts do have sanctuary lamps there which they are allowed to light. They also have Coptic processions within the church, stopping at every altar for acts of adoration, intercession and benediction. On the eve of Easter the Greek Orthodox patriarch, accompanied by an Armenian Orthodox monk, enters the church of the Resurrection for the ceremony of the Holy Fire. From the chapel of the Angel the fire is passed through the southern and northern openings to the pilgrims. The Copts receive the Holy Fire through the southern opening. Then the Holy Fire is taken to the Coptic Orthodox metropolitan, who during the ceremony has remained in the Coptic chapel of the Blessed Virgin Mary to the west of the Holy Sepulchre. After having received the Holy Fire, the Coptic archbishop carries it to the Coptic pilgrims. Then the Greeks, Armenians, Syrians and Copts make a procession three times around the church.[43] This procession is repeated on Easter Sunday morning at 4 a.m. Such annual celebrations have enormous significance in churches which think not merely in years but in centuries. The continuity of archbishop and community is of an importance barely imaginable to a westerner.

Throughout the centuries, the Copts have lived cheek by jowl in the Holy City with the sister church of Ethiopia. Any account of the Egyptian Christian presence in Jerusalem must include some notice of this bitter and tragic relationship. It cannot be the function of this chapter to offer all the documentary evidence relating to the conflicting claims of the Copts and Ethiopians to the site known as the Dair al-Sultan (monastery of the Sultan) on the roof of the church of St Helena, and to the chapels of the Four Living Creatures and of the Archangel Michael. Both churches claim jurisdiction of the Dair al-Sultan, and, at different times, both churches have managed to convince external arbiters that they were the rightful owners. The Ethiopian case has been eloquently presented in careful, scholarly polemic by Sister Abraham,[44] an internationally distinguished scholar who has lived in Jerusalem for many years, and an academic examination with a Coptic bias is provided by Professor Otto Meinardus.[45] A general statement concerning recent Coptic–Ethiopian relations, with a notice of contemporary developments in Jerusalem, will assist anyone turning to the conflicting accounts which are usual when dealing with the Dair al-Sultan.[46]

The apostle of Ethiopia was Frumentius, a Syrian known as *Anba Salama*, the Father of Peace, or *Kasate Berhan Salama*, the Revealer of Light. Because Frumentius was consecrated by St Athanasius (*c.* AD 350), the Egyptian church claimed authority over the southern church. The Copts exercised control over Ethiopia for many centuries by appointing an expatriate as bishop, even though he rarely understood the language, culture and psychology of the Ethiopians.[47] This imposition was never wholeheartedly accepted in Ethiopia. The last Egyptian Copt to rule the Ethiopians died on 22 October 1950, after which the ascetic Abba Kyrillos appointed an Ethiopian as patriarch-catholicos. The Copts also agreed that they would not establish any bishoprics or titles in the Diaspora without first consulting the Ethiopian church:[48] we shall see that this was to have serious consequences affecting the church in Jerusalem.

From the beginning of Coptic–Ethiopian relations many problems usually associated with the relations between the developed and the developing world have been effective agents of alienation and separation. Paternalism, nationalism and racism have played their part in the story. Certainly the Ethiopians are a proud people who recognize their own cultural history as being equal to that of Egypt. The Copts have occasionally harboured the extremely unpleasant notion that they have preserved the ethnic racial purity of Pharaonic Egypt, so that they can be distinguished from the Muslim majority. The Copts share with many other peoples a suspicion of black people, especially when the black peoples are not subject and obedient. For centuries this incipient and unacknowledged racism has been part of the problem in the relations between Ethiopian and Egyptian Christians. It has often seemed very odd to the Ethiopians that Coptic bishops who crumbled before the might of Islam in the Nile valley were so aggressive and assertive when dealing with black Christians on the shore of Lake Tanna.

The conquest of the Copts by Islam weakened the claims of Alexandria over Ethiopia. To the southern Christians it seemed that Ethiopia, 'a sovereign Christian state',[49] where the Abuna and his flock could walk with their heads held high was at least as significant as Egypt, where the Copts were oppressed, a *dhimmi* people, under the sword of Islam. This history of ambivalent relations between Copt and Ethiopian is very long and most unedifying, acrimony always surrounding the comparison made between the freedom of established Christianity in the Ethiopian Empire and the subjection of the Copts in the Islamic state. The Ethiopian Orthodox church invariably found that it was numerically much stronger than the church in Egypt. The Ethiopians have been eager to exploit this fact and to assert the need for complete independence in the light of political developments throughout Africa. Leadership of Christian Africa is also felt to be at stake: the Copts have been enthusiastic missionaries in East Africa, but Ethiopia continually reminds commentators that the Egyptian church is arabophone, and culturally and ethnically distinct from most of Africa.

Two men, one a Copt and the other an Ethiopian, did more than any others to restore Christian relations between the Alexandrian church and the church led from Addis Ababa. They were Haile Selassie I (1891–1975) and Pope Kyrillos VI, Coptic pope of Alexandria and 116th patriarch in the see of St Mark (1902–71). They shared a vision of oriental Orthodox unity and achieved much in a relatively short period. Pope Kyrillos visited Ethiopia in 1960. Pope and emperor presided over the only oriental Orthodox assembly at Addis Ababa in 1965, and Haile Selassie delighted the Copts by attending their liturgy in Cairo during a state visit in 1969. If both had lived longer the tragic experience of the Ethiopians under Marxism and its aftermath, especially in Eritrea, would have been quite different. Haile Selassie outlived Kyrillos by a few years, but he was dethroned in 1974 and murdered in 1975.[50]

From the inception of his patriarchal ministry in 1959 there were rumours that Pope Kyrillos would meet Emperor Haile Selassie in Jerusalem. The rumours were reinforced by the preface (1960) to the important monograph *The Copts in Jerusalem* when Professor Otto Meinardus seemed to address them both:

> It is . . . hoped that this study of the historical position of Dair as-Sultan may help to solve some of the problems with regard to property-claims, and that thereby a more satisfactory settlement may be reached . . . The author feels assured . . . that . . . His Holiness Amba Kirillus VI will come to an agreement on this thorny question with His Majesty Haile Selassie, if both parties are embued with the Spirit of Christian charity, and eschewing all recourse to legal documents and action, wherein worketh not the righteousness of God.[51]

The appeal was apparently unheard. There were, in any case, more pressing issues for church and empire.[52]

Ironically, it was during the period when Kyrillos and Haile Selassie were working so closely together that the situation at the Dair al-Sultan was at its worst for many years. Just before the accession of Pope Kyrillos, the Coptic metropolitan and his priests had been expelled from Jerusalem. The Jordanian government had taken over control of east Jerusalem after the British mandate and the Arab–Israeli war of 1948, but the Arab republic of Egypt had broken off diplomatic relations with King Hussein and the Hashemite kingdom of Jordan, and the Copts were, not for the first or last time, pawns in Arab politics.[53] *Al-Ahram* of 4 January 1959 reported that the expelled clergy had been given visitors' visas in time for the Orthodox Christmas on 6/7 January. The visas were renewable.

The site now changed hands, and keys, on a number of occasions. In early February 1959 the Jordanians ordered the site to be handed to the Ethiopians.[54] The Copts complained that the Treaty of Berlin in 1878 had guaranteed the site to them. The Copts again held some of the keys to the site. On 22 February 1961 the Jordanian government once more decided that the Ethiopians owned the site and ordered the Copts to give up the keys.[55]

According to Pedersen, Cairo now applied pressure and the keys went back to the Copts.[56] On 2 April 1961 the Jordanians found in favour of the Copts and, as Meinardus has it, 'the Dair as-Sultan was returned to the original owners, the Copts'.[57] In its Christmas Eve report on 6 January 1963 the Cairo Coptic newspaper *El Watani* reported its satisfaction that the Copts were still *in situ* at Dair al-Sultan.

Outsiders are always tempted to scoff at the farcical element in the tale, but tragedy often follows quickly in the wake of comedy. In February 1966 al-Sayyid Anwar al-Khatib became governor of Jerusalem.[58] Anwar al-Khatib had installed electricity and running water. The Copts objected to this disturbance of the status quo. Physical violence ensued in which a number of Ethiopians were seriously hurt. This was, unbelievably, whilst the Ethiopians were engaged in the 1967 Easter processions. Pedersen claims that the Copts had gathered an arsenal of stones for some time in anticipation of this confrontation.[59] It is a matter of record that the police were called to intervene. Police protection became the norm. In the Six Day War of June 1967 the Israelis took control of the Old City and the question of Dair as-Sultan passed to another political jurisdiction.

By the night of Easter 1970 the opposing factions were again ready for open struggle which led to a Coptic appeal to the High Court of Israel. The Ethiopians now held the keys, leaving the passageways open but controlling the chapels. On 16 March 1971 the Israeli High Court decided in favour of the Copts but allowed the Israeli government to set up a commission to examine the problem. Golda Meir accepted this suggestion and appointed Abba Eban as a commission member. The situation has now continued for a quarter of a century: the Copts have the High Court judgement, the keys to one gate, and one of their priests occupies a monastic cell on the site, whilst the Ethiopians have the remaining keys including those to the two chapels. Coptic appeals in 1977, 1980, April 1981, December 1984 and more recently in 1994 have confirmed their rights but have not resulted in any action. Arbitration by Judge David Bacher also broke down in February 1982.

Pope Shenouda has prohibited Coptic pilgrimages to the Holy Land for as long as the Israelis do not intervene for the return of the Dair as-Sultan to the Copts. He has reiterated this interdiction from his desert exile in 1981, through subsequent years and more recently at Easter 1996. He has been ignored by some Copts. Records in the 1960s show that tens of thousands of Copts were usually in Jerusalem for Easter. The pilgrimage has a vital place in Coptic popular religion. In Easter 1995 it was calculated that 15,000 Copts went to Jerusalem despite the interdiction of the patriarch.[60] Monks of the monasteries of St Macarius in the Wadi Natrun and from other parts of Egypt have been openly critical of the patriarch, and some have led pilgrim groups to the holy places. In September 1995 Pope Shenouda reacted angrily to suggestions in the Egyptian press that he was excommunicating people who went on pilgrimage.[61] 'It is a question of church discipline, that we

support our rights before the Israelis.' But Shenouda's ban on pilgrimages to
the Holy City was continually raised in Egypt in a debate which included
wider criticisms of the pope. In April 1995 an official government journal,
published in English and Arabic, debated the issues and the patriarch claimed
that his critics were backed by tour companies who were angry because of his
refusal to let Copts travel to Jerusalem.[62] Both Shenouda and Amba Abra'am
are anxious to establish that their criticisms are always directed against Israel
rather than the Ethiopians.[63] It is true that Amba Abra'am has been more
acceptable to the Ethiopians than any other hierarch in living memory. He
has held out a hand of friendship, but his work has been undercut by tragic
events outside Jerusalem.

Relations between the Coptic Orthodox Church and the Ethiopian
Orthodox Church had been seriously effected by the Marxist revolution and
the martyrdom of Orthodox Ethiopia under Mengistu. The Ethiopians found
that the Copts had little understanding of the impact of communism on the
old empire and even less sympathy: Ethiopian refugees customarily found
more sympathy and help amongst the Catholics and Anglicans. Nevertheless,
Pope Shenouda was willing to establish ecclesiastical norms with Addis
Ababa and a protocol of reconciliation was drawn up and ratified by both
synods.[64] Whilst preparing the protocols, bringing them before the synod and
signing them, Pope Shenouda was also preparing to establish an autonomous
Orthodox church within the jurisdiction of the Ethiopian patriarch-catholicos. In response to requests from Eritrea, Pope Shenouda III consecrated five
Eritrean abbots as bishops on 19 June 1994, the feast of Pentecost, with the
promise of the establishment of an autocephalous Eritrean Orthodox church
led by a patriarch appointed by the Coptic patriarch. The Ethiopians believed
that the Copts had reneged on the agreement of 1959 and on the protocols of
1994. Protests from Addis Ababa were received in Cairo.[65]

The five Eritreans had come to Cairo wearing the traditional Ethiopian
pillbox headdress. Just before their consecration the Copts dressed the bishops in the *qalansuwa* and *'imma* – the monastic dress of the Coptic revival
now so prominent in Jerusalem.

The effect of these consecrations upon the church in Jerusalem was entirely
negative. Relations between the Ethiopian church and the church in Egypt
broke down,[66] but the situation is always fluid and unpredictable and it is wise
to reserve judgement on the outcome of these most recent developments.

Jerusalem is continually present for the Coptic Orthodox Christian wher-
ever he or she may be. The Coptic Synaxarium has four major festivals with
specific readings relating to the holy places. On 26 September (16 of the
Coptic month *Tut*) the Copts commemorate the consecration of the church of
the Resurrection by St Athanasius the Apostolic (*c.*296–373). The Egyptian
patriarch was assisted by the patriarchs of Constantinople and Antioch at a
time long before the divisions of Chalcedon in 451. On the following day, 17
Tut/27 September, the discovery of the Holy Cross (AD 326) by St Helena

(*c.255–330*) is honoured in the liturgy. On 12 *Bashons*/20 May the manifestation of a Cross of Fire over the site of Golgotha in AD 351 is observed. On 10 *Barmahat*/19 March the Copts make annual celebration of the restoration of the Holy Cross to Jerusalem. The Cross, discovered by St Helena in the fourth century, had been stolen by the attacking Persians in 614, but was rescued by the Byzantine Emperor Heraclius (575–641) and brought back into the Holy City in 629.[67]

At the time of writing the liturgical memory of Jerusalem is all the memory most Copts have of the city, because the patriarchal prohibition of pilgrimage remains in force and the problem of Dair al-Sultan is unresolved, but Coptic monks in the *qalansuwa* can be seen everywhere in Israel and in the Palestinian territories.

Notes

[1] Aziz Atiya, *The Copts and Christian Civilisation*, The Fredk. Wm. Reynolds Lecture. Delivered at the University of Utah (Salt Lake City, 1979). In this lecture, and in his *A History of Eastern Christianity* (London, 1968), 119 f., Professor Atiya employed the same metaphor: 'Like a great and solitary Egyptian temple standing sorrowfully on the edge of the desert and weathering sandstorms over the years until it became submerged by the accretions of time, the ancient Coptic Church led its lonely life unnoticed on the fringe of Christian civilisation . . . Like the same massive temple, too, it has proved itself to be indestructible. In the last few decades . . . its sons have started removing the sands of time from around the edifice, which has shown signs of shining again.' See also Aziz Atiya (general ed.), *The Coptic Encyclopaedia*, 8 vols (New York, 1991); Otto Meinardus, *Christian Egypt: Faith and Life* (Cairo, 1970); Takao Yamagata, *Coptic Monasteries at Wadi Natrun in Egypt* (Tokyo, 1983); John Watson, *Abba Kyrillos: Patriarch and Solitary* (Pennsylvania, 1996); John H. Watson, *Among the Copts* (Brighton, 2000); O. F. A. Meinardus, *Two Thousand Years of Coptic Christianity* (Cairo, 1999).
[2] Cf. Pieternella van Doorn-Harder, *Contemporary Coptic Nuns* (Columbia, SC, 1995), 90–100.
[3] The two halves allude to an incident when St Antony had his cowl torn in two during a fight with demons. According to the Copts the shape of the cowl resembles a bib for young children and recalls the childlike simplicity of St Antony and the words of Jesus when he said, 'Truly, I say to you, whoever does not receive the kingdom of God like a child shall not enter it' (Mark 10:15). In the Islamic world the embroidered crosses stress the monk's removal from the world.
[4] See esp. Saad Michael Saad, *Christian Minorities in a Pluralistic Situation* (Chicago, 1984), 23–8.
[5] Otto Meinardus photographed the metropolitan and the Coptic priests in Jerusalem for his 1960 monograph: not one is wearing the cowl. In *Snaps of Pope Kyrilios VI* (64pp. undated but purchased in Cairo, 1989: publishers Pope Kyrillos Publications, with captions in Arabic, French, German and English) the patriarch is photographed at least sixty times, not once with the *qalansuwa*.
[6] An international directory of Orthodox bishops, *Orthodoxia*, is compiled and edited biennially by Dr Nikolaus Wyrwoll at the Ostkirchliches Institut, Regensburg, Germany. The information used here is taken from the editions of 1986–7 and 1996.
[7] Otto F. A. Meinardus, *Monks and Monasteries of the Egyptian Deserts*, rev. edn (Cairo, 1989), 120.
[8] Alain and Evelyne Chevillat, *Moines du désert d'Égypte* (Lyon, 1990).

⁹ There is no single comprehensive study in English of the history of the Coptic presence in Jerusalem, but Otto F. A. Meinardus has placed us all in his debt with his carefully considered contributions to the subject over the last four decades. Apart from primary sources which were available in the library of the Central College of the Anglican Communion at Canterbury, now presumably at Pusey House, Oxford, the major sources of dates and information – though not of interpretation – in the present essay were obtained from the following works by Otto F. A. Meinardus who has conscientiously treated the question of the Dair al-Sultan over the last quarter century: *The Copts in Jerusalem* (Cairo, 1960); 'The Copts in Jerusalem and the question of the holy places', *Coptic Church Review*, 16 (1995), 9–25; *Christian Egypt: Faith and Life* (Cairo, 1970), 436–67; 'The Copts in Jerusalem and the question of the holy places', in Anthony O'Mahony with Göran Gunner and Kevork Hintlian (eds), *The Christian Heritage in the Holy Land* (London, 1994), 112–28.

¹⁰ The monastery of the Sultan, Dair al-Sultan, will feature later in this chapter. Nobody knows why it has its name. Some believe the site to have been a gift of one of the Mameluke sultans (the dynasty reigned in Egypt and Syria from 1250 to 1517), others that it was founded by Roxelana, the Russian Orthodox wife of the Ottoman sultan Suleiman 'Qanuni', the Law-Giver, known in the West as 'the Magnificent' (1520–66). Cf. Meinardus, *Copts in Jerusalem*, 47.

¹¹ R. E. Wilson, *Picturesque Palestine, Sinai and Egypt*, 2 vols (New York, 1881).

¹² Meinardus, 'The Copts in Jerusalem', 20–1.

¹³ Meinardus, 'The Copts in Jerusalem', 23, bases his statistics on information received from the metropolitan.

¹⁴ Quoted in Kenneth Cragg, *This Year in Jerusalem* (London, 1982), 110. Khodr was addressing a theological consultation in the Lebanon on issues arising from the Palestinian problem.

¹⁵ Cragg, *This Year*, 111.

¹⁶ Benedicta Ward, *Harlots of the Desert* (London, 1987). The phrase occurs in the life of St Pelagia the Harlot, 74. Cf. John H. Watson, *The Transfigured Cross* (Pennsylvania, 2002), 54–5.

¹⁷ Benedicta Ward, *Harlots*, tells the tale in 'St Mary of Egypt: the liturgical icon of repentance', 26–56.

¹⁸ Meinardus, *The Copts in Jerusalem*, 113.

¹⁹ See Meinardus in *The Christian Heritage in the Holy Land*, 114.

²⁰ See especially Bat Ye'or, *The Decline of Eastern Christianity under Islam: From Jihad to Dhimmitude* (London, 1996), 43–68.

²¹ Meinardus, *The Copts in Jerusalem*, 11.

²² George C. Anawati, 'Un papyrus chrétien en Arabe', *Mélanges Islamiques* (Cairo–Paris), II (1954), 98.

²³ Aziz Atiya (ed.), *History of the Patriarchs of the Egyptian Church* (Cairo, 1959), 2, 358.

²⁴ Meinardus, *The Copts in Jerusalem*, 114.

²⁵ Meinardus, states that the Latins were particularly hostile to the Copts and Syrians: *The Copts in Jerusalem*, 13. This view, however, must be set against the important work of Bernard Hamilton, *The Latin Church in the Crusader States: The Secular Church* (London, 1980), 188–211, 332–60.

²⁶ Kenneth Cragg, *The Arab Christian* (London, 1991), 181.

²⁷ See Bernard Lewis, *The Middle East* (London, 1995), 91; and Albert Hourani, *A History of the Arab Peoples* (London, 1991), 84.

²⁸ Aziz Atiya, *History of Eastern Christianity*, 94–6.

²⁹ Hourani, *A History of the Arab Peoples*, 125, and Aziz Atiya, *History of Eastern Christianity*, 95.

³⁰ Cragg, *The Arab Christian*, 182.

³¹ Timotheus P. Themelis, *Les Grecs aux Lieux Saints, Jérusalem* (Jerusalem, 1921). This work is cited by Otto Meinardus in all his books and essays on Jerusalem. A copy could be seen at St Augustine's Library, Canterbury in 1986.

[32] Meinardus, *The Copts in Jerusalem*, 19.

[33] Ibid., 22.

[34] Ibid., 29.

[35] Ibid., 37.

[36] Ibid., 81.

[37] Meinardus, *The Christian Heritage in the Holy Land*, 117.

[38] Salvatore Tedeschi, 'Etiopi e Copti al concilio di Firenze', *Annuarium Historiae Conciliorum*, 2 (1991), 380–407.

[39] Josef Metzler, 'Bemühungen der S. C. Propaganda Fide um die Wiedervereinigung der Koptischen Kirche mit Rome', *Euntes Docete*, 17 (1964), 94–108.

[40] See the two volumes by Charles Libois, *Égypte (1547–1563)* (Rome, 1993) and *Égypte (1565–1591)* (Rome, 1998).

[41] A. Goodrich-Freer, *Inner Jerusalem* (London, 1904), 123.

[42] Meinardus, *The Copts in Jerusalem*, 35.

[43] Meinardus, *The Christian Heritage in the Holy Land*, 122–3.

[44] Kirsten Stoffregen Pedersen (Sister Abraham), 'The Qeddusan: the Ethiopian Christians in the Holy Land', in O'Mahony et al. (eds), *Christian Heritage in the Holy Land*, 129–48.

[45] Ibid., 112–28.

[46] A fuller account of the relations between Copts and Ethiopians can be found in my essay 'Abba Kyrillos: patriarch and solitary', *Coptic Church Review*, 17, 1 and 2 (1996).

[47] Otto Meinardus, *Christian Egypt*, 349.

[48] Watson, *Abba Kyrillos*, 23.

[49] Pedersen, 'The Qeddusan', 131.

[50] An unforgettable account of Haile Selassie's final days as emperor can be found in Ryszard Kapuscinski, *The Emperor* (London, 1983).

[51] Meinardus, *Christian Egypt*, 7.

[52] See Karekin Sarkissian, *The Witness of the Oriental Orthodox Churches* (Beirut, 1968).

[53] For a discussion of Egyptian regional policy see P. J. Vatikiotis, *The History of Modern Egypt* (London, 1976), 405ff.

[54] Meinardus, 'The Copts in Jerusalem', 22.

[55] Pedersen, 'The Qeddusan', 147.

[56] Ibid.

[57] Meinardus, 'The Copts in Jerusalem', 23.

[58] Let the reader notice that Pedersen does not tell us of this man's employment by the Ethiopians, whilst Meinardus is quick to note that he had 'served the Ethiopians for 15 years as advocate'. Pedersen, 'The Qeddusan', 147; Meinardus, 'The Copts in Jerusalem', 23.

[59] Pedersen, 'The Qeddusan', 147.

[60] See Syndesmos Orthodox Press Service no. 59 (April 1995), 1–4; cf. *Sourozh*, 60, (London, May 1995), 50.

[61] In a private meeting with the writer at the Dorchester Hotel, London, September 1995.

[62] *Egypt Today* (April 1995), 87–91, by Lee Keath.

[63] Meinardus quotes the metropolitan to this effect in 'The Copts in Jerusalem', 26.

[64] The present writer was able to study these documents at Deir Amba Bishoi in the Western Desert in April 1994. The Copts have not published them, but the Ethiopians have: Kahsay G. Egziabher (Amharic) and Yohannes G. Selassie (English) in *Ecumenism in the Ethiopian Orthodox Tewahido Church* (Addis Ababa, 27 September 1995), 43–8.

[65] Ernst Chr. Suttner, 'Eritreas Eigenstaatlichkeit und die Kirchen', *Una Sancta*, 49 (1994), 106–24.

[66] See Meinardus, 'The Copts in Jerusalem', and Watson, *Abba Kyrillos*, 28.

[67] For details concerning the Coptic Synaxarium see the footnotes in Aziz Atiya, *History of Eastern Christianity*, 31.

6

PILGRIMS AND ASCETICS FROM AFRICA: THE ETHIOPIAN CHURCH AND COMMUNITY OF JERUSALEM

Kirsten Stoffregen Pedersen

It has been suggested that the Christians in the Holy Land could be divided into three categories: the original local church, the pilgrim churches, and the missionaries. While the local church of course is the founding church of Jerusalem, the mother of all other national churches, the pilgrim churches are national churches which originated with Jerusalem pilgrims, some of whom remained for the rest of their lives in the holy places without taking any active role in the country in missionary or social work, unlike the third group.

It is quite clear that the ancient Ethiopian Christian community in Jerusalem belongs to the group of pilgrim churches, which reminds us that we should not understand that expression as describing Christians who visit the holy places merely for a shorter or longer period and then go back to their country of origin. Nothing prevents the individual pilgrim from returning, but in actual fact few of the members of the pilgrim churches do so, nor do these churches ever tend to disappear from the Holy Land. Quite the contrary: their members have throughout history shown great fortitude and determination to stay whatever happens.

The first we hear in post-biblical literature about Ethiopians in the Holy Land presents them to us as pilgrims. It is in two short passages in letters from disciples of St Jerome in Bethlehem in the closing years of the fourth century AD. Sts Paula and her daughter Eustochium write to their friend Marcella in Rome, encouraging her to visit the Holy Land:

> Anyone who was in Gaul before would want to get here as quickly as possible. Even the Briton, although far removed from our world, if he has persevered in his faith will leave his western sun to seek out these places which are known to him only through their fame and the narrative of the Scriptures. What need is there to list the Armenians, Persians, people from India and Ethiopia, and from Egypt itself, rich in monks, Pontus and Cappadocia, Coele, Syria, Mesopotamia and all the multitudes of the East?[1]

A very similar letter to another friend, Leta, contains this description:

> The military standards carry the emblem of the cross. This symbol of execution and salvation decorates the purple robes of kings and the glittering jewels of

their crowns. Now even Egyptian Serapis has become a Christian. The god Marnas, trapped in Gaza, mourns and is constantly afraid that his temple will be overthrown. From India, Persia and Ethiopia every day we welcome crowds of monks. The Armenian has laid down his quiver. The Huns learn the psalter. The frosts of Scythia are warmed with the heat of faith. The rosy-cheeked, fair-haired Getae carry their churches about with their armies, and it may be that they fight us on equal terms just because they equal us in faith as well.[2]

In the second letter we see that among the Ethiopian pilgrims were ascetics, *monachi*, and this tended to be the case with all later pilgrims' caravans. It was mostly those ascetics, single men and women with no responsibility for a family, who remained in the Holy Land.

Ethiopian Traditions regarding Ancient Ethio-Judaean Relations

A traditional Ethiopian, asked about the origins of his national church, will always start with the queen of Sheba.[3] In his view, Ethiopia was converted to Old Testament Judaism around 1,000 years before it embraced Christianity. Typically, one of the newest books on the history of the Ethiopians in Jerusalem, Archbishop Matthewos's *Däbrä Seltan bä-Iyärusalem* (in Amharic) (Jerusalem, 1988 EC/September AD 1996)[4] opens with a short description of the results of the queen's visit to King Solomon. Several cycles of legends have developed around that short, remarkable Old Testament story, and in Ethiopia one version has been written down in the royal chronicle *Kebrä Nägäst* (Glory of the Kings) which became popular in the thirteenth century and has repeatedly been copied since. According to the *Kebrä Nägäst*, King Solomon and the queen had a son born in Ethiopia to whom she gave the name Menilek (from *ben melekh* – son of a king). The young Menilek visited his father in Jerusalem. Solomon wanted him to be his successor on the throne of Judah, but Menilek saw it as his destiny to return to Ethiopia. All the first-born of Israel followed him, and at the last moment the young priests laid hands on the Ark of the Covenant and brought it from Jerusalem to Ethiopia, where it is believed still to be kept in the church of St Mary of Sion in the ancient royal city of Axum.[5]

The queen of Sheba personally embraced Judaism during her stay in Jerusalem as King Solomon's guest. She expressed her will to return there on pilgrimage and to send her servants, if she herself could not come. For this purpose she asked for, and obtained from the king, a place in Jerusalem where Ethiopian pilgrims could be accommodated.

The archbishop continues with the traditional description of the arrival of Christianity in Ethiopia. This is of course based on the story of the baptism of the Ethiopian eunuch (Acts 8:26–40) and is less adorned with non-biblical additions. The Ethiopians do not pay attention to the disturbing name (or title) of the queen whom the eunuch served as a treasurer. Candace is in reality connected with Meroë rather than with Axum.[6]

In order to understand the development of the Ethiopian community in the Holy Land we shall have to recall what happened in Ethiopia during more than 2,000 years of Ethiopian presence in Jerusalem. It is characteristic of the pilgrim churches in general that events in their countries of origin always influence their life in the Holy Land.[7]

When we said 'more than 2,000 years', this was no exaggeration. 'Eretz Kush' – Ethiopia, in Greek translation – is mentioned in the Old Testament forty-eight times, and while the queen of Sheba was a guest and pilgrim, 'Ebed-melekh the Ethiopian (Jer. 38:7–39:18) seems to have been permanently established at the Judaean court.

Christianity reached Ethiopia during the first three centuries of the Christian era, and when Frumentius and Edesius arrived at the court in Axum at the beginning of the fourth century, the ruling family embraced the Christian religion of these two young Syrians. We know about this development from Rufinus,[8] and his account is supported by archaeological evidence from both the stelae of Axum and the finding there of coins bearing the sign of the cross from the time of King Ezana.

The language of the kingdom of Axum was a purely Semitic language, Ge'ez, which is still today the official language of the Ethiopian Orthodox church. The alphabet – or rather the syllabarium – with which this and other Ethiopian languages are traditionally written is of Sabaean origin. The contact of Ethiopia with Arabia across the Red Sea has obviously always been close, and the kings of Axum reigned in Yemen and took up the defence of Christians in southern Arabia when a Jewish king there, Dhu-Nuwas, persecuted them. An Ethiopian attack, supported by the Byzantine emperor, brought an end to his kingdom in 525.

In the early seventh century the rise of Islam brought great and swift change to the Middle East and North Africa. As a reason for the strange fact that the Islamic armies did not attack Ethiopia, the story is told that the disciples of the Prophet Muhammad found refuge at the court of Axum when they were being persecuted in their homeland in the 620s.[9] It is of course possible that this story is true and the reason a good one, but it should also be kept in mind that the mountainous country of Ethiopia with its many natural fortresses, the so-called 'ambas', is difficult to conquer.

Ethiopia remained Christian, but Axum lost its importance as a centre of commerce through its Greek-built port city of Adulis. The centre of power receded westwards following the rise of Islam, and became concentrated during the tenth to twelfth centuries in the region of Lasta and in the hands of the Zägwe dynasty. This was replaced in 1267 by the so-called Solomonic dynasty, which claims descent from King Solomon through Menilek I.

This dynasty gave Ethiopia some remarkable rulers in the fourteenth and fifteenth centuries. 'Amdä Seyon I (1313–44) was able not only to keep the surrounding Muslim emirates from the borders of his kingdom, but also to conquer new territory. Zär'a Yaëqob (1434–68), himself a theologian, carried out a religious reform. Ethiopia was respected and even feared in Egypt because of its geographical position on the sources of the Nile.

The relative stability of the high Middle Ages became seriously endangered only at the beginning of the sixteenth century. The Ottoman Turks were gaining power in the Middle East, and Ethiopia's Muslim neighbours gained in audacity from the new religious–political balance of power. A crisis over commercial routes during the reign of the young emperor Lebnä Dengel (1508–40) developed into a religious war under the leadership (on the Muslim side) of the Somali Ahmad bin-Ibrahim al-Ghazi – nicknamed by the Ethiopians 'Gra ñ' (the Left-handed). He was a major military leader and succeeded in conquering most of Christian Ethiopia, forcing the people to embrace Islam, and burning and destroying churches, monasteries and numerous Christian books and icons after his victory at Shembera Kure in 1529.

Fortunately for Ethiopia, the Portuguese had found a sea route to the African Christian kingdom towards the end of the fifteenth century.[10] When a Portuguese delegation visited the court of Lebnä Dengel in 1520, the king did not see any profit for his country in allowing them to build fortresses on the Red Sea coast, but after Grañ's victory he sent messengers to Portugal to ask for military help. This was immediately granted, and 400 men under the leadership of a son of Vasco da Gama, Cristobal da Gama, were dispatched to Ethiopia with the best weapons of the time.

In the first battle Cristobal da Gama was captured and executed by the Muslims, but at Wayna Daga to the east of Gondar the united Ethio-Portuguese army finally managed to overcome Grañ in 1543. The Muslim leader fell in the battle, and his army was thereafter soon expelled from Ethiopian territory.

Emperor Fasilades (1632–67) established a new capital in Gondar. During the Middle Ages Ethiopia had no capital – the emperor lived in a camp which moved around to the various provinces of his territory. In the mid-seventeenth century, Gondar became an important centre both for the government and for Ethiopian learning, music and art. The Gondar emperors gathered around them the most gifted and learned people of the country, and the result was a short period in which the arts flourished.

In the long run, however, continued isolation was not profitable. Another problem was the trickling into Ethiopia of the pastoral Oromos, or Gallas, as the Semitic-speaking Ethiopians called them. The Oromo language is Cushitic, and prior to their migration into Ethiopian territory they adhered to a traditional African religion. Arriving in Ethiopia, some of them embraced either Christianity or Islam, and soon they began to win political influence, particularly by marrying their daughters into Ethiopian noble and royal circles. Emperor Yoas (1755–69) spoke his mother's Oromo tongue. Strangely enough, it was he that summoned the northern ruler, Ras Michael Suhul of Tegre, to the capital to help him against Oromo intrigues at the court. Ras Michael came, did help, and then had the emperor assassinated. Yoas was replaced by Emperor Yohannes II, who, however, was both enthroned and removed from the throne in 1769. During the so-called 'era of the princes' (zämanä masafent) the puppet emperors had no true power, while the provincial governors were continuously waging war on each other.

This unhappy period of civil war in Ethiopian history came to an end only in 1855, when a young military genius, Kassa Haylu of Qwara, managed to win the throne under the name of Tewodros II (1855–68). Emperor Tewodros succeeded in centralizing the government, although most of his other attempts at modernization came to very little. The power of government remained in the hands of his successors Yohannes IV (1871–89), Menilek II (1889–1913), Empress Zäwditu (1916–30) and Haile Selassie I (1930–74). The Marxist revolution in 1974 abolished the monarchy, and the communist interlude lasted from that year until May 1991.[11]

The Hierarchical Situation of the Ethiopian Church

In the field of church politics one of Emperor Haile Selassie's most important achievements was the success of his diplomatic work for the independence of the Ethiopian national church. It had been the custom that the head of the church was appointed and consecrated by the patriarch of Alexandria, where the first head of the Ethiopian church, the Syrian Frumentius (Abba Sälama) had been consecrated around the year 325. The patriarch would choose a Copt for the task, not a native Ethiopian, and this arrangement had caused many spiritual, organizational and political difficulties for the Christian kingdom through the ages. It was of course by no means unique in the history of the world Church – it must remind us of the relations of the national churches of Bulgaria, Greece, Romania, Russia and Serbia with the patriarchate of Constantinople during many centuries of the life of those churches.[12]

What was particular to the Ethiopian church was the fact that its relations with the Coptic church (the patriarchate of Alexandria) were regulated by the so-called Arab/Nicene canons, a collection of eighty canons erroneously believed to have issued by the Council of Nicaea (AD 325).[13] These had been translated into Arabic in the eighth century. About the relationship between the Coptic patriarch of Alexandria and the metropolitan of Ethiopia, canon 36 says:

> The Ethiopians ought neither to create nor to elect a patriarch, because, on the contrary, their prelate should be under the authority of him who holds the see of Alexandria. There may be among them, [one] in the place of the patriarch, and he should be called catholicos; but he has no right to create archbishops, as the patriarch has. Because of the patriarch he has neither the honour nor the authority. If it happens that there be a council and that this prelate of the Ethiopians be present, let him take the seventh place, after the

prelate of Seleucia [Ctesiphon, today Baghdad]. If authority be given to him to create archbishops in his province, he will, however, not be permitted to appoint any of them [the Ethiopians]. Anyone who shall not obey, the synod excommunicates him.[14]

A movement for independence began to grow in the Ethiopian church at the beginning of the twentieth century. When a new Coptic metropolitan was appointed for Ethiopia in 1929, it was agreed that he should be authorized to consecrate bishops from among the native Ethiopian clergy, and five such bishops were indeed appointed and consecrated. In 1948 a new agreement was signed by which a native Ethiopian metropolitan should be chosen upon the death of the then reigning Coptic Abunä Gerlos. He died in 1951, whereupon the Ethiopian Abunä Bäsilewos was enthroned as metropolitan. In 1959 the autonomy of the Ethiopian national church was further confirmed by the elevation of Abunä Bäsilewos to the rank of patriarch.[15]

The Ethiopian Community in Jerusalem from the Fifth to the Thirteenth Century

From the era prior to the crusades little is known about the Ethiopians in the Holy Land. The German bishop Willibald of Eichstätt (d. 786) met one on his way from one holy place to another in Galilee. But we do not know anything about a more or less organized Ethiopian community in Jerusalem during the Byzantine and early Islamic periods.[16] It is likely that Enrico Cerulli is right in his opinion, expressed in vol. I of his magisterial study *Etiopi in Palestina* (Rome, 1943), that the Ethiopian ascetics living in Jerusalem in those days probably found accommodation with the Copts and Syrians in the Coptic monastery of St Mary Magdalene near Herod's Gate. It is not until the thirteenth century that we meet the Ethiopians in Jerusalem as an easily distinguishable community; from that time on the reports concerning their history become increasingly numerous and exact.

When the bishop of Jerusalem, Juvenal, at the Council of Chalcedon in 451 declared himself in favour of the dyophysite doctrine[17] and was appointed patriarch of the simultaneously established patriarchate of Jerusalem, the monophysites of the Holy Land could no longer accept him as their leader. It therefore became customary that the Syro-Jacobitic patriarch of Antioch appointed and consecrated a bishop for those Christians in Jerusalem.

The Syrian historiographer Barhebraeus (1226–86) tells a story which throws some light on the situation of the Ethiopans in Jerusalem in the thirteenth century.[18] In 1237 a dispute broke out between the Coptic patriarch Cyril III ibn Laqlaq (1235–43), and the Syro-Jacobitic patriarch of Antioch, Ignatius, when the former – quite contrary to common usage – appointed and consecrated a Coptic bishop for Jerusalem. An Ethiopian monk from the

Holy City, Abba Thomas, tried to draw profit for himself from the situation by asking Patriarch Ignatius to consecrate him bishop of Ethiopia. The Syrian was willing to do so, but owing to resistance to the plan in Jerusalem it finally came to nothing.

The Situation of the Ethiopians in Jerusalem 1300–1520

We know about the history of the community during the Middle Ages mainly from two sources: (a) from Ethiopian writings, that is, letters from the Ethiopian emperors to their subjects and brethren in the faith in the Holy Land, including dedications in the manuscripts they donated to the monastery; and (b) from the *itineraria*, travelbooks of many European pilgrims. We must keep in mind that the medieval Ethiopian kings were politically powerful. Medieval Europe knew about a Christian kingdom beyond the territory of the Muslim powers,[19] where a priestly king, 'Prester Yohannes', was believed to reign, but direct contact between Europe and Ethiopia in those days was difficult, so that it was an extraordinary experience for Europeans to meet Ethiopian Christians face to face in Jerusalem.[20]

Well-known dispatches from Ethiopian emperors to their community in Jerusalem were those of Yagbe'ä Seyon (1284–95), 'Amdä Seyon (1313–44) and Zär'ä Yaëqob (1434–68). Yagbe'ä Seyon sent a letter and gifts to the community in Jerusalem in the year 1290 by way of Cairo. The seventeenth-century German *éthiopisant* Hiob Ludolf mentions and quotes the Ge'ez dedication of a *mäshafä nägäst* (Book of Kings) which Emperor 'Amdä Seyon gave to the Ethiopian monastery in Jerusalem; and Emperor Zär'ä Yaëqob sent a *mäshafä sinodos*. During his reign an Ethiopian delegation was dispatched from Jerusalem to Rome to attend the Council of Ferrara–Florence in 1439–41.[21]

Of the numerous European testimonies to an Ethiopian presence in Jerusalem during the Middle Ages, the following are perhaps the most interesting. In 1283 the Dominican friar Burcardus of Mount Zion described the Ethiopians as 'the most pious among the orientals'. Two Franciscans, Fra Simon and Fra Hugo Illuminator, from Ireland tell us of an Ethiopian liturgical service they attended in Jerusalem in 1323. Among the first of those who inform us about the places where such services were celebrated was the Franciscan Niccolò da Poggibonsi, who visited the Holy Land in 1347. According to his report, the Ethiopians at that time possessed two chapels inside the church of the Holy Sepulchre, namely those of St Mary of Golgotha and of St Michael.

Leonardo Frescobaldi (1348) and Oglier d'Anglure (1395–6) speak of four chapels which were then in the hands of the Ethiopians. From the travelbook of the German pilgrim Sebald Rieter the Younger, who visited Jerusalem in 1479, we know that the Ethiopian monks at that time possessed and inhabited a monastery situated on Mount Zion around the so-called Cave of David, where according to one tradition King David composed the penitential psalms.

The situation of the Ethiopian community in Jerusalem was in general quite good during the Middle Ages. It enjoyed the support of the Ethiopian emperors, who were then sufficiently strong to be able to protect the Christians in the Holy Land. When in 1422 Sultan Barsebai closed the church of the Holy Sepulchre, Emperor Yeshaq of Ethiopia (1414–29) began to put pressure on the Muslims in his empire. Ethiopian emperors reacted to persecution of Christians on the part of Muslim rulers on other occasions with the threat to cut off the flow of the Nile, so that its waters would not reach Egypt if the persecution was not stopped.[22]

The Ethiopians in the Holy Land 1520–1855[23]

The Turkish conquest of Jerusalem in 1517 and Ahmad bin Ibrahim Grañ's invasion of Ethiopia soon afterwards brought about a sudden and drastic decline in the situation of the Ethiopian ascetics at Jerusalem. The connection with their country of origin was interrupted and they remained without the means to pay the taxes and bribes which the new rulers in the Holy Land demanded from non-Muslim inhabitants.

A French pilgrim, Maître Denis Possot, who visited the country in 1530, bore witness to the fact that the Ethiopian monks already then lived in their tiny huts at Däbrä Seltan (Deir es-Sultan),[24] the oldest of the Ethiopian monasteries in the Holy Land today, situated on the roof of the chapel of St Helena, one of the chapels of the church of the Holy Sepulchre. Possot describes in his book, *Le Voyage de la Terre Sainte*, how he and a small group of French pilgrims visited that place 'where Abraham fulfilled his duty of sacrificing Isaac; and the chapel is guarded by the black people called Abyssinians. And there also stands an olive tree which is still today as beautiful as it was when Abraham was about to offer up his sacrifice.'[25]

Däbrä Seltan is also described as being in the hands of the Ethiopians in the *Itinerário da Terra Santa* of the Portuguese Franciscan Pantaleão de Aveiro, who spent a year and eight months in the Holy Land from April 1563 to November 1564.[26] Like Denis Possot, he mentions the olive tree and its connection with Abraham. Fra Pantaleão also describes the chapel called St Mary of Golgotha situated in the forecourt of the church of the Holy Sepulchre, on the right hand of the pilgrim as he or she enters, as still being in the possession of the Ethiopians. These are furthermore said to play an important part in the ceremony of the Holy Fire on Holy Saturday. Fra Pantaleão tells us that the Turkish soldiers admitted only two Ethiopians into the chapel of the Holy Sepulchre, and that they came out again after a considerable time with their lighted candles. From the Franciscans living in Jerusalem he had heard that previously the Greek patriarch of Jerusalem and an Armenian bishop named Andrew had been allowed inside, and that the Greeks greatly resented the change, which Fra Pantaleão found difficult to explain. In his *Itinerário* we also find the Ethiopians participating in the ceremonies on the Mount of Olives on the feast of the Ascension, a privilege they have since lost together with that of participation in the ceremony of the Holy Fire.

Inside the church of the Holy Sepulchre the Ethiopians are said to occupy one chapel in the rotunda and another which is known as the chapel of the Mocking of Christ (chapters XXVI and XXXV). The whole of chapter XXXII of the *Itinerário* is an account of the Ethiopian community, which the Portuguese Franciscan describes with great sympathy, and often with admiration. In chapter XXII he also speaks of an Ethiopian martyr who was burnt by the Moors in the forecourt of the church of the Holy Sepulchre, leaving a footprint in one of the stone slabs 'as though on soft wax'.

In spite of the fact that, according to Fra Pantaleão, the Ethiopians had in the 1560s not yet lost all their privileges in the holy places, their situation was far from good. Poverty, hunger and misery brought it about that several Ethiopian monks at that time left Jerusalem and sought refuge in Europe. We find them in those days in Austria, in Florence and Rome, and even in Spain. It is probable that many of those Ethiopian manuscripts from Jerusalem which are today to be found in the Vatican and Italian libraries reached Europe at that time with refugees from the Holy Land.[27]

Another positive result of Ethiopian monks' flight to Europe was the encounter of Ethiopian and European scholars. Two such scholars met in Rome at the end of the fifteenth century: the German Johann Potken, *praepositus* of the church of St Gregory at Cologne, and the Ethiopian monk from Jerusalem, Abba Thomas Wäldä Samuel Bähtawi (the hermit). Both of them spent several years in Rome. When Johann Potken on one occasion had attended an Ethiopian service there, his interest was aroused to such a degree that he set about trying to find an interpreter who could translate for him the Ethiopian liturgical texts from 'the Chaldean language', as he called it. In actual fact it was of course not Chaldean, but Ge'ez.

Potken complains that not even among the Jews of Rome was he able to find an interpreter with knowledge of that language, but in the end he met Abba Thomas, and a long-lasting collaboration between the scholars started, with prolific results. Together they edited and published the first book printed in Ge'ez: the Psalms of David, published in Rome in 1513.

Some thirty years later another Ethiopian monk from Jerusalem arrived in Rome. This was Abba Täsfä Seyon, who prepared for publication the four Gospels and some anaphoras (eucharistic texts), printed in Ge'ez in Rome in 1548. One year later, a Latin translation of the anaphoras became available in print.

From the testimony of European pilgrims it is well known that the Ethiopian monks and nuns in Jerusalem lived in appalling poverty from the sixteenth to the nineteenth century. Even so, most of them stayed in the holy places, and every new generation brought new pilgrims to Jerusalem, though many perished on the way. The journey from Ethiopia to the Holy Land was made on foot or with primitive means of transport through the deserts of Nubia, Egypt and the Sinai. And when they arrived, the Holy City itself proved to be far from a paradise. For well over a century and a half the Ethiopian ascetics there lacked the means to feed themselves, and they used to receive a daily meal from their Armenian brethren in the faith, who in exchange took over some of their privileges in the holy places.[28]

Enrico Cerulli has expressed the opinion that the Ethiopians were absent from Jerusalem during the eighteenth century.[29] He is, however, not right in this. The Amharic manuscript Qutr 77, written in the 1890s by Aläqa Wäldä Mädhen Arägawi about the history of Däbrä Seltan, records a dispute in 1774 EC (AD 1782) between the Ethiopian monks in the monastery and a Coptic guest, Ibrahim Juhari, over the right of possession there.[30] A Russian pilgrim, Hieromonk Meletij from the Sarov hermitage, describes in his travel memoirs how during his pilgrimage in 1793–4 he witnessed a similar dispute in the same place.[31]

The origin of that unfortunate dispute between the two African communities in Jerusalem, the Copts and Ethiopians, which has not yet been settled even today, may have to be sought much earlier than in the eighteenth century. Abunä Matthewos places it as early as the time of Salah al-Din in the twelfth century. Salah al-Din is said to have turned the property over to the Copts, and when he did not give a clear positive answer to the Ethiopian protest, the Ethiopian King Näakuto lä-Ab, nephew of King Lälibela of the Zägwe dynasty, turned to Pope Alexander III in Rome (1159–81) for help. The pope is said to have sent a dispatch to Jerusalem with a certain hakim Philippos in which he ruled that the property of Däbrä Seltan (Deir es-Sultan) belonged to the Ethiopians and was to be given back to them. In the early twelfth century the buildings put up by the crusaders on the roof of the St Helena chapel must still have been standing, but we have as yet no evidence of either the Copts or the Ethiopians ever having inhabited these.

Today neither of the two communities can prove its right of possession by means of legal documents, for in 1838 a plague came to Jerusalem and all except two of the Ethiopian monks and nuns then living in the monastery died. The Copts and Armenians burnt everything found in the library of the Ethiopians, for fear, they said, of contamination.[32]

An important point in the juridical development of the case is the fact that the Turkish authorities in 1846 apparently did not regard Däbrä Seltan as Coptic property. When the Copts in that year tried to revive a dispute between the Greek Orthodox and the Ethiopians in Jerusalem in an Ottoman Turkish law court, the court rejected the application on the grounds that between the Coptic property and the Orthodox property in dispute lay the Däbrä Seltan and al-Dabbaga wall.[33]

The Ethiopians gained support and good advice from Bishop Samuel Gobat when he took up his post as the second Protestant bishop in Jerusalem

in 1846. On his way to his mission in Ethiopia in 1826 he had learnt the
Amharic language from the monks in Däbrä Seltan, and throughout his life
he remained a faithful friend to the Ethiopians. The British consul, James
Finn, also took pains to help the Ethiopian community in the Holy Land.
That becomes clear from the correspondence between the British consulate in
Jerusalem and the Foreign Office in London concerning the situation of the
community. The letters have been published several times and can be found in
Enrico Cerulli's *Etiopi in Palestina*.[34] They are an important source for our
knowledge of the situation of the Ethiopians in Jerusalem in the middle of the
nineteenth century.

The Russian Orthodox church also took an interest in the troubled
Ethiopian community in the Holy City. The Russians concentrated their
endeavours around the search for legal documents concerning the ownership
of Däbrä Seltan, and the most important result of their work is the paper
produced by the Russian professor of international law, Baron Boris Nolde,
'Consultation concernant les droits de la communauté abyssine en
Palestine'.[35]

The Situation of the Ethiopian Community
in Jerusalem 1855–1941

The situation of the community improved during the second half of the nineteenth century, and that improvement is closely connected with the
centralization of the Ethiopian government in the hands of the emperor.[36]
The destructive civil wars came to an end, and the government found time
and financial means for the work of reconstruction. Emperor Yohannes IV
(1872–89) showed great interest in the Ethiopian community in Jerusalem.
He bought land outside the walls of the Old City towards the north-west, not
far from the newly erected Russian cathedral. There he began in 1884 to
build a large round church. Yohannes IV fell in the battle of Mätämma
against the Sudanese Mahdists in 1889, but the building of the church in
Jerusalem was completed by his successor Menilek II (1889–1913) and the
consort of the latter, Queen Taytu. In 1893 the new church was consecrated
under the name of Kidanä Meherät (the Covenant of Mercy, one of the great
feasts of the Virgin Mary in the Ethiopian church year). The monastery
surrounding the church was called Däbrä Gännät (Mount Paradise or the
Paradise monastery).

Menilek and Taytu supported the community throughout their lifetime,
and other Ethiopian rulers and rich benefactors followed their example.[37]
Two relatives of Empress Zäwditu (1916–30), Lady Dästa Nessibu and Lady
Amarätch Wälalu, became nuns in Jerusalem and endowed the monastery
with several properties, among which were the Ethiopian monastery in
Jericho, which during the lifetime of Lady Amarätch Wälalu was one of her
private houses.

Queen Taytu and Empress Zäwditu built palaces for themselves in the vicinity of Däbrä Gännät. Taytu's house was ready in 1903 and in 1936 was rented to the British mandatory government to serve as a radio station, a task it is still fulfilling today under Israeli authority. Empress Zäwditu built her palace on Prophets' Street with the intention of retiring there as a nun – a hope which was not realized. The house was ready in 1928, but the empress died on 2 April 1930 at Addis Ababa without reaching Jerusalem.

The consort of Haile Selassie I, Queen Männän, also supported the Ethiopian community in the Holy Land. She gave her crown to the monastery, following the example of Menilek II, and in 1933 she founded the monastery of the Holy Trinity on the bank of the Jordan at the traditional site of Christ's baptism. Ethiopian hermits had been living there for centuries.

When the Italians invaded Ethiopia and occupied the country under the Fascist dictatorship of Benito Mussolini after their victory in May 1936, Haile Selassie went into exile with his consort and numerous courtiers.[38] The first station on their way was Jerusalem, where they arrived on 8 May by way of Djibouti and Haifa. The emperor and Negest Männän stayed only for a short time in the Holy Land. Most of their years of exile were spent at Bath in England. But many of their courtiers and nobles stayed on in Jerusalem.

On 16 November 1938 an agreement was signed in Rome by the British ambassador to Italy and the foreign minister of the Mussolini government, which was to have harsh consequences for the Ethiopian community in Jerusalem.[39] During the summer of 1939 the Italian consul in the city began to claim that the house of Empress Zäwditu on Prophets' Street, which had hitherto been Ethiopian state property, now, after the Italian conquest of Ethiopia, belonged to the king of Italy. The consul brought that claim to the attention of the British mandatory authorities which had been governing Palestine since 1917. The British administration hesitated to act, and the Ethiopians in Jerusalem mounted a determined opposition. Emperor Haile Selassie found a courageous and capable lawyer in a young Jewish immigrant from Copenhagen, Nathan Marein (1900–82). In July 1939 Marein took upon himself the task of representing the interests of the Ethiopians in the Holy Land. He managed to bring the matter to a Jerusalem law court and to keep the litigation going, until Italy entered the Second World War on 10 July 1940 on the side of Nazi Germany and the Italians overnight became enemies of the British.

Thirty Ethiopians in the Jerusalem monastery became 'enemy aliens' because they had accepted Italian citizenship, and together with all other Italians in the country they were relegated to internment camps at Muzra'a, Sarafand and Jericho. But the danger that the Italians might manage to appropriate Ethiopian property in the Holy Land was over. After the return of Haile Selassie to Addis Ababa on 5 May 1941, Nathan Marein became a legal adviser to the emperor, in which capacity he spent twenty-five years in Ethiopia.

At Däbrä Seltan the Ethiopian monks and nuns were still living in appalling circumstances. Because of their dispute with the Copts, only the government could carry out repairs in the monastery, as required by the Order-in-Council of 1924, dealing with the question of the holy places. There was neither electricity, nor running water or modern sanitary installations in the monastery compound. Since the Copts had in 1890 locked the two small chapels which the two communities had been sharing, the Ethiopians had to celebrate their eucharist services in a tiny room with space only for the cele-brating priests. The rest of the community had to stand outside in sun, rain or snow. During Holy Week and the Easter days they were allowed by Ottoman decree to set up a tented chapel for their pilgrims.

On 22 February 1961, the Jordanian government issued a decree by which Däbrä Seltan, including the two chapels which had remained locked since 1890, was declared Ethiopian property, and the Copts were ordered to hand the keys over to the Ethiopians. For forty days the Ethiopians could at last once again enjoy the possession of a chapel in their monastery, but then the Jordanian government yielded to pressure from Cairo and reversed the deci-sion. The chapels were given back to the Copts and the matter was frozen. When as-Sayid Anwar al-Khatib became governor of Jerusalem in February 1966, he had electricity, running water and modern facilities installed at Däbrä Seltan. Because of this, the Ethiopian Easter procession of 1967 was greeted by their Coptic brethren in the faith with a rain of stones. The Jordanian police had to intervene to restore peace, and since then the Ethiopians have every year celebrated Easter under police protection.

One of the results of the war between Israel and its Arab neighbour states was the division of Jerusalem, an arrangement which caused many difficulties for the Christian communities. The churches suddenly found themselves with communities, churches and chapels, monasteries, schools and hospitals in two states. Most of the Ethiopian monasteries were now situated in Jordan, while Däbrä Gännät and several other properties were within Israeli territory. Such was the situation until the Six Day War in June 1967, when the Israeli army conquered the Old City of Jerusalem and the rest of the Jordanian terri-tory on the West Bank.

During the night of Easter 1970, the Ethiopians managed to change the locks in the doors of the two locked chapels, the upper one of the Four Living Creatures and the lower one of St Michael. Since that night they have thus once again had a small sanctuary where they can celebrate their services. The Copts are not in need of those chapels and did not use them, because they had a church and two chapels on the roof, and another chapel inside the church of the Holy Sepulchre.

However, the then Coptic bishop in Jerusalem, Amba Basilius, immediately turned to the Israeli High Court with an accusation against the Ethiopian archbishop and members of the Israeli government, and on 16 March 1971 the court ordered the Ethiopians to give the keys to the Copts. The decision, however, had a condition. Under the above-mentioned Order-in-Council concerning the holy places, the government could set up a commission to examine the basic rights of possession in the monastery. The Israeli government decided to do so, and in the meantime the chapels have remained in the hands of the Ethiopians, even though the Copts have several times tried to regain possession. In 1962 the Jordanian government proposed a compromise, and the Israeli government did the same in 1976. The proposals were rejected by both parties, and thus no permanent solution of the problem has been found to this day.[40]

Until 1951 the head of the Ethiopian community in Jerusalem bore the title of *mämher* (teacher, master). At that time Abunä Philepos was appointed leader after having been consecrated a bishop. Since 1973 the head of the community has had the rank of an archbishop. The first Ethiopian archbishop in Jerusalem was Abunä Matthewos (1972–7 and again 1992–8).

The monastery today comprises seven houses: in the Old City of Jerusalem are situated Däbrä Seltan and the residence of the archbishop, which the community acquired in 1872; Däbrä Gännät is in west Jerusalem; in Jericho the community has owned a monastery since the 1920s, and at the traditional site of Christ's baptism, the monastery of the Holy Trinity since 1933; the site of the monastery of Meskabä Qeddusan (Resting-Place of the Saints, because of the cemetery connected with it) was acquired in Bethany (Al-'Azariya) by Emperor Haile Selassie for the community in the 1950s. Abunä Philepos put a wall around it at that time, and Abunä Matthewos built the church dedicated to St Täklä Haymanot and two houses in 1974. In January 1990 the Däbrä Sälam monastery was founded in Bethlehem by Abunä Atenatewos (1984–92).

The Ethiopian community in Jerusalem is no museum-piece. It is very much alive and has plans, in spite of the fact that it is still far from being wealthy, to build and found a guest-house where the numerous pilgrims can be fed and at least partly accommodated, a house for the elderly and a theological school. We may hope that the upward trend which has been in evidence since the 1850s can continue.[41]

Notes

[1]   S. Eusebii Hieronymi Opera, Sectio I, Pars I: Epistulae, ed. I. Hilberg, CSEL, vol. 54 (Vienna, 1910), 339–40.
[2]   S. Eusebii Hieronymi Opera, Sectio I, Pars I: Epistulae, ed. I. Hilberg, CSEL, vol. 55 (Vienna 1912), 292.
[3]   1 Kings 10:1–10 and 1 Chron. 9:1–9.
[4]   For the background to the history of the Ethiopian presence in Jerusalem see my 'The historiography of the Ethiopian monastery in Jerusalem', in G. Goldenburg (ed.), Ethiopian Studies: Proceedings of the Sixth International Conference, Tel Aviv, 14–17 April, 1980 (Rotterdam and Boston, 1986), 419–26.
[5]   Issac Ephraim, 'The Hebraic moulding of Ethiopian culture', Mosaic, 6 (1965), 8–15, and E. Ullendorff, Ethiopia and the Bible (Oxford, 1988).

6   On the background to the formation of the Ethiopian Christian traditon see Taddese Tamrat, *Church and State in Ethiopia, 1270–1527* (Oxford, 1972); Tafla Bairu, 'The establishment of the Ethiopian church', *Tarikh*, 2, 1 (1967), 28–41 and Issac Ephraim, 'Social structure of the Ethiopian church', *Ethiopian Observer*, XIV (1971), 240–88.

7   See the following studies by Anthony O'Mahony on the Ethiopian community in Jerusalem: 'The Ethiopian community in Jerusalem: pilgrims, politics, holy places and diplomacy until 1840', *Chronos*, 2 (1999), 29–53; 'Between Islam and Christendom: the Ethiopian community in Jerusalem before 1517', *Medieval Encounters: Jewish, Christian and Muslim Culture in Confluence and Dialogue*, 2, 2 (1996), 140–54; and 'Pilgrims, politics and holy places: the Ethiopian community in Jerusalem until ca. 1650', in Lee I. Levine (ed.) *Jerusalem: Its Sanctity and Centrality to Judaism, Christianity and Islam* (New York, 1999), 467–81.

8   *Historia ecclesiastica*, i. ix.

9   On the impact of the world of Islam upon Ethiopia see Haggai Erlich, *Ethiopia and the Middle East* (Boulder, 1994), 3–40; J. S. Trimingham, *Islam in Ethiopia* (Oxford, 1952); Joseph Cuoq, *L'Islam en Éthiopie des origines au XVIe siècle* (Paris, 1981); Hussein Ahmad, 'The historiography of Islam in Ethiopia', *Journal of Islamic Studies*, 3, 1 (1992), 15–46; and the collected studies of E. Cerulli: *L'Islam di ieri e di oggi* (Rome, 1971); and *idem*, 'Ethiopia's relations with the Muslim world', in *UNESCO General History of Africa* (Paris/Berkeley/London, 1988), 575–85.

10   A. J. R. Russell-Wood, *A World on the Move: The Portuguese in Africa, Asia and America, 1415–1808* (Manchester, 1992), 12–19. See also Francis M. Rogers, *The Quest for Eastern Christians: Travels and Rumor in the Age of Discovery* (Minneapolis, 1962).

11   Haile Maryam Larebo, 'The Ethiopian Orthodox church', in P. Ramet (ed.), *Eastern Christianity and Politics in the Twentieth Century* (Durham, NC, 1988), 375–99; and 'The Ethiopian Orthodox church and politics in the twentieth century', *Northeast African Studies*, 9 (1987), 1–17, and 10 (1988), 1–23.

12   Otto Meinardus, 'A brief history of the abunate of Ethiopia', *Wiener Zeitschrift für die Kunde des Morgenlandes*, 58 (1962), 39–65; and S. Tedeschi, 'L'Etiopia nella storia dei patriarchi alessandrini', *Rassegna di Studi Etiopici*, XXIII (1967–8), 232–71.

13   P. Mauro da Leonessa, 'La versione etiopica dei canoni apocrifi del concilio di Nicaea', *Rassegna di Studi Etiopici*, II (1942), 34–6.

14   See Giovanni Vantini, *Christianity in the Sudan* (Bologna, 1981), 77–8.

15   Abba Ayele' Taklahaymanot, 'The Egyptian metropolitan of the Ethiopian church: a study on a chapter of history of the Ethiopian church', *Orientalia Christiana Periodica*, 54 (1988), 175–222.

16   Otto Meinardus, 'The Ethiopians in Jerusalem', *Zeitschrift für Kirchengeschichte*, 76 (1965), 112–47 and 217–32; and my 'The Qeddusan: the Ethiopian Christians in the Holy Land', in A. O'Mahony, with Göran Gunner and Kevork Hintlian (eds), *The Christian Heritage in the Holy Land* (London, 1995), 129–48.

17   Doctrine concerning the two natures of Jesus Christ. The dyophysite school teaches that the divine and human nature of Christ are separate from each other, while the so-called 'monophysites' (the Armenian, Coptic, Ethiopian, South Indian (Malabar) and Syrian-Jacobitic churches) teach that the two natures are united in Christ.

18   See P. Renaudot, *Historia Patriarcharum Alexandrinorum* (1700), 579; J. M. Neal, *History of the Patriarchate of Alexandria* (London, 1847), II, 31; E. Cerulli, *Etiopi in Palestina: Storia della comunità Etiopica di Gerusalemme*, 2 vols (Rome, 1943 and 1947), I, 62–76.

19   Charles F. Beckingham, 'The achievements of Prester John' and 'The quest for Prester John', in *Between Islam and Christendom: Travellers, Facts and Legends in the Middle Ages and the Renaissance* (London, 1983), 3–24, and 291–310; Edward Ullendorf and C. F. Beckingham, *The Hebrew Letters of Prester John* (Oxford, 1982); and C. F. Beckingham and Bernard Hamilton (eds), *Prester John, the Mongols and the Ten Lost Tribes* (London, 1996). On the impact of Ethiopia and Prester John upon European

imagination see Jean Delumeau, *History of Paradise: The Garden of Eden in Myth and Tradition* (New York, 1995), 71–96.

[20] On the relationship between Ethiopia and Europe see the important studies by Renato Lefevre, 'Riflessi Etiopici nella cultura Europea del Medioevo e del Rinascimento', *Annali Lateranensi*, VIII (1944), 9–89; IX (1945), 331–444; and XI (1947), 255–342.

[21] Salvatore Tedeschi, 'Etiopi e Copti al concilio di Firenze', *Annuarium Historiae Conciliorum*, 2 (1991), 380–407.

[22] European travellers to Palestine often reported exaggerated accounts of the decisive role which Ethiopia could play in a united Christian front against the Islamic powers of the eastern Mediterranean. A constant theme in these accounts since the fourteenth century has been the absolute control which the Ethiopians were believed to have over the flow of the Nile. On the association of Ethiopia and the origins of the Nile in European thought see O. G. S. Crawford, 'Some medieval theories about the Nile', *Geographical Journal*, 114 (1949), 6–29; and Elisabeth-Dorothea Hecht, 'Ethiopia threatens to block the Nile', *Azania*, XXIII (1988), 1–10.

[23] See my *The History of the Ethiopian Community in the Holy Land from the Time of Tewodros II till 1974* (Jerusalem, 1983).

[24] See my 'Deir es-Sultan: the Ethiopian monastery in Jerusalem', *Quaderini di Studi Etiopici*, 7–8 (1987–8), 33–47.

[25] (Paris, 1532; 2nd edn, published and annotated by Ch. Shefer, Paris, 1890).

[26] I owe thanks to Anthony O'Mahony for having drawn my attention to C. F. Beckingham's article 'Pantaleão de Aveiro and the Ethiopian community in Jerusalem', *Journal of Semitic Studies*, VII (1962), 325–38; and to 'The Itinerário of Fr. Pantaleão de Aveiro' by the same author, *Revista da Universidade de Coimbra*, XXVII (1979), 3–11.

[27] On relations between the Papacy and Ethiopia and the Ethiopian presence in Rome see Renato Lefevre, 'Documenti pontifici sui rapporti con l'Etiopia nei secoli XV e XVI', *Rassegna di Studi Etiopici*, V (1946), 17–41; *idem*, 'Documenti e notizie su Tasfa Seyon e la sua attività romana nel secolo XVI', *Rassegna di Studi Etiopici*, 24 (1969–70), 74–133; and *idem*, 'Note su alcuni pellegrini etiopi in Roma al tempo di Leone X', *Rassegna di Studi Etiopici*, XXI (1965), 16–26; M. Chaine, 'Un monastère éthiopien à Rome au XVe et XVIe siècle: San Stefano dei Mori', *Mélanges de la Faculté Orientale*, V (1911), 1–37; S. Euringer, 'S. Stefano dei Mori in seiner Bedeutung für die abessinische Sprachwissenschaft und Missionsgeschichte', *Oriens Christianus*, III, serie X (1935); and P. Mauro da Leonessa, *Santo Stefano Maggiore degli Abissini e le relazioni romano-etiopiche* (Vatican City, 1929).

[28] R. Pankhurst, 'The history of Ethiopian–Armenian relations', *Revue des Études Arméniennes*, n.s. 12 (1977), 273–345; 13 (1978/9), 259–312; 15 (1981), 355–400.

[29] Cerulli, *Etiopi in Palestina*, II.

[30] See my 'A 19th century Amharic manuscript about the story of the Ethiopians in Jerusalem', in Thomas Hummel, Kevork Hintlian and Ulf Carmesund (eds), *Patterns of the Past, Prospects for the Future: The Christian Heritage in the Holy Land* (London, 1999), 157–66.

[31] See Catherine Pillet de Grodzinska, 'Premières notions sur l'Éthiopie parvenues en Russie de la fin du 14ème à la fin du 18ème siècle', *Quaderni di Studi Etiopici*, 6–7 (1985–6), 37.

[32] S. Tedeschi, 'Profilio storico di Dayr as-Sultan', *Journal of Ethiopian Studies*, 2 (1964), 92–130.

[33] The correspondence of the British consulate in Jerusalem concerning the Ethiopian community in Jerusalem was published as *Correspondence respecting Abyssinians at Jerusalem (1850–1867) Presented to the House of Lords by command of Her Majesty* (London, 1868). Cf. Cerulli, *Etiopi in Palestina*, II, 213–31.

[34] Vol. II, 274–347.

[35] Published in Paris, March 1925.

[36] Heinrich Schollar, 'The Ethiopian community in Jerusalem from 1850 to the

Conference of Dar el-Sultan 1902: the political struggle for independence', in G. Goldenburg (ed.), *Ethiopian Studies*, 487–500.

[37] For Empress Taytu's close relationship with the Ethiopian community in Jerusalem see Getatchew Haile, 'Empress Taytu and the Ethiopian property in Jerusalem', *Paideuma*, 35 (1989), 66–82; and Chris Prouty-Rosenfeld, *Empress Taytu and Menelik II: Ethiopia, 1883–1910* (London/Trenton, 1986), 247–56.

[38] *The Autobiography of Emperor Haile Sellassie I: 'My Life and Ethiopia's Progress', 1872–1937*, translated and annotated by Edward Ullendorf (Oxford, 1976).

[39] M. G. Caravaglios, 'La Santa Sede e l'Inghilterra in Etiopia durante il secondo guerra', *Africa*, (1980), 217–54; Calvin E. Shank, 'The Italian attempt to reconcile the Ethiopian Orthodox church: the use of religious celebrations and assistance to churches and monasteries', *Journal of Ethiopian Studies*, X (1972), 125–36.

[40] Walter Zander, 'Jurisdiction and holiness: reflections on the Coptic–Ethiopian case', *Israel Law Review*, 17 (1982), 245–73.

[41] See my 'The revitalization of the Ethiopian church in the Holy Land', in D.-M. A. Jaeger (ed.), *Christianity in the Holy Land* (Jerusalem, 1981), 197–211.

7

BETWEEN EASTERN AND WESTERN CHRISTENDOM: THE ANGLICAN PRESENCE IN JERUSALEM

Thomas Hummel

The Anglican presence in the Holy Land as an ecclesial organization began in the early nineteenth century under the influence of the missionary zeal of the London Society for Promoting Christianity amongst the Jews.[1] This evangelical impulse to preach the gospel to the Jews and to restore the Jews to the promised land was the initial impetus for an Anglican engagement in an area so distant in miles and exotic in character. Since the Reformation in England had first attacked pilgrimages for political reasons (especially those to Canterbury and Rome), and then for religious reasons (the rejection of earned indulgences), there had been little English interest in the earthly Jerusalem. Spiritual and metaphoric pilgrimages were commonplace in Anglican devotional literature, but the destination was the transcendent, heavenly Jerusalem not the small, squalid, provincial town of that name huddled behind magnificent walls in the hills of Ottoman Palestine.[2]

But if the catalyst for Anglican contact with the Holy Land was the conversion of the Jewish residents of Jerusalem as a sign of the coming completion of God's Kingdom it was not the only or even the major factor that accounted for the rapid rise to social, religious and political, if not numerical, significance of the Anglican community in Jerusalem.[3] The primary ingredient in the complex mixture of motives was the geopolitical reality that Palestine was on the land route to India, and therefore who controlled the Middle East (Syria, Mesopotamia, Afghanistan) was of immense importance to the British government. This political consideration did not set the agenda for the Anglican church's presence in the Holy Land, but it did help convince the government in most cases to assist rather than hinder the variety of activities and personnel working in the name of the Anglican church.[4]

Although when the Anglicans and Prussians created a joint bishopric in 1841[5] there was a titular head of the Anglican community in the Holy Land, the work of that community took a variety of forms and frequently represented very different and often contradictory agendas. The London Society for Promoting Christianity amongst the Jews (LSJ) was interested primarily in the spiritual welfare (conversion) and physical condition (health and income) of the Jewish population. The bishop, especially the second, Samuel

Gobat,[6] became more focused on the spiritual, intellectual and physical well-being of the native Christians, and with the help of the Church Missionary Society (CMS)[7] began schools, hospitals, clinics and, most controversially, native Protestant churches. Many of the bishops in England, however, saw the Anglican bishop in Jerusalem as an opportunity to reach out to the eastern Christians and to discover and polemically exploit a non-papist expression of the ancient Christian tradition. As the development of steamships, railroads and the construction of the Suez Canal opened the area for tourism, the Anglican church in the Holy Land became an orientation facility for those English on religious tours which were even beginning to be called pilgrimages. With the rise of biblical criticism and its seeming attack on the credibility of the Bible there arose an interest among scholars to explore the Holy Land and use it to demonstrate the historicity of the 'Book'. In this endeavour British scholars played a crucial role and augmented the number and variety of projects in which the Anglican church in its many guises was involved. The conquest of Jerusalem and Palestine by the British in 1917 opened up another aspect of the Anglican presence, this time as an interpreter between the various religious and political communities in Palestine, especially the Christians, and the British mandate government. The withdrawal of the British government and the creation of the state of Israel and the West Bank territory under Jordanian rule meant that the significance of the Anglican presence on the local scene shifted to relief and educational work, as well as trying to put its rather fractured identity into some kind of order. The Anglicans in Jerusalem are at present a multitude of communities: the Palestinian Anglican churches, a pro-Zionist charismatic mission to the Jews (Christ Church), a centre for Anglican relations with eastern Christians, Muslims and Jews, an institution supporting pilgrimages and advanced study of the Bible and the Holy Land (St George's College), and finally but not least a collection of schools, hospitals and clinics serving primarily the local Palestinian population. If these various aspects are hard to reconcile it is indeed the consequence of a history that is equally divergent and it is the evolution of this Anglican presence that this article will seek to illuminate.

Origins: 1822–1841

The London Society for Promoting Christianity amongst the Jews began in 1808 as part of the ministry of Joseph Frey, a converted Jew who was doing missionary work in the East End of London and who wanted to emphasize an outreach programme to the Jews who lived there. Because his ideas, which included institutions to help in education and training, were not sufficiently supported by the London Missionary Society (LMS) he began the LSJ and immediately attracted the attention and support of notable personages among the Evangelical community, including Charles Simeon, William Wilberforce and, because of his future contributions the most important,

Anthony Ashley (Lord Shaftesbury). Although it began as an ecumenical venture, the non-Anglicans withdrew in 1815 and the LSJ became an Anglican institution.[8] The vision of the society which captured the imagination of the Evangelical community was that 'God was going to use England to play a leading role in helping to restore the Jewish people to their homeland and to their Messiah'.[9] It was, therefore, only a matter of time before the LSJ tried to bring its work to Jerusalem itself. The converted German Jew Joseph Wolff went to Jerusalem in 1822 in order to test the water for the society. His report emphasizing the openness of the Jewish rabbis to discussion of the gospel led the LSJ to plan a mission. A visit by the Revd W. B. Lewis in 1824 led to a proposal to develop not only a mission station but also a Protestant church. The hostility of the Muslim Ottoman authorities to a new Christian church, of the indigenous Christians to a Protestant presence and of the Jewish leaders to a missionary ministry aimed at them made Lewis realize that there would need to be a British political presence to surmount this resistance, so he suggested a British consulate.[10] With Lewis's departure from Jerusalem Dr and Mrs George Dalton arrived, sent by the LSJ to do medical work (which helped Dr Dalton gain acceptance by the Ottoman administration) and evangelical probing. In 1826 he was joined by the Revd John Nicholayson, a Dane trained by the LSJ. Dalton soon died and Nicholayson inherited his work (and his wife). For the next few years Nicholayson worked on and off in Jerusalem and Lebanon but made little progress. In the meantime the political climate had changed. Muhammad Ali of Egypt occupied Palestine, and in order to garner western support he opened Jerusalem up to foreign residents, including missionaries. Nicholayson saw his opportunity and by 1833 he was settled in the Holy City with two other missionaries and requesting the British to establish a consulate and a bishopric.[11] The need for these two institutional supports was to help guarantee a toleration for 'an English church' in Jerusalem, a holy Muslim city, and respect from the resident Christian communities.

While waiting for the consulate and bishopric, and with the relative freedom granted by Muhammad Ali's regime, Nicholayson began to conduct a series of services in German, English and Arabic which included Christians and not just converted Jews; in addition, he illegally bought property to build a church (also illegal).[12] The expanded nature of the mission to include other Christians and an ecclesiastical and political component is the beginning of a confusion about the purpose of the Anglican presence and the expression of a patronizing attitude towards local authorities and dignitaries, both Muslim and Christian, that would haunt the Anglicans in the future.

The consulate was the first of Nicholayson's requests to be honoured, partially as the result of the strong advocacy by Lord Shaftesbury (related by marriage to Lord Palmerston, at that time foreign secretary).[13] Palmerston, pursuing the traditional British policy of upholding the Ottoman presence in the Middle East to keep it out of the hands of any rival European power, especially Russia, supported the consulate but wanted it done in a low-key manner. Since Palestine was under the control of Muhammad Ali, who himself was, at least in theory, under that of the sultan in Constantinople, the arrangements necessitated a delicate three-way negotiation. The firman (decree) by the Sublime Porte was granted in July 1838, and William Young was sent to Jerusalem as vice-consul with instructions to assist British interests, including the LSJ mission, but to be as inconspicuous as possible so as not to create hostility in the Muslim local government. By March 1839, however, Young was adding his voice to calls for a Protestant church and for the British to accept responsibility for the protection of the Jewish population, just as France had for the welfare of the Catholics and Russia for the Orthodox community.

While the LSJ and its supporters at home and in Jerusalem pushed for greater British engagement in the Holy Land, another Anglican organization, the Church Missionary Society, interpreted the defeat of Napoleon as an opportunity to expand Protestant influence in the Mediterranean.[14] From its new local base in Malta it envisaged a missionary effort that included not just Roman Catholics in this area but also the Muslim and Jewish populations of the eastern Mediterranean, as well as a reformation of the eastern Christian churches. So the CMS began to support the LSJ's request for an English church and bishop in Jerusalem as an outpost of its mission to eastern Christians, and through them to the majority Muslim population.[15]

The reconquest of Palestine by the Ottomans in 1840, with help from the western powers including the British navy, had been partially made possible because the Ottoman government had promulgated the Hatti Serif of Gulhane. This decree promised a reform of the government and equality before the law of all citizens, Muslim and non-Muslim alike. These two factors, a new reformist orientation, at least in theory, by the central Ottoman government and the help which Britain provided in the reconquest made not only the continuation of the Anglican presence but its expansion seem possible.

The next step, as indicated by both the LSJ and the CMS, was to have an Anglican bishop. This would give leadership to the missionary community and also provide the Protestants with the same prestige as that of the other Christian communities in Jerusalem with their ecclesiastical hierarchies. The initiative for realizing this goal, however, came from an unexpected source. Frederick William IV of Prussia wanted to create a united Protestant church in Europe with an apostolic episcopate. He looked at the Anglican church as a model and proposed beginning the process by establishing a joint Protestant bishopric in Jerusalem. This would set a precedent for such a union away from the ecclesiastical jealousies of the two churches and would give the Protestants the presence in the Holy Land which their political power and their evangelical purity deserved.[16] Frederick William's envoy, Bunsen, also interested in the conversion of the Jews, met with the archbishop of Canterbury, and with the support of Lord Shaftesbury and others in government circles as well as the interest of Queen Victoria and Prince Albert, who were keen on relations with Germany, ensured that the arrangements were quickly made. The Prussians and British were to take turns nominating the candidate, and all holders of the see would be consecrated by the archbishop of Canterbury, who would also be able to impose a veto. The major domestic opposition was from the Anglo-Catholics in Britain, most notably John Henry Newman, who saw this as an attempt to influence the English church in a Protestant direction, and from Prussian churchmen who feared the opposite. The concern of the High Church party did, however, force the Anglicans to define the bishopric not only as a missionary enterprise but also as an emissary to the eastern Churches. The bishop, when created, was therefore titled the Anglican Bishop in (not of) Jerusalem.

The planned joint bishopric was also opposed by the Ottoman authorities in Constantinople, who saw the dangers in another Christian religious figure with foreign allies being added to the already crowded religious scene in Jerusalem. Besides, Muslim sensibilities were already strained by the numerous requests by Christians for expanded rights and privileges. The British ambassador at the Sublime Porte agreed that this was not the time or the issue to push with the Ottoman government, and in the end no official recognition was granted. Consequently, the first bishop had to go as a private citizen, albeit delivered by a British warship – although it took a considerable effort to persuade the British government to accord such an ambiguous dignity.

The man who was appointed to the post as first Anglican–Prussian bishop in Jerusalem was Michael Solomon Alexander,[17] a former missionary of the LSJ, a Prussian Jewish rabbi who had emigrated to England and converted to Anglicanism. He had since become a professor of Hebrew at King's College London. Here was a candidate who fitted perfectly with the LSJ agenda. When he left for his new see he took with him a letter from the archbishop of Canterbury to the leaders of the Christian communities in Jerusalem assuring them that the bishop was not going to interfere in their jurisdictions and would accord them respect and honour.[18]

Before the Anglican bishop even arrived, it was evident that the seeds for discord had been sown. The primary agenda was that developed by the LSJ of providing succour, physical and spiritual, to the Jewish community.[19] But the CMS also wanted to use the opportunity to reach out and enlighten the eastern Christians and give them the evangelical zeal necessary to witness to their Muslim neighbours.[20] The British government wanted to increase the British presence and influence in the Middle East, but not to the point of alienating the Ottoman Empire, whose existence was a check on Russian expansion.[21] The High Church patristic-orientated Anglicans and the Anglo-Catholics, if they accepted the bishopric at all, sought to use the Jerusalem connection to explore the theology and polity of ancient Christian communities never under papal control or the 'corrupting influence' of medieval Roman Catholic devotional developments.

Early Years: 1841–1845

When Alexander arrived in Jerusalem accompanied by Hugh Rose, British consul in Beirut, he inherited a mission with a small Hebrew congregation and a few indigenous Christian converts. Nicholayson was also overseeing the building of a chapel which was being constructed illegally. During his short tenure (21 January 1842–26 November 1845) Alexander worked primarily on creating institutions (hospitals, craft schools, a Hebrew college and an inquirers' home) to help evangelize among the Jewish community. Some converts were made, but the more telling reaction was the strong defensive response by the Jewish community, which threatened to excommunicate anyone who had social intercourse with the mission or its institutions. A Jewish–Christian Protestant church had been planted in Jerusalem but it had to live in exile from its Jewish neighbours and relatives, who rejected its members as outcasts and traitors.

The second most important aspect of Alexander's career in Jerusalem was the lobbying effort he and the LSJ mounted to convince the British government to extract from Constantinople permission to build a church. Sir Robert Peel had replaced Lord Melbourne as prime minister in 1841, and Lord Aberdeen had replaced Palmerston as foreign secretary. The new government was less enthusiastic about the bishopric, and even suggested to William Young, the vice-consul, that he should not get too involved in supporting Alexander. On a number of occasions Alexander's lack of tact in dealing with local sensibilities led to disputes with both Young in Jerusalem and Rose in Beirut. But Alexander did manage to convince both that the failure to gain permission for a Protestant church, when the French and Russians had their own churches, was an insult to the prestige of the British and Prussian nations. The French and Russians, as well as native Christians and Muslims, for a host of different reasons, did not want a Protestant church in Jerusalem. In the face of such widespread opposition, it took a concerted diplomatic effort by Britain and Prussia in Constantinople to obtain permission to get the central government both to approve the project and then to force it upon a reluctant governor in Jerusalem.[22] The final permission came just months before Alexander's death. By the time of his death there was a congregation of thirty-one in Jerusalem and permission to build a church but also an alienated Jewish community, an alienated local governor, and distrustful Catholic and Orthodox communities. The only church in Jerusalem that was on good terms with the Anglican bishop was the Armenian Orthodox, which probably saw the Anglicans as an ethnically based national church like themselves and therefore of no threat, and possibly even as allies in the constant struggle with the Greek and Latin churches over rights to the holy sites. Besides, the Armenians were the landlords of the British.

When Alexander arrived in 1842, only the Armenians had a resident patriarch. The Greek Orthodox patriarch lived close to the corridors of power in Constantinople, leaving supervision to the Greek monks of the Holy

Sepulchre, and the Latin patriarch had become an honorific title only, while Roman Catholic interests were looked after by the Franciscan order and an official called the custos. Alexander, when he arrived, had pointedly refused to call upon the Latin (Roman Catholic) representatives, and his relations with the Greeks seemed to be perfunctory There were, however, repercussions in ecclesial circles from the residency of an Anglican bishop. In 1845 the Orthodox patriarch transferred his residence to Jerusalem, and in 1847 Pope Pius IX revived the Latin patriarchate and appointed a patriarch who moved to the Holy City. In the ecumenical mission field Alexander's work seems to have elicited competition and defensiveness, not co-operation and collegiality.

Anglicans Take Root: 1847–1881

With the death of Bishop Alexander, it was the Prussians' turn to name a candidate. Their choice was Samuel Gobat, a German-speaking Swiss from Basle who was brought up in the Swiss Reformed church but ordained an Anglican in Malta to serve as a CMS missionary in Ethiopia. He later returned to Malta to work in the CMS college. An Arabic-speaker, Gobat was intimately acquainted with the society's vision of evangelizing the Muslim East through the reinvigoration of the eastern Christians with the unadulterated power of the gospel of Christ. It was this Protestant evangelical zeal representing the CMS that upset the Anglo-Catholics when they learned of his appointment. In fact, it was so controversial that his consecration was held in private to avoid a public protest.[23]

Gobat left for Jerusalem in 1847, promising the English church that he would not seek to convert Christians in Palestine to Protestantism. It has been charged by Tibawi and others that Gobat was being basically duplicitous, because when he arrived in the Holy Land he engaged in an explicit strategy to recruit within the Christian community. According to Tibawi, the plan involved gathering around him 'native Bible readers' and encouraging them to develop a spirit of inquiry by reading the Bible in small groups. Then, when these groups were sufficiently primed with probing questions, they would apply to the bishop or a Protestant clergyman for guidance. They would then be encouraged to request schools to help foster this inquisitive spirit in a more systematic and community-wide manner. If these inquirers managed to alienate their own clergy, as they often did, and discovered themselves persecuted, they could then request permission for supervision from the Protestant clergy, and when they were excommunicated they could be received into the Protestant church as members. Gobat protested that it was not a recruitment but an act of charity to allow these people to become Protestants and have an evangelical service in Arabic. Tibawi, however, claims that Gobat not only knew what was happening but orchestrated it.[24]

There is no doubt that Gobat's methods of encouraging the questioning of ancient church tradition in the name of the Bible led to a small but growing

Arabic Protestant church, and that his infusion of CMS and German missionaries into Palestine to create schools, hospitals and clinics created an environment ripe for cultural as well as religious conversion. By 1856, less than ten years after his arrival, Gobat had six schools in the Holy Land teaching 260 children, only sixty of whom were Jewish. The others were of Christian parents, mostly non-Protestant. Education was one arena where Gobat felt he could transform Palestine.[25]

But none of this seems to necessitate Gobat being dishonest about his interpretation of the situation. He, like most of the other Protestants, believed the Orthodox and Catholic churches to be in the grip of superstition, and that what was needed was the liberating effects of hearing the gospel pure and unencumbered. That the Protestant reading of the Bible was itself an interpretative framework embedded in its own tradition and culture did not occur to him. Gobat probably believed that to encourage the reading of the Bible would elicit a reformation of the eastern churches – that he would not need to convert Christians because the eastern churches would reform themselves in the face of the self-evident nature of the biblical message. Taking on converts was just a momentary expedient while the larger reform movement developed. The immensity of Gobat's *naïveté* and his overbearing imperialism should not obliterate his confidence in the religious righteousness of his vision and his dedicated commitment to its realization.

Whether or not Gobat was duplicitous, his approach created a host of problems and many opponents. By moving the thrust of his ministry away from the LSJ agenda of promoting Christianity amongst the Jews, and by importing the CMS missionaries and their agenda, Gobat created a split between the Anglican bishop and the LSJ and its mission that has never been completely bridged. Also the effect of the conversion of native Christians to Protestantism alienated the Orthodox and Catholic communities in the Holy Land, especially after the Protestants were made a millet in 1850 and could therefore have the same status as the other communities. It equally enraged the Anglo-Catholic community in England which was at this time growing in numbers and influence. There was even a petition campaign against Gobat, which the archbishops of Canterbury and York and the bishop of London felt obliged to disown.

Gobat's lack of sensitivity also alienated the Muslim population, which saw the growing presence of Protestant institutions and their imperiousness as a threat to the religious identity of the Holy Land. In one episode in Nablus, Gobat had the church bells rung and flags flown to celebrate the government decree which granted religious freedom. This resulted in a riot and the ransacking of the English mission and the houses of the Protestants.[26]

Gobat also found himself at odds with the English consul, James Finn (1846–62). Although married to the daughter of the man who turned down the first Jerusalem bishopric (McCaul), and friend and supporter of the LSJ, Finn had problems with Gobat's methods and his attitude. Finn felt that

Gobat was not always furthering British and Anglican interests, and that his recruitment and support of German missionaries and institutions was splitting the Protestant community. In fact, almost all of the Anglican figures central to the work of the Church in Jerusalem had up to this point been foreign-born. The split between the German and Anglican components of the bishopric had been there from the beginning, but when in 1851 German nurses and missionaries, invited by Gobat, began to arrive, and with the appointment of a German chaplain by the Prussian king in 1852, and the granting of a plot of land for a Lutheran church to the visiting Crown Prince of Prussia next to the Holy Sepulchre, followed by the arrival of a large colony of German settlers (German Templars), the gap began to become unbridgeable. Finn's concern reflected the dual fear that Gobat was alienating the native Christians, the Ottoman government and indigenous Muslims, and also promoting German more than British interests.

The conflict between Finn and Gobat led to multiple complaints by each side to the foreign office, and finally, since he was the only person the British government could control, and to avoid further embarrassment, Finn was reassigned, although he resigned instead. Finn, however, cannot be allowed to fade too quickly from the scene because, besides his autobiography *Stirring Times* describing, albeit in a rather self-serving way, his time in Jerusalem, he was instrumental in contributing to two areas where the British presence and therefore to some extent the Anglican presence would be influential in the future. One was the creation of the Jerusalem Literary Society, for the study of the Holy Land for purposes of agricultural development, but also to find proof and illustrations of the truth of the Bible. Back in Britain the same spirit was behind the establishment of the Palestine Exploration Fund in 1865 under the leadership of the archbishop of York. Its purpose was: (1) to explore 'Jerusalem and many other places on the Holy Land by means of excavations' to throw light upon the history of the Jewish people; (2) to 'carry out such systematic survey as will establish the true geographic and geological character of that remarkable region'; (3) to collect the animals, plants and minerals of the Holy Land for a natural history; and (4) to make provision so that 'the Biblical scholars may receive assistance in illustrating the sacred text from the careful observation of the manner and habits of the people of the Holy Land'.[27]

The second of Finn's contributions was to help assist the growing number of British citizens who were visiting the Holy Land by arranging safe passage. One such tourist/pilgrim was the Prince of Wales, who visited in 1862. But this was just the beginning of the opening up of the Holy Land to English pilgrims. In conjunction with the opening of the Suez Canal in 1869 Thomas Cook conducted a tour to the Holy Land. In the years to come Cook's alone would shepherd thousands through the sacred sites. What most visitors found reinforced their prejudices about the backwardness of Muslim culture, the superstitious nature of eastern Christianity and the superiority of their own culture and religion. They were especially distressed by the iconography which decorated all the major biblical sites. The tomb of Christ was a free-standing building within the church of the Holy Sepulchre made of marble and encrusted with holy pictures. The ceremonies there, especially the Holy Fire on Holy Saturday, were viewed as riotous and superstitious events. This was because of the tradition that the taper taken into the darkened tomb by the Greek patriarch was said to be lit miraculously, and the jubilation that preceded and followed the event was not decorous behaviour by the standards of the English church. Golgotha was encased in a platform so that one had to look through holes to see the holy hill, and again the predominant visual focal points were eastern Christian icons. These English pilgrims complained of the crass commercialism and distasteful desecration of the sacred spots, and found their inspiration in the landscape instead. This at least could still evoke the biblical scenes. So the Mount of Olives, the Sea of Galilee, Mount Tabor were the Protestants' favourite sites. When General Gordon argued for the Garden Tomb outside the walls of the Old City as the true site of the burial of Jesus, Protestants agreed, not because its validity was more historically based but because it looked and felt like the tomb their Bibles had described.

Similarly the poverty, dirt and technological backwardness of the towns and the barrenness of the countryside were viewed as a consequence of the lack of ambition inculcated by Islamic ideas of fate. They were even commented upon as divine punishment for the failure to embrace the Lord who had lived and died in that very land.[28] So when these pilgrims worshipped in the finally completed Christ Church according to the Anglican prayerbook, and visited the Anglican missions with their schools, hospitals and even churches, they heartily approved. They believed that the English Protestants were bringing the gospel and modern progress to the Holy Land – redeeming it from its religious and cultural backwardness. But these attitudes on the part of the pilgrims represented only slightly more crass versions of those held by the English missionaries, including the bishop. Pilgrimage would be one area where the Anglican presence would expand and be transformed to meet the needs of the visitor for assistance in interpreting and understanding not only the places they were visiting but the people and culture they were encountering during their stay.

By the time of the death of Gobat in 1879 the Anglicans might have been in Jerusalem, but they were hardly of the city. The bishop's death meant it was the British turn to appoint the next incumbent, and they chose Joseph Barclay who had headed the LSJ mission in Jerusalem until 1870. It was an appointment which was to highlight a concern for the founding goals of the mission, which had been underemphasized during Gobat's tenure. But times had changed and the future growth of the Anglican presence did not lie in the Jewish community. Under Bishop Barclay the division of the Protestant community into German, Arabic and Hebrew-English congregations took place, and Barclay himself focused on the English and Jewish congregations. When he died in 1881 after less than two years, the Germans took the opportunity to end the joint bishopric and establish a separate leadership for their communities. The English reluctantly agreed, and since the Anglicans did not have sufficient finances to support a bishopric on its own, they decided to explore whether there should be an Anglican bishop, and if so to rethink what his mission should be.

Bishop Blyth and a New Spirit: 1887–1914

The loss of German support for the Jerusalem bishopric and its controversial character amongst the High Church wing of Anglicanism led many to believe that it would cease to exist. Benson, the archbishop of Canterbury, however, wanted it continued, but possibly moved to Beirut. A letter from the Greek Orthodox patriarch in Jerusalem requesting that the Anglican bishopric be not only preserved but located in Jerusalem helped provide Benson with the ammunition to counter High Church objections. The Greek Orthodox patriarch for his part seemed to find hope that the Anglicans would be useful allies in their battle with the Latins (Roman Catholics) over rights to the holy sites, and would also enlist British support for Christian communities with the Ottoman government. Benson solved the financial problem by pressuring the LSJ and CMS to contribute £300 each for the bishopric's expenses. Both of those societies, therefore, expected a man who was sympathetic to their missionary goals. Having managed the support of the Orthodox patriarch and the support (financial) of the missionary societies involved, Benson had the revival of the bishopric announced. The reasons given were threefold: (1) the need for a bishop to supervise the English churches and schools in the Middle East; (2) the need to provide episcopal oversight of the 'preaching of the Gospel to Jews, Arabs and other non-Christian inhabitants of those countries'; and (3) the need to develop further relationships with the eastern Christians. It was specifically stated that converting members from other churches was *not* in the spirit of the bishopric, although encouraging religious inquiry was not ruled out of place.[29] The purpose of this announcement was to try to cover both the LSJ and the High Church objections to poaching on Greek Orthodox territory. The final statement, on encouraging inquiry, which was the justification used by Gobat for allowing native Christians to become Anglicans, could even be seen as a nod in the direction of the policies of the CMS. But if the announcement was an attempt to be all things to all parties, the intention of Benson was not, and with the selection of the new bishop, George Francis Popham Blyth,[30] a man was found who was, in the words of Benson, 'sufficiently high church in the noblest way to be trusted to reverence other churches and put his foot on proselytism . . . and sufficiently Evangelical . . .'[31] It is obvious that for both Benson and Blyth there was to be a major shift in emphasis towards the role of the Anglican bishop as envoy to the eastern churches and away from conversion of Christians and possibly Jews as well. The LSJ and CMS waited to see what would happen. Many heard rumours of Blyth wearing eucharistic vestments and feared a ritualist was being sent to oversee the work of strongly Evangelical missionaries.

When Blyth arrived in Jerusalem in 1887 it quickly became obvious that one of his main priorities was the establishment of good relations with the Greek Orthodox. He was welcomed by the Greek patriarch, who had lobbied for an Anglican bishop, and the Anglicans were accorded the right to hold services in the Orthodox chapel of Abraham in the Holy Sepulchre.[32] Although this right had been granted in 1885, Blyth was the first Anglican bishop in Jerusalem to take possession of the gift and the hopes it represented. Because Blyth saw himself as the envoy of the whole of the Anglican church to the eastern churches he felt the need of a more impressive and spacious establishment than the simplicity of Christ Church. Blyth's first plan was to expand Christ Church into a collegiate church (he did not want to create a separate cathedral in the same city as the Holy Sepulchre) with a dean and canons. The reaction of most of the Christ Church staff was to find such a plan pompous and out of keeping with the missionary spirit of the LSJ or the CMS. When the LSJ passed a resolution rejecting Blyth's proposal he began to plan financing and building a complex of his own, separate from Christ Church and its LSJ connection.[33]

This marked the beginning of the breach with both the LSJ and the CMS, the latter of which even came to the point of excluding Blyth from their local conferences. Although there were voices such as the Revd Kelk of the LSJ in Jerusalem who feared the implications for the Church of a division between the missionary societies and the bishop, their separate agendas made the breach virtually inevitable.[34]

Blyth's instrument in gaining financial independence was the Jerusalem and East Mission (JEM) and as the resources became available he bought land on Nablus Road in east Jerusalem and eventually built a collegiate church and a compound with residences for the bishop, dean and canons and school buildings. The style was English Gothic, and this was made even clearer when Edward's Tower (a version of the Magdalene College, Oxford tower) was constructed on the site in 1910. Here was an impressive establishment that could appropriately represent Anglicans in the Holy Land, and it was a church where Anglicans could display to the other Christians of the East that theirs too was a church with an apostolic heritage, with an ancient liturgy and ceremonies of suitable solemnity. If St George's, as this collegiate church was named, was to make the English feel at home and represent the catholicity of Anglicanism, it was a success. But to those Evangelical missionaries who wanted the Anglicans to represent the 'purity of Protestantism' in a land of 'corrupt' Christianity, the new bishop and his compound seemed an unfortunate development.

As evangelicals, they believed in the authority of Scripture over that of the Church, and tried to keep ceremony to a minimum. The preaching of the Word of God was the most important thing. Apostolic succession, vestments, candles and Catholic ceremonial (including the eastward position) were specifically rejected as being 'Romish'. And when we recall the reasons why Christ Church was built with its modest interior design, with its attempt to portray the Jewish roots of Christianity, the conflict become even clearer. Christ Church and the evangelicals intended to introduce the simplicity of Christian worship, to interest the Jew, the Moslem, and the Eastern Christian, whereas Blyth intended to reintroduce Catholic practices into the Church in Jerusalem, so as to reconcile the Anglicans with the Eastern Churches.[35]

Increasingly the Anglican presence in Jerusalem began to splinter into three parts: (1) the work of the LSJ amongst the Jews with their schools, hospitals and outreach organizations as well as the Hebrew Christian congregation at Christ Church; (2) the mission work of the CMS with its schools, hospitals and churches drawing primarily on converted native Christians; and (3) the ecumenical work of developing relations between the Anglicans and the eastern churches centred at St George's collegiate church. This threefold division became more complex in the early 1900s as both the Hebrew Christians and the Arab Anglicans developed associations to free themselves from the LSJ and CMS respectively. To a large extent these associations also kept their distance from the bishop, recognizing his spiritual authority but managing their own affairs and institutions. The Palestine Native Church Council was the voice of the Arab Anglicans and gained for them a great deal of autonomy. Meanwhile the importance of St George's as an international embassy of Anglicanism increased with the appointment of six bishops, one each from Britain, Canada, Australia, South Africa, India and the United States, as honorary canons of the collegiate church. St George's was also becoming the spiritual centre for the increasing number of English living, working and visiting Jerusalem.

Bishop Blyth died in 1914 on the eve of a war that was to reshape the Middle East and see the Jerusalem Anglicans go from outcast sympathizers of an enemy power to members of the established church of the occupying power. The church Blyth left at his death ironically was probably stronger and better able to cope with the withdrawal of English personnel during the war because of its divisions and the autonomy of the Hebrew Christian and Arab Anglican associations. Blyth's legacy was manifold, but probably the international role of St George's was the one most purposefully bequeathed. The divergent agendas embodied in the establishment of the original bishopric were not solved by Blyth, but they were separated, and the ecumenical component brought to the fore as never before, and it was this aspect that now captured the imagination of most Anglicans in Britain and America. Those who saw the restoration of Israel as a prophetic prelude to God's new kingdom were no longer the dominant voice among Anglicans interested in

Jerusalem, but they too were encouraged by the possibilities created by the development of Zionism, the Balfour Declaration and the transfer of Palestine to British political control.

The War Years

The new Anglican bishop, Rennie MacInnes, was appointed in 1914 but could not take up his post because of the war and the entry of the Ottoman Empire on the side of Austria and Germany. The British subjects in the Holy Land were for the most part forced to leave their posts, and indigenous Anglicans were generally looked upon with suspicion. As the war moved into the Middle East, the Turkish army's need for food, coupled with a locust infestation, created famine conditions in Palestine, and thousands died. In the midst of this the American consul Glazebrook helped provide civilian relief and looked after British interests and property. The Hebrew Christian and the Anglican communities kept themselves going with difficulty, but bit by bit their institutions were appropriated by the Turkish government. St George's was closed down completely as a symbol of British presence, and when the Turkish authorities were told that 'cannons' were buried in St George's its pavements were dug up, but only the bodily remains of some collegiate canons were found.[36]

Despite threats to the contrary the Turkish army decided not to fight a battle over Jerusalem and withdrew quietly. The mayor of Jerusalem went out to meet the British with a large white sheet on 9 December 1917, and General Shea entered the city. The documents of surrender were signed at St George's on Bishop Blyth's desk.[37] On 11 December General Allenby entered the city on foot, and from the steps of the citadel by Jaffa Gate and opposite Christ Church declared the 'liberation' of the city and proclaimed that the religious status quo would be preserved. Four hundred years of Turkish rule had ended, and for the first time since the crusades a Christian power controlled the Holy City. What would this mean for the city, for the religious communities – especially the Jews who had been promised a homeland – and the Anglicans, the established church of the conquering power?

The British Mandate: Bishops MacInnes and Brown, 1914–1942

During the war the Anglican presence was greatly diminished, but with the British conquest it was possible for the new bishop to return and for the rebuilding of morale and structures to begin. At first the British government was hesitant to allow the missionaries to return before a political settlement could be arranged. The desperate need for relief, however, persuaded them to relent, and Bishop MacInnes was prepared with a plan. On his appointment in 1914 MacInnes began approaching the various missionary groups with interests in Palestine, and by 1917 he had organized the Syria and Palestine

Relief Fund. The British military government, needing the help, allowed the missionaries to return. Bishop MacInnes came to Jerusalem in 1918 and the Relief Fund immediately began to provide soup kitchens and medical care, not only to the impoverished local citizenry but also to the Armenian refugees who had fled from the Turkish genocide and sought shelter with the Armenian community and convent in Jerusalem.[38] Once the issue of relief was settled the bishop had to grapple with the restoration of the various buildings, institutions and morale of the shattered, scattered church. Most of the work of the church had ground to a halt with only a few native Arab clergy left. Christ Church had been closed, the services had stopped, and the teachers of the local schools were gone – either exiled by the Turks or lost to the war. Bit by bit the churches were reopened and hospitals began again to serve the population. Schools in the major towns were also re-established, though the village schools tended to be entrusted to the public education system established by the mandatory government.

By 1920 the British were given a mandate to control Palestine, and a civilian government was created. The British mandate meant that the Anglican community would again be divided into three distinct groups. The first was the increasing number of British citizens who would live in the Holy Land, many of them working for the mandatory government and attending the Anglican church. These usually found the collegiate church of St George with its Englishness an appropriate oasis. The native Arab Anglicans were also a strong community, encouraged by the educational and social advantages of a connection with the religious culture of the occupying power. The mandatory government went out of its way not to give the Anglican church any advantages (the government refused to recognize the Anglicans as an official religious community with autonomous social laws). In fact the size of the Anglican church in 1939 was only a few hundred more than in 1920. There were however, definite advantages in an English education at an Anglican school, and therefore many Arabs, Christians and Muslims attended these institutions, which nurtured much of the leadership of the Palestinian nationalist movement. The third group were the Hebrew Christians, and the missionaries of the LSJ, now renamed the Church's Mission to the Jews (CMJ), and their supporters in England were excited by the British mandate in Palestine, seeing it as a prelude to the restoration of Israel to the Jews as promised in the Balfour Declaration, which had been a theological concern of theirs since the foundation of the mission in 1808. The long-hoped-for return of the Jews to their homeland seemed to be not only a theological vision but a realistic political expectation. This support for the restoration of Israel, and therefore for Zionism, increasingly alienated the Hebrew Anglicans and their supporters centred in Christ Church from both the English and Arab Anglicans centred at St George's. The restorationists were looked upon with suspicion not only by the other Christians (both Anglican and Orthodox), but also by the Jews, who felt converting Jews to Christianity would alienate them from their own community and reduce their nationalist commitment. So the mission work of the CMJ was attacked by the Jewish, Muslim and Christian communities.[39]

As the conflict in Palestine grew between the Jewish community and its desire for a homeland, and the Arab community and its fear of being displaced, the Anglicans themselves split on the appropriate approach to take. The CMJ was active in promoting the restoration and, as a CMJ pamphlet contended,

> In the Old and New Testament alike we can trace the purposes of God . . . Of all the many races connected with the Holy Land in its long history one race stands out pre-eminently as the great means of blessing the whole world. We believe we find in this revelation a promise that the land shall be restored to this race, and that once again blessing shall come to the world through the Jews.[40]

The bishops were less enamoured of the policy. In the case of MacInnes, a former CMS missionary to Egypt, this was not because he rejected the theological idea but because his work among the eastern Christians and the Arab Anglicans made him sensitive to the practical problems of allowing a large influx of Jewish settlers. In fact many of the major figures in promoting Arab nationalism were either Arab Anglicans or educated in Anglican schools. It became important for them to see the struggle for Arab nationalism as not a religious but a political one. The English living in Palestine tended also to agree with the bishop that the creation of a Jewish homeland would raise political problems for the government and increase instability in the region, and would be an injustice to the Arab population. As the mandate continued and the Arab and Jewish communities became involved in communal violence, this fissure within the Anglican community grew. By 1936 Bishop Brown and three others were able to submit a paper to the Royal Commission of Inquiry under Robert Peel which in part states:

> The past history, and present treatment, of the Jews in Europe is a reproach to the name of Christendom. But the reproach is not wiped out, nor can the problem be solved by shifting the responsibility of Christendom in the matter on to a predominantly non-Christian people, the Arabs of Palestine . . .
>
> The Jewish problem of Europe therefore must be solved by the Christian Powers at their own expense and not at the expense of Palestine. . . The Jewish claim to Palestine on the basis of prophecy is declared throughout the New Testament to have been abrogated. 'They are not all Israel who are of Israel.' 'God is able of these stones to raise up children to Abraham.'[41]

Here Bishop Brown goes even beyond MacInnes and rejects the theological premise of the idea of restoration.

The political issue of the Jewish homeland was central to the mandate years, but was not the only or even the primary concern of the Anglican community.

For Bishop MacInnes the role as envoy to the eastern churches was a central one, and he worked very hard to help build up the Orthodox church in Jerusalem and further the theological conversation between the two churches. At one point he managed to get the Orthodox patriarch in Jerusalem provisionally to recognize the validity of Anglican orders (ordination), which excited many English churchmen who saw Orthodox recognition of the catholicity of Anglicanism as a counter to Roman Catholic rejection of those claims. He also travelled extensively to garner support for the Anglican church in Jerusalem including a trip to the General Convention of the Episcopal church in 1922. The American church responded by sending a regular contribution from a special collection taken on Good Friday. In 1924 the American church decided to send a priest, Charles Bridgeman, to assist at St George's, teach at the Armenian seminary and help create an Orthodox school of theology. At first the bishop in Jerusalem was suspicious of this American who was officially under the jurisdiction of another bishop, but in time the relationship flourished and Bridgeman was made a canon of the collegiate church. MacInnes also helped in settling a number of disputes among various eastern churches, especially a schism in the Syrian Orthodox church.[42]

Both Bishops MacInnes and Brown were frequently requested to approach British authorities on behalf of a concern of a particular religious community or to act as mediators between contending communities, as was the case when the Latins and Orthodox had a dispute over who cleaned and therefore controlled the windows on the north side of the church of the Nativity in Bethlehem. The connection with the British government was one reason for this use of the Anglican bishop, but it was also because of the work the Anglican bishops had done to foster ecumenism and their lack of desire to control or have a presence in the most sacred sites. MacInnes also helped create a local council of churches that eventually evolved into the Middle East Council of Churches. But this ecumenism was not exclusively orientated towards Christians; canons were created who were experts in Islam and Judaism to foster better relations with those two communities. This foreshadowed the establishment of St George's College where Anglicans from throughout the world come to study the Bible and the Christian, Jewish and Islamic traditions that intersect in the city.

The persecutions in Europe prior to the Second World War created more pressure to allow Jewish immigration, and therefore created greater resistance in Palestine, but with the onset of the war itself a fragile ceasefire was made between most of the Jewish, Arab and British groups. It was while on an automobile journey during the war that Bishop Brown was killed in an accident in 1943. His successor was Weston Henry Stewart, one of the archdeacons of the Jerusalem diocese and therefore someone deeply knowledgeable and already on the scene. It was Bishop Stewart who would have to cope with the upheavals created by the 1948 war for Israel's independence and the subsequent partition of Palestine.

War and Partition: 1948–1967

The end of the Second World War created once again great pressure to allow large numbers of displaced Jewish refugees to settle in Palestine. The Anglo-American Commission of Inquiry was sent to study the situation and make recommendations. It was an opportunity to show Anglican loyalty to the cause of Arab nationalism. *Bible Lands*, the magazine of the Anglican bishopric, wrote on the occasion:

> One of the significant events of 1946 in Palestine was the appearance before the Anglo-American Commission of Inquiry of a joint delegation of the Christian-Arab communities. The aim of this delegation was to present the Christian Arab case and to demonstrate their solidarity with one another and with their Muslim brethren. They were whole-heartedly with the Muslim Arabs in their opposition to what they regarded as the threat of a Jewish state.[43]

One of the main delegates to the inquiry was the Revd Najib Cubain, the president of the Arabic Evangelical Episcopal congregations and later the first indigenous Arab-Anglican bishop. The new bishop, Stewart, while expressing sympathy for the plight of the European Jews and condemning anti-Semitism, attacked the idea of restoration. In a memorandum Stewart writes:

> There is a not uncommon tendency today, both in England and America, to base large Zionist claims on the Old Testament history and prophecies, and thereby win support from many Christians whose respect for the Bible is perhaps greater than their understanding of it . . . The Christian doctrine of the New Testament is that the new spiritual Israel of the Christian Church with its descent by the spiritual birth of baptism, is the sole heir to the promises, themselves also spiritualized, which had been forfeited by the old Israel after the flesh, with its descent by human generation.[44]

As *de facto* partition began taking place the Arab-Anglicans and the Anglican bishop supported the resistance to a Jewish state and partition. The members of the CMJ, with their mission to the Jews, were increasingly distrusted on both sides, and their properties were divided between Christ Church in the Old City, with its predominant Arab population, and the hospital in Jewish west Jerusalem. With the UN vote for partition in 1947 and the subsequent war in 1948

> the CMJ missionaries were placed in a very difficult situation, especially those associated with Christ Church. Because of siege conditions, the Jewish community was very suspicious of anyone not considered to be 100% with them. This meant unfair dismissal from jobs of some Hebrew Christians. They were also taken off for interrogation by the Hagannah or by the Stern group and sometimes suffered severe handling.[45]

In the end the Hebrew Christians were flown out for their own safety.
With the end of the mandate and the withdrawal of British troops, Israel

declared its independence and the war began in earnest. By the time the cease-fire was arranged most of the Arab-Anglicans living in Israel had fled as refugees to the West Bank and Jordan, Jerusalem had become a divided city, with the Old City and east Jerusalem under Jordanian and west Jerusalem under Israeli control. St George's was in the Jordanian sector, and Bishop Stewart became actively engaged in relief work, helping to feed and then house the numerous refugees. He demonstrated his solidarity with the Arab predicament by even helping to build new mosques for the Muslim refugees, assisting in the relief work of the eastern Christian communities, and starting work on four refugee villages.[46]

With increased indigenous control of the Arab-Anglicans in Jordan, a physical separation from the remaining Israeli Arab-Anglicans and the reduction of the English congregation of the mandate period, the Anglican bishop in Jerusalem re-emphasized his role as Anglican envoy to the eastern Christians and as a facilitator for ecumenical dialogue among Christians, and of Christians with Jews and Muslims.

Meanwhile the CMJ missionaries had Christ Church as a mission church to the Jews, with a whole decorative motif using Hebrew and Jewish symbols, in an area with no Jewish population. They began to work out of St Paul's, formerly an Arab-Anglican church in west Jerusalem, but after the war of 1948 the anti-British, anti-Arab, anti-Jewish-Christian atmosphere of Israel made their life difficult.

In post-partition Jordan there was a great deal of pressure to have an indigenous Arab-Anglican bishop, and this corresponded to similar movements throughout the Anglican church in the former British colonies. The retirement of Bishop Stewart in 1957 provided the perfect opportunity to institute change.[47] In negotiations between the archbishop of Canterbury (Geoffrey Fisher) and the Arab-Anglicans in Jordan (since 1947 called the Evangelical Arab Community) it was decided to create an archbishopric of Jerusalem and the Middle East with five dioceses: Jerusalem; Egypt; Iran; the Sudan; and Jordan, Lebanon and Syria. The new archbishop would have oversight of the church of Jerusalem and Israel, and be the envoy of Anglicanism to eastern churches, Islam and Judaism. The bishop of Jordan, Lebanon and Syria would control all of the congregations in the West Bank, Jordan, Lebanon and Syria.

The implication was that the archbishop would continue to be British, and the new bishop of Jordan would be an Arab-Anglican. Angus MacInnes, son of the former bishop, Rennie MacInnes, was appointed archbishop, and Najib Cubain was elected bishop of Jordan, Lebanon and Syria. The question of where the new bishop was to be based became an important one because there was still some resentment by Arab-Anglicans who 'regarded the establishment of an archbishopric headed by an English archbishop as a means for continuing Western dominance over the indigenous bishop'.[48] There were a number of attempts to convince the CMJ to give Christ Church to the new bishop as his seat, which in light of the lack of any Jewish residents of the Old City had a certain logic. MacInnes even offered to trade St Paul's church in western Jerusalem for Christ Church. The CMJ agreed to let Christ Church be used by Bishop Cubain, but not to relinquish ownership, nor to let its Jewish iconography be replaced. The Arab community found that unacceptable, and in the end both the bishop and archbishop were centred at St George's.[49]

Besides being the seat of two bishops and a school, St George's also became the home in 1962 of a theological college to train clergy and provide courses for visiting students from around the Anglican communion. St George's hostel was also established as a home for the students and for pilgrims visiting Jerusalem. As the opportunities for traditional mission work contracted, the archbishopric became increasingly an embassy of Anglicanism in the Holy Land, centring on educational and ecumenical ventures.

The 1967 War and Its Consequences

The nearly twenty years of partition between east and west Jerusalem ended with the Israeli victories in the Six Day War of 1967. The Old City with its holy shrines, east Jerusalem with its Arab population and the seat of the Anglican archbishop and bishop, and the whole of the West Bank including Bethlehem, Nablus, Hebron and Ramallah (the strongholds of Palestinian Anglicans) came suddenly under Israeli control. At first this was assumed to be a temporary situation, and the desire was for the Arab-Anglicans to show solidarity with their fellow Palestinians. As a result, many Anglicans became actively engaged in political resistance movements. It also increased the already existing demand by the Arab-Anglicans to end the anomaly of an English archbishop controlling the church of Jerusalem. The incumbent at this point was Archbishop George Appleton. His difficulty was to maintain the flexibility necessary to work with the Israeli government and Israeli Anglican congregations, to keep a relationship with the CMJ and the pro-Zionist Hebrew Christians, to represent the worldwide Anglican church in Jerusalem, and to be of pastoral and episcopal support to the Palestinian Anglicans and their pain and aspirations. The CMJ wanted to keep the existing arrangement with a western archbishop having oversight of Jerusalem. They feared that an Arab bishopric would be in danger of politicizing the church and alienating the Israelis. Many western Anglicans feared that the ecumenical concerns of the bishopric, especially the dialogue with Judaism, would be compromised. But in 1973, with the help of the interested parties and the Anglican Consultative Committee, a new constitution was negotiated. The diocese of Jerusalem and Israel was amalgamated with the diocese of Jordan, Lebanon and Syria, with an Arab bishop who would represent Anglicanism in the Holy City. The other dioceses of the Middle East (Cyprus and the Gulf States; Iran; Egypt and North Africa) became autonomous, and with the exception of Cyprus were to have indigenous bishops. The head of the Middle East province would then be elected from the four diocesan bishops. When Archbishop Appleton retired, the archbishop of Canterbury selected the retired bishop of London, Robert Stopford, to oversee the transition to the new constitution, which took effect in 1976 (slightly altered in 1978) with the consecration of Bishop Haddad as the first Arab-Anglican bishop in Jerusalem.

Meanwhile the CMJ were beginning to reclaim Christ Church as the centre of their unique ministry to the Jewish population and a witness to their restorationist theology. Whereas most of the Anglican church in Palestine found the results of the 1967 war disconcerting and discouraging, the restorationists celebrated as Israel came to control the whole of the Holy City and their traditional homeland of Judaea and Sumeria (the occupied West Bank). The more the Jerusalem bishopric became arabized, the more concerned the CMJ and the Hebrew Christians (strong supporters of Zionist expansionism) became. The CMJ worked to maintain their independence from the bishop and to keep control of their original home in Christ Church. During the 1975 constitutional changes the CMJ were allowed to retain ownership of their properties and to pursue their mission. They would, however, become increasingly alienated from the Anglican presence centred at St George's. This alienation hardened even more as the occupation by Israel became more permanent.

From Intifada to Peace to Intifada

In the early years following the 1967 war it seemed as if the return of the occupied territories would be a matter of time. As the occupation became long-term, and Israel began to build settlements in the West Bank and in and around Arab east Jerusalem, it became increasingly clear that the Arabs would soon be a vanishing minority if current trends continued. The Christian churches were especially disturbed by the emigration of Arab Christians out of Jerusalem and the West Bank as it became harder to find educational, occupational and housing opportunities in their homeland. This fear of losing control of the land for ever, and frustration at thirty years of occupation, led to the Intifada or uprising. This movement to make Israel pay a price for its occupation and to try to stop the advance of settlements caught the imagination of the Arab residents, Muslim and Christian. Since 1984 Samir Kafity had been the Anglican bishop, and as the Intifada expanded he joined with other Christian bishops and the patriarchs (Greek, Latin, Armenian) to condemn Israeli occupation. Christian communities which had long struggled with each other over the rights to the holy places began to join together to keep Israel from unilateral appropriation. In this struggle the Anglicans at St George's were in the forefront but completely out of step with the loyalties and theological concerns of Christ Church. The contribution of

Canon Ateek, pastor of the Arabic congregation of St George's, to the development of a Palestinian liberation theology is one example of the ongoing Anglican influence.[50]

As a fragile peace made possible by the pressure of the first Intifada, the end of the Cold War and the end of the Iran–Iraq war began to take hold between Israel and the Palestinian Authority, the most difficult issue was: who would control Jerusalem? The Anglicans in Jerusalem are also split between those who would like one city with both Israeli and Arab capitals (St George's) and those who feel Jerusalem is now a Jewish city with a decreasing Arab minority (Christ Church). Meanwhile the ecumenical and educational work continues through St George's College and the pilgrim hostel. It has become the tradition for the dean of St George's church to be British, the dean of St George's College an American, and the bishop to be an Arab, with bishops from all over the Anglican communion to be honorary canons of the collegiate church. Currently, Jerusalem's Christian communities are again in the throes of conflict, with the outbreak of the second Intifada and the Israeli response.

Conclusion

The Anglican presence in numerical terms has never been great in the Holy Land, and in many ways it did not seek to be so. The desire to convert the Jews, which was the initial impetus, was not so much to create Anglicans as to establish or re-establish a truly Hebraic Christian Church, which it was thought would closely resemble an evangelical Protestant one. The desire to find contacts with the eastern churches, and for some the desire to reform those churches and convert the Muslim population, also tended to envisage a church which would be evangelical and reformed but not necessarily Anglican. The desire to establish western educational, medical and economic help was probably the most imperialistic aspect of the Anglican presence. For most of their presence in Jerusalem, lasting over 150 years, the Anglicans have sought to give to the Holy Land what they felt was needed, and if they usually assumed that what was needed was for the people, institutions and beliefs to be more like their own, that is how most people think. The Anglicans came to Jerusalem with very mixed agendas and it is hardly surprising that they are still in the process of trying to sort it all out. But for good and/or ill, and for all the reasons we have been looking at, the Anglicans have made a major impact on modern Jerusalem. Now they find themselves on all sides of the political map. The conversion vision of the original missionaries is unfulfilled but the importance of being in the Holy City, and in some way of it, is recognized by the Anglican Communion as an important aspect of its mission.

Notes

[1] For a general history of the society see W. T. Gidney, *The History of the London Society for Promoting Christianity Amongst the Jews, from 1809 to 1908* (London, 1908).

[2] See my 'The sacramentality of the Holy Land: two contrasting approaches', in David Brown and Ann Loades (eds), *The Sense of the Sacramental: Movement and Measure in Art and Music, Place and Time* (London, 1995), 78–100.

[3] On English Protestant attitudes to the Jews, Nabil Matar, 'The idea of the restoration of the Jews in English Protestant thought: between the Reformation and 1660', *Durham University Journal* (1985); 'The idea of the Jews in English Protestant thought, 1661–1701', *Harvard Theological Review*, 78, 1–2 (1985), 115–48; M. Verete, 'The restoration of the Jews in English Protestant thought 1790–1840', *Middle Eastern Studies*, 8, 1 (1972), 3–50; and for the Jewish community in Jerusalem, Tudor Parfitt, *The Jews in Palestine, 1800–1882* (London, 1987).

[4] Kenneth Cragg, 'The Anglican church', in A. J. Arberry (ed.), *Religion in the Middle East: Three Religions in Concord and Conflict* (Cambridge, 1969), 1, 570–95.

[5] Studies relating to the formation of the bishopric: J.-M. Hornus, 'L'évêché anglo-prussien de Jérusalem (1841–1881): controverses autour de sa création (1841)', *Proche-Orient Chrétien*, 13 (1963), 130–49 and 234–58; 14 (1964), 184–201 and 307–34; idem, 'La fondation effective de l'évêché anglican de Jérusalem et son premier titulaire (5 Oct 1841–23 Nov 1845)', *Proche-Orient Chrétien*, 19 (1969), 194–219; 'Les missions anglicanes au Proche-Orient avant la création de l'évêché de Jérusalem', *Proche-Orient Chrétien*, 12 (1962), 255–69; P. J. Welch, 'Anglican churchmen and the establishment of the Jerusalem bishopric', *Journal of Ecclesiastical History*, 8 (1957), 193–204; and Wilhelm H. Hechler, *The Jerusalem Bishopric: Documents with Translation* (London, 1883).

[6] S. Gobat, *Samuel Gobat, Bishop of Jerusalem: His Life and Work* (London, 1884).

[7] E. Stock, *The History of the Church Missionary Society* (London, 1889).

[8] Kelvin Crombie, *For the Love of Zion* (London, 1991), 13–16.

[9] Ibid., 13.

[10] Ibid., 18–19; A. L. Tibawi, *British Interests in Palestine, 1800–1901* (Oxford, 1961), 7–8.

[11] Tibawi, *British Interests*, 14.

[12] Ibid., 15.

[13] Ibid., 35.

[14] For the general context of Protestant politics see Caesar E. Farah, 'Protestantism and politics: the 19th century dimension in Syria', in David Kushner (ed.), *Palestine in the Late Ottoman Period* (Leiden, 1986), 320–40; and Joseph Grabill, *Protestant Diplomacy and the Near East: Missionary Influence on American Policy, 1810–1927* (Minneapolis, 1971).

[15] Tibawi, *British Interests*, 24–7.

[16] Lester G. Pittman, 'The Protestant bishopric in Jerusalem and the Eastern Question' (unpublished master's thesis for the University of Virginia), 3. See further L. Pittman, 'More than missionaries: the Anglican church in Palestine 1918–1948' (unpublished paper, Washington, 1995); and 'The formation of the episcopal diocese of Jerusalem 1841–1948: Anglican, indigenous and ecumenical', in Thomas Hummel, Kevork Hintlian and Ulf Carmesund (eds), *Patterns of the Past, Prospects for the Future: The Christian Heritage in the Holy Land* (London, 1999), 105–13, at 85–104.

[17] Brian Taylor, 'Alexander's apostasy: first steps to Jerusalem', *Studies in Church History*, 29 (1992), 363–72.

[18] Pittman, *The Protestant Bishopric*.

[19] Albert M. Hyamson, *The British Consulate in Jerusalem in Relation to the Jews of Palestine, 1838–1914* (London, 1939).

[20] Shaul Sapir, 'The Anglican missionary societies in Jerusalem: activities and impact', in

Ruth Clark (ed.), *The Land that became Israel: Studies in Historical Geography* (New Haven, 1990), 105–19.

[21] Alexander Schölch, 'Britain in Palestine 1838–1882: the roots of the Balfour policy', *Journal of Palestine Studies*, 22 (1992), 39–56; and M. Verete, 'Why was a British Consulate established in Jerusalem?', *The English Historical Review*, 85 (1970), 316–45.

[22] Crombie, *For the Love of Zion*, 51–5; Tibawi, *British Interests*, 68–73.

[23] Tibawi, *British Interests*, 88.

[24] Ibid., 89–95.

[25] Ibid., 96–100.

[26] Tibawi, *British Interests*, 115–16.

[27] Quoted from Tibawi, *British Interests*, 185.

[28] Ruth and Thomas Hummel, *Patterns of the Sacred: English Protestant and Russian Orthodox Pilgrims of the Nineteenth Century* (London, 1995); and T. Hummel, 'English Protestant pilgrims of the 19th century', in Anthony O'Mahony, with Göran Gunner and Kevork Hintlian (eds), *The Christian Heritage in the Holy Land* (London, 1995), 160–80.

[29] Crombie, *For the Love of Zion*, 122–3.

[30] E. Blyth, *When We Lived in Jerusalem* (London, 1927).

[31] Quoted from Tibawi, *British Interests*, 222.

[32] Saul P. Colbi, *Christianity in the Holy Land Past and Present*, (Tel Aviv, 1969), 116.

[33] Crombie, *For the Love of Zion*, 126.

[34] Ibid.

[35] Ibid., 127.

[36] Ibid., 153.

[37] Ibid., 162.

[38] Ibid., 166.

[39] Ibid., 194.

[40] Quoted ibid., 176–7.

[41] Quoted ibid., 197–8.

[42] See my 'Canon Bridgeman: an Anglican emissary to the eastern church', in Hummel, Hintlian and Carmesund (eds), *Patterns of the Past, Prospects for the Future: The Christian Heritage in the Holy Land* (London, 1999), 105–13, and the material cited there from the Jerusalem and East Mission archives at St Anthony's College, Oxford.

[43] Quoted in Crombie, *For the Love of Zion*, 206.

[44] Quoted ibid., 207.

[45] Ibid., 216.

[46] Daphne Tsimhoni, *Christian Communities in Jerusalem and the West Bank Since 1948: An Historical, Social and Political Study* (Westport, 1993), 113; and *eadem*, 'The Anglican (Evangelical Episcopal) community and the West Bank', *Oriente Moderno*, 2 (1983), 251–8.

[47] Ibid., 142–3.

[48] Ibid., 149.

[49] Crombie, *For the Love of Zion*, 233.

[50] Naim Ateek, *Justice and Only Justice: A Palestinian Theology of Liberation* (New York, 1989); N. Ateek, Marc H. Ellis and Rosemary Radford-Ruether (eds), *Faith and the Intifada: Palestinian Christian Voices* (New York, 1992); N. Ateek and Michael Prior (eds), *Holy Land – Hollow Jubilee: God, Justice and the Palestinians* (London, 1999); N. Ateek, Cedar Duaybis and Marla Schrader (eds), *Jerusalem: What Makes for Peace? A Palestinian Christian Contribution to Peacemaking* (London, 1997); N. Ateek, 'An Arab-Israeli's theological reflections on the state of Israel after 40 years', *Immanuel*, 22–3 (1989), 102–19; N. Ateek, 'Who is the Church? A Christian theology for the Holy Land', in O'Mahony, with Gunner and Hintlian (eds), *The Christian Heritage in the Holy Land* (London, 1995), 311–20.

EDUCATION, CULTURE AND CIVILIZATION: ANGLICAN MISSIONARY WOMEN IN PALESTINE

Inger Marie Okkenhaug

The arrival of the new bishop, George Popham Blyth, and his family in Jerusalem in 1887, symbolizes the reconstitution of the Jerusalem bishopric and the foundation of the Jerusalem and East Mission, which furthered the Church of England's ambitious educational project in the Holy Land. The bishopric built schools for Palestinian children, offering education from nursery and eventually up to a college degree. The educational scheme included both sexes. This chapter will, however, look at the development of Anglican female education under Bishop Blyth in Ottoman Palestine and its expansion into a prominent position within the British mandate. What role did female education play in the Anglican church's work in the Holy Land and what kind of education did they offer girls? What role did the mission-based education for women play under the British administration?

The chapter will be based on sources from the Jerusalem and East Mission (JEM)[1] and will concentrate on uncovering this so far unused material. There are few studies on missionary education from Syria/Palestine in the period before 1948, apart from Billie Melman's *Women's Orient*,[2] which deals with female missionaries, and A. L. Tibawi's studies of British and American religious and educational enterprises.[3] Derek Hopwood's work on the Russian church and schools in the area should also be mentioned.[4] The main aim here is not a comparison of Anglican education and other evangelical institutions in Palestine, but rather an attempt to gain insight into the Jerusalem and East Mission's scheme for female education from the late 1880s until the end of the British mandate in 1948.

Mission and Education in Ottoman Syria

During the nineteenth century there was an increase in European presence in Palestine, both economically and religiously, with strong political overtones; France, Russia, Italy, Great Britain and the Austro-Hungarian Empire, as well as America, wanted influence in the decaying Ottoman state. Mission-based philanthropic institutions were encouraged as part of the competing Powers' establishments in the region, and by 1900 such enterprises were a common factor in Jerusalem especially, but also in other areas of Palestine. As Alexander Schölch's study of nineteenth-century Palestine shows,[5] the European powers endeavoured to build up and expand their presence in Palestine particularly by religious-cultural penetration. 'To this end, each energetically supported the philanthropic, cultural, and missionary activities of its own citizens.'[6] The position of the Holy Land in the western religious mind made it attractive as an area to acquire influence by means of a 'religious protectorate'.

The Ottoman government did not permit Christian missionary activities. This anti-foreign policy was, however, to change with the Egyptian occupation of Syria in 1833. Muhammad Ali's expansionist policy resulted in a six-year Egyptian rule of Syria (including Lebanon and Palestine) that led to an opening-up of the area. The Egyptians were willing to allow missionaries to settle in the Holy Land, despite opposition from many of the local Christian communities. In 1840 Syria revolted against its Egyptian rulers. In order to safeguard the Status Quo of the Ottoman Empire, England, Russia, Prussia and Austria fought together with Turkey against Egypt until July 1841, when Muhammad Ali was obliged to surrender all claims to Syria and Palestine. Turkey had no choice but to accept the help of the European powers, and she accepted their demands, which meant that these European nations, in addition to France, established firm footholds in the land.[7] This hospitable policy of the Ottomans created a surge of philanthropy and proselytizing in Palestine and southern Syria during the middle decades of the nineteenth century.

Russia and France were soon to take the lead in the race to gain influence by means of 'protecting' minorities. Russia was the traditional 'protecting power' of the Orthodox Christians, both in Palestine and the Middle East generally, while France held the same position for the Catholic Christians. Schools were an important part of this religious influence, and Russia and France made the largest contribution to education. The Protestant powers, England and Prussia, needed an institutional base in the Holy Land to compete with the Orthodox and the Catholics.[8] This was created with the establishment of an Anglo-Prussian episcopal see in Jerusalem in 1841.[9] Its protégés, Jews and Protestants, were placed under the political protection of England.[10]

The first Protestant church in the Ottoman Empire, the Christ Church in Jerusalem, was built by the London Society for Promoting Christianity amongst the Jews (LSJ) in 1840. As it was strictly forbidden in Islamic law to build new churches or new synagogues, the church was ultimately permitted as the private chapel of the British consul.[11]

During this period the general level of education in Ottoman Syria was very low. The schools that already existed were of an elementary type and, whether Muslim or Christian, concentrated on restricted religious studies. The only schools of higher learning aimed at an ecclesiastical education. This was, however, to change to some degree with the Egyptian occupation of Syria, which led to the introduction of a wide programme of primary education for boys, based on the educational system of Muhammad Ali's Egypt. From 1834 on there were three main sources building up educational institutions in Syria: the Egyptian administration with its state schools at primary level, the foreign missions, French and American (later British, German, Russian and Italian) and the local ecclesiastics. Egyptian rule lasted only six years, but its secular education for Muslims lived on after 1840.

The first foreign missionaries who had settled in Syria at the beginning of the seventeenth century had been Catholic, and mostly of French origin, and their activities had been limited to the establishment of a few schools and seminaries. In 1820 the first American missionaries arrived in Beirut. These were Protestants, and since there was no Protestant community in Syria, they had to convert members of other Christian sects. This activity created bad feeling among the local Christian communities, but the hostility must have been overcome, because by 1860 the American Presbyterians had established thirty-three schools in various parts of Syria, Lebanon and Jerusalem. These institutions were attended by approximately 1,000 pupils, of whom nearly one-fifth were girls.[12] In 1866 they established the Syrian Protestant College in Beirut, where the language of instruction was Arabic.

The Russians, via the Imperial Palestine Society, established schools in and around Jerusalem, Nazareth, Ramallah, Jaffa and Haifa, and began teaching in Arabic. The revival of the Greek Orthodox church in Palestine and its reaction to the Protestant missionaries were strongly supported by Russian money and enterprise. Until then the Greek Orthodox had taught mostly in Greek, a language the locals could not understand. Russians provided Orthodox Christians with education in Arabic and as much independence as possible from the control of the Greek church. The Russian schools also introduced students to Arabic literature and folklore.

These educational institutions were aimed mainly at boys, and female education was almost universally neglected. The first school in Syria to have a building constructed to serve as a school for girls was established in Beirut in 1834 by the American Presbyterian Mrs Eli Smith. Later other missionary organizations also opened schools for girls. In 1868, with the support of the Protestant bishop of Jerusalem, Samuel Gobat, German deaconesses from the Kaiserworth Institute built a large school for Arab girls, outside the city walls, known as Talitha-Kumi (Young Girl, Arise).[13]

A Protestant educational enterprise for Jewish girls was established by the LSJ, which opened separate schools for Jewish girls and boys near the Christ Church compound. In 1892 a new large girls' boarding school was opened, where two years later there were thirty-five boarders, all of them Jewish. At the girls' day school there were between fifteen and forty-nine pupils. After promulgation of excommunication by the rabbis (when the LSJ hospital was built), many girls left the school. As a result, some Christians and Muslims were admitted to compensate for the loss. During this period, the LSJ gave high priority to educational work for girls, and the organization opened the Girls' Industrial School in 1900. The largest building project of LSJ during this period was, however, the new girls' day school (the present-day Barclay building at Christ Church) which was completed in 1902.

The first Protestant bishop (the Christian Jew Michael Solomon Alexander) in Jerusalem established a college in 1842, whose primary object was the education of Jewish converts. Druses and other Gentile converts were also accepted. Alexander's successor, the Swiss Samuel Gobat (1846–79) introduced the Berlin Missionary Society to Palestine, as well as supporting the work of the Church Missionary Society, which established a large number of schools in Palestine.[14]

By the 1880s the CMS was by far the largest Protestant mission in Palestine, both in material resources and in large-scale work. The CMS had begun its work in Syria and the Holy Land in the early 1820s, and from the start there was an ambitious educational scheme designed to prepare the way for direct missionary work. By around 1860 there were four girls' and three boys' (Anglo-German) Protestant schools in Jerusalem. Tibawi argues that the exact number of schools outside Jerusalem is difficult to ascertain, because of frequent failures resulting in closure. These were mostly single-teacher schools with anything between ten and fifty pupils. Outside Jerusalem it was difficult to organize schools for girls, and most of these schools were for boys only. By 1882, however, the total number of schools was thirty-five with 1,635 pupils.[15]

Beside the CMS institutions, the LSJ and the Kaiserworth, there were other Protestant organizations that opened schools for boys and girls. The English Society for Promoting Female Education in the East opened and maintained schools in Nazareth and other centres. The (Scottish) Tabeetha Mission (known as the Miss Arnott School after the teacher who started it, Miss Walker Arnott) opened and maintained a school for girls in Jaffa, and the American Friends (Quakers) opened a girls' school and later a boys' school at Ramallah.[16] By 1880 there were over 100 different schools run by and representing different countries, scattered all over the area.[17]

Bishop Blyth and the Jerusalem and East Mission

While the LSJ to a large extent concentrated its missionary work on the Jewish population only, the CMS described its aim in the Middle East as the 'diffusion of Christian truth among the Jews, Mahometans, and pagans'.[18] Since direct missionary work among the Muslims was contrary to the law of the country, the aim of these early missionaries was the propagation of 'Christian knowledge'. Christian education was deemed to be the sure way of converting people, but any education combined with Christian instruction would not be tolerated by Turkish authorities if it were offered to Muslim children. A strategy of educating the children of the eastern Christians was then adopted, for it was believed that, influenced by the pure form of Christianity, they would convert Muslims.

This policy changed, however, in 1887, when the Germans withdrew from the joint bishopric and the Anglican church was free to revive the bishopric. The High Church party in England became engaged in the future of the Jerusalem bishopric, and this influential group opposed the CMS and the LSJ's evangelical approach.[19] As proselytizing of Christian Arabs in any form was officially condemned, it was stressed that the primary aim of the bishopric had originally been and still was evangelization of the Jews, Muslims and Druses.[20] The Anglican bishop should primarily be diplomatic, only partly pastoral and missionary. The appointment of George P. Blyth (who held the see from 1887 to 1914) whose 'temperament and training fitted him for a much closer sensitivity to the mind and ethos of the Eastern Churches',[21] gave substance to the 'embassy' concept of the Anglican presence. The diplomatic approach was to be developed during Blyth's time in Jerusalem and was also to characterize the bishop's relations with the Muslim and Jewish communities. This was, however, to alienate the bishop from the CMS missionaries in Palestine.

Blyth wanted to coordinate the missionary work and to direct it, without actually controlling it. Here he collided with the interests of the CMS, whom Blyth accused of continuing an aggressive proselytizing of Muslims, a policy that threatened to jeopardize all the work of the Church of England. After several disputes, Blyth established a new organization in 1887; this was the Jerusalem and East Mission (JEM), which was completely controlled and directed by the Anglican bishop himself.[22]

The Anglican Compound

In 1888 Bishop Blyth acquired land north of the Damascus Gate outside the city walls, where during a ten-year period, a group of buildings were erected around the Anglican collegiate church (consecrated in 1898). This area, called St George's Close, was to be a purely Church of England institution, completely independent of the LSJ and CMS.

The Anglican centre included the bishop's residence, a training centre for clergy, catechists and teachers, and the choir boarding school for boys who trained as clerics. Blyth's first educational venture, however, was the establishment of a girls' orphanage, St Mary's Home (with a preference for orphans and for Jewesses), attached to his own residence. It was founded by him in 1889, together with Miss Alice Blyth, one of the bishop's sisters, with ten Jewish girls who boarded, and were clothed and taught free of charge. Miss Blyth was the first lady superintendent until she died at Jerusalem in

1895. In 1900 there were twelve girls, who were received without payment. In addition there were eighteen girls who paid a fee either through their parents or from scholarships.[23] In 1907/8 there were thirty girls, who were all baptized.[24] The subjects taught were English, Arabic, French and music, and the institution was also a training school for teachers and nurses. To St Mary's Home was attached a free day school for children of the neighbourhood. It started in 1888 with around 100 girls between the ages of four and fifteen, a number that had grown to 120–30 thirteen years later.[25] These children were usually not baptized, as Christian girls were usually not received because there were already free schools for them.[26] The free day school for girls was for several years under the personal charge of an English woman, before she handed it over to the JEM.

As was the case with the boarding school for girls, baptism was a condition of admission to the choir school. But to be admitted to the day primary school for boys, opened in 1899, later known as St George's Boys' School (or Madrasat'ul Mutran, the bishop's school), baptism was not a condition. St George's was developed as a fee-paying school for children coming from well-to-do homes. It was important for it not to be seen as competing with other mission schools, as was noted by the bishop: 'St George's Day School for Boys of the better classes, who can pay fees: there being plenty of free Schools for boys at Jerusalem'.[27] It was run on the model of preparatory and public schools in England. During this early period the children came mostly from poor Jewish homes, but there were also some Greek Orthodox children admitted with the consent of the patriarch.

Outside Jerusalem, the bishopric's missionary and educational activity were mainly in Haifa, where the bishop initiated a mission to the Jews with a dispensary and a school, and the building of St Luke's church, consecrated in 1889.

Working Parties for Jewish Women

From the early nineteenth century on, proselytizing of Jews was a central theme in the Evangelical-inspired Anglican church. The Evangelical movement saw the Scriptures, including the term 'millennium' as revealed text to be read literally. Within the Church of England there were groups called pre-millenarists who believed that the regeneration of Jews, or of oriental non-Protestant Christians, should occur before millennial times, and precipitate the awakening of the orient. The idea of mission was central to pre-millenarianism, and the different Evangelical societies in the Middle East, especially the above-mentioned LSJ but also the CMS, were motivated by these ideas.[28] The assertion that Palestine was truly the God-given home of the Jews, to which they sooner or later would return, gained wide currency among the British public. During the latter part of the nineteenth century, the idea of the 'restoration' of the Jews was joined with imperialist tendencies.[29]

When the newly re-established bishopric in Jerusalem chose to initiate its proselytizing with working parties for Jewish women, it must be seen as a result of the relatively central role the doctrine of the 'restoration of the Jews to the Holy Land' played within certain strata of the British establishment as well as in public opinion. The JEM gave priority to organized teaching of needlework to Jewish women as a means to improve social conditions and Christian influence. In doing this, they chose to continue a tradition from the early nineteenth-century English missionaries.

In the Middle East, so-called 'working parties' for Jewish women had existed since the early decades of the nineteenth century, organized by evangelical missionaries in Syria as well as in Egypt.[30] Elizabeth Ann Finn, the wife of the British consul in Jerusalem from 1845 till 1863, had an Evangelical background, and as a 'staunch millenarist' she was involved with several charity projects for indigent Jews.[31] Finn cooperated with Anne Gobat, the wife of Bishop Gobat, and combined evangelization (Bible reading, the distribution of suitable reading material, sermonizing) with social aid to women.[32]

In 1843 the LSJ established a 'House of Industry' in Jerusalem, which was a school where Jewish men learned a trade and received religious instruction.[33] There was also a parallel female part to the 'House of Industry', originally established and run by Miss Cooper, a 'benevolent English lady'.[34] This Jewesses' Institution aimed at helping the poor Jewish women of Jerusalem. This was the first example of vocational education for women in Jerusalem. When Miss Cooper died in 1859, she bequeathed the Institution to the LSJ.

The JEM working parties for Jewesses had the same object as their predecessors, evangelization combined with utility. In the St George's compound Jewish women were taught needlework while they had the gospel read to them.[35] These women were all Arabic-speaking Jewesses, native Palestinian and Middle Eastern Jews and from the poorer elements of the Jewish population.[36]

It has been argued that western female-reform ideology dictated the presence of dependent clients.[37] This is however an issue that the JEM was conscious of avoiding. The traditional Jewish community depended on money from the Diaspora to survive. The women were the breadwinners, while the men studied the Torah. This economic aspect was a concern for the Anglican mission, which stressed the importance of teaching the women a craft. The women sewed uniforms for the bishop's schools, paid for by the mission, in order to improve the economic conditions of Jewish families. The production was based on local patterns and techniques which were familiar to the women. The attraction of original handicraft from the Holy Land was probably also an asset for a potential 'oriental craft' market in England. Whether the Anglican missionaries did succeed in improving the material conditions of these women on a permanent basis is difficult to ascertain. The response from the Jewish women was initially good and in Jerusalem Deaconess Berkeley had sixty women who came for instruction, while there seemed to be even more women wanting to join than they had capacity to take on.[38]

The good attendance was, however, dependent on the consent of the religious leaders, the rabbis. From the beginning of their work, the LSJ met strong opposition from the Jewish community, especially to their schools and work among women. This was also the case of the JEM work among the Jews. At one time the JEM working party in Haifa had only one girl attending. The reason for the other Jewish women staying away was the rabbis' *herrem* (sentence of excommunication) against all who went to the missionary's house. The Jewish rabbis resisted all attempts to proselytize Jewish women, and excommunication was a real threat. Jewish opposition to the work of the mission increased, especially among the secular Jewish immigrants who came to Palestine in the early 1880s, and the hostility that had always been shown to the women attending the working-party classes spread to the inmates of St Mary's Home.[39]

St Mary's Home had originally been seen as a good way of reaching Jewish children. In around 1897 there were five Jewish girls living in St Mary's Orphanage, but because of anti-mission feeling among the Jewish population in Jerusalem, all were taken out of the school, never to be replaced. The Jewish community were not interested in a Christian education for their girls, and the bishop had to confess that though 'preference was always given to Jewish children, there were not many of them'.[40] This was not an exceptional reaction from the Jewish community. The new and large girls' boarding school opened in 1892 had a similar experience. By 1894 there were some thirty-five boarders, all of them Jewish. Attendance at the girls' day school during this time varied between fifteen and forty-nine, depending upon the Jewish feasts and the vigilance or laxity of the rabbis.

Crombie writes that in 1905 there were only seven Jewish boys over the age of seventeen who were baptized, while the girls at the LSJ's Industrial School were threatened by the rabbis and 'feared the wrath of their parents, and dread[ed] the curse which would be pronounced upon them'.[41] Barbara Tuckman as well as Melman has shown that the evangelical aim of converting Jews was not successful.[42] Both mention that the LSJ, despite being one of the most active Evangelical mission societies in Palestine during this period, had between sixty and just over one hundred converts over a period of half a century, during which the Jewish population of Jerusalem soared from under 2,000 to 10,000.[43]

Other independent female organizations and philanthropists had minimal success in attracting converts, either Jews or indigenous Christians. According to Melman, the converts came from the margins of the community, socially as well as economically, and the strongest inducement to conversion seemed to be financial. Tibawi argues that 'the motives for the conversion were seldom pure', but often prompted by material gain or political protection.[44]

Besides the economic improvement in the material condition of the poorer parts of the Jewish community, Melman points to another quite revolutionary result: the working parties separated women's work from the home and removed them from the patriarchal segregated household.[45] This 'territorial revolution' also affected the lives of the girls and young women at the JEM female educational institutions, not only Jewish but Muslim and Christian as well, as will be discussed next.

The Anglican Schools

In contrast to his predecessor, Blyth's educational strategy was dominated not by proselytizing, but rather by the 'embassy' aspect. This meant that his educational work was based on a principle of 'influence through living a Christian life' and, unlike the other mission societies, the JEM schools were not separated for Jews, Christian and Muslim children. Education through the medium of English was to overcome linguistic differences, a principle that was vindicated throughout the twentieth century.

The day school was free of charge, and attracted children from the poorer elements of the population. Only a minority of the students, perhaps one-quarter, came from homes that were able to feed them. The rest were fed by the school. The headmistress, Deaconess Ruth Berkeley, emphasized the poverty of the girls when writing for an English audience about 'the very poorest to whom we give a meal in the middle of the day; bread and olives or whatever is cheapest and in season'.[46]

The ideal of economic self-sufficiency was also part of the day school's programme. The previously mentioned working parties for Jewish women had been part of the institution of St Mary's. The same concept of teaching young girls and women to make lace, which was bought by the school, was used as part of the educational programme in order to give the women a chance to make an income. The children were offered basic skills in Arabic, English, geography, arithmetic, plain sewing and needlework.[47] A central part of the education was Scripture reading, in both Arabic and English. According to Hill Lindley, most Protestant missionaries placed a high value on basic literacy because reading the Bible was so central to their understanding of Christianity.[48] The Anglican girls' school emphasized Scripture reading and Bible sessions for all grades, and even the youngest girls had to learn texts from the Bible by heart, in English as well as Arabic, despite lacking knowledge of the language. It was this part of the education that was shown off to the school's visitors: 'Before each group stood a Christian Syrian teacher who made her scholars recite and sing . . . the little ones said the 23rd Pslam in English, a great feat as they do not understand English, then they repeated portions of Scripture in their own language very nicely and sang some Arabic hymns.'[49] In one instance the Muslim girls are described as the least bright of the girls at the day school, with the Protestant (here Christians that are not Orthodox or eastern Christians) girls on top and the eastern Christians in the middle. But in later descriptions this has changed: 'The scriptural knowledge is excellent, the Moslem and Jewish girls showing an equal if not superior knowledge to that of the Christians.'[50] The Muslim girls' ability to learn by heart is also commented upon.

Hygiene was one issue that was stressed as an important part of the girls' education. The local population, regardless of nationality and religion, were perceived as dirty and living in unhygienic surroundings. L. A. Flemming shows how in India the missionaries' attempt to change attitudes towards health and hygiene was a result of reform ideas concerning personal cleanliness and family hygiene common among the western middle classes in the late nineteenth century.[51] In Britain this development was seen in the state as well as private schools, where part of the educational profile around the turn of the century was to make the children wash and dress neatly if possible. In urban areas, pupils from the lower classes were encouraged to use the public baths, and reports tell of improvements in the children's health and academic progress as a result of improved personal hygiene.[52]

This strategy was adopted by the Anglican girls' schools in Palestine, where the first task was to clean the exterior of the possible converts. Cleanliness and tidiness were stressed in the journals read by the home audience: 'little Syrian children are fascinating, especially when they are clean, which they always are at the Day School.'[53]

St Mary's Boarding School was presented as the showcase of the bishopric in Jerusalem. In 1899 there were ten girls living in the 'Home', while only two years later, the number of children educated and clothed there had risen to thirty. This increase signifies the important role the boarding school played in the JEM's educational work. Its main aim was to educate local women, Jews as well as Christians, and train them to carry on the missionary work as teachers and nurses. The JEM boarding schools had a clear class profile. In Cairo, at the Anglican St Mary's it was important to get hold of the 'children of the middle classes, those of professional men and business men'.[54] The same was true for the St Mary's Home in Jerusalem, where only girls from 'good' families able to pay the entrance fee were accepted, or those on scholarships, donated by supporters in England and USA.[55] An example from 1904 shows that because few parents were able to pay the annual fee there was a base of eighteen girls, while the school could take thirty. Two years later the number of pupils had risen to thirty-one. Because of lack of funds, the school could not accept any more girls even though there was a waiting list.[56] Some of the better-class children from the day school, however, were allowed to join the boarding school as day pupils. This social stratification was very much intentional. The JEM wanted to educate the children of the local middle classes because of their potential social and political influence, something that will be discussed later.

The Home offered a better-quality education, and there were more subjects taught than in the day school. On examination days the Home pupils were examined in many more subjects than the day pupils: 'Miss Blyth examined them in composition, grammar, geography, arithmetic and catechism, Miss Furnival in English writing, reading, dictation and recitation . . . as well as Prayer Book and needlework.'[57]

Susan Hill Lindley argues that, in general, Protestant missionaries were eager to found boarding schools, and especially boarding schools for girls, 'in hopes that more sustained and pervasive influence of the teachers would result in more effective evangelism and the formation of "Christian Character"'.[58] Kumari Jaywardena has found the same strategy in her study of Methodist boarding schools for girls in Sri Lanka, where the students were seldom allowed leave from the school, because it was thought they should be kept away from heathen influence until old enough to form a steady 'Christian character'.[59] For the JEM mission, the boarding school of St Mary's provided great prospects for influencing the students, where the training of character was given the highest priority.[60] This was the primary arena in which the new Christian woman would be created: 'the gem of all the future hope is the education of girls – education in its broadest, deepest meaning – the building of character far more than mind; the training that gives them a higher aim and a greater scope than the last generation knew.'[61]

In the English school system, domestic economy and general home-making skills (including needlework), were made obligatory for girls by the early 1870s. This strategy for female education was adopted by Protestant missionaries, for example in India, where the 'new Christian Woman' that the missionaries wanted to create in their institutions was strongly orientated to domestic roles.[62] At St Mary's Home one finds the same emphasis on domestic chores as central in the 'character training' or socialization of the Palestinian girls. The entire housework was done by the girls: dormitories, schoolrooms, passages, dining hall, etc., being taken in turn by each girl for a fortnight at a time.

There might have been an economic reason for using the girls as free labour. The Anglican mission organization was always in need of money, and at this time most English women missionary-teachers were honorary workers who were not paid, but lived on their own means. The feeling that the pupils themselves should contribute was probably a factor behind the emphasis on household chores. The general educational principle should, however, not be ignored. In England school textbooks encouraged girls to be self-sacrificing, domesticated and highly moral.[63] These virtues were also taught to the Palestinian girls in the Anglican schools: 'We try to develop what is best in our children so that they may become true and earnest women, and help to raise and brighten their homes in the future.'[64]

Woman as Spiritual Catalyst

Deborah Kirkwood, who has analysed Protestant missionary women in south Central Africa during the nineteenth century, argues that, for the Protestant mission, 'contact with, and the instruction of, the women was seen as a key to the consolidation of the gains made in the conversion of men.'[65] Melman's research from the Middle East shows, however, that the Evangelical ideal of women's moral superiority was transferred to the local women, who, after being influenced by Protestant Christianity, would become social and religious transformers, regenerating the Ottoman Empire morally and spiritually.[66] This role as spiritual catalyst is also characteristic of the JEM: 'To our girls we already owe much of the awakening of their brothers and cousins to the fact that if the women are not educated the men must suffer in character, in power, and in personality.'[67]

These ideas were not only Evangelical but were held by most British teachers at the time. The English Board of Education stressed that domestic training should lead the scholars not only to 'set a higher value on the housewife's position' but also 'to understand that the work of women in the homes may do much to make a nation strong and prosperous'.[68] The extended, national aspect was adapted to a Middle Eastern setting by the JEM. The Palestinian woman possessed the potential for indirect influence on political and social issues, and interestingly the Middle Eastern woman is seen as having more influence on her sons and husband than have western women on theirs: 'Mothers are the makers of men, and as nowhere in the world have women more power in the inner domestic life than in the East, so nowhere is their ignorance more fatal. They are clogs to every advance . . . How many boys might have gone away and done well instead of becoming idlers and café loungers, if their mothers had not kept them at home.'[69]

The JEM felt they had found common ground with the local population. Not only were the girls eager to attend the mission schools; there was also considerable support and approval from the local men: the girls 'are greedy to be taught, [and] their brothers are more than eager to help them'.[70] The Anglican educated woman was not a threat to the Middle Eastern ideal of mother and wife. The aim was not to challenge the traditional life of the eastern woman, but to improve her in her domestic roles as mother and wife, thus standing on common ground with Arab reformers of the time.

Intellectuals (men) in the cosmopolitan centres of the Ottoman Empire were voicing a demand for giving women more educational opportunities, opinions that were reflected in the literature of the time. One of the best known, Kasim Amin (1865–1908) who lived in Egypt, asserted that only if women were educated could they fulfil their function in modern society. Namik Kemal (1840–88) saw educated women as an integrated part of a modern society. 'We know that in civilised countries the women, like the men, are educated.'[71] These Ottoman intellectuals made a link between women's status and the degree of a society's development and civilization.

These ideas of the modern woman were also found among the young men at St George's. Anglican-educated Palestinians wanted an educated wife to substantiate their modern identity, a fact that the JEM used as an additional argument in justifying the priority given to girls' schools.

> One of our old boys, who has sisters at St Mary's said to me . . . 'for every boy's school in the country, I would make ten girl's schools, if I had the money. Our women hold us back, and we cannot reason with them for they do not understand'. Another said 'I want my sisters to be interested in many things, and my wife, when I marry, to be my friend'. And another, bringing us a girl whom he implored us to take, said, 'Take her, beat her, kill her if you like but make her into a woman who can think.'[72]

The Christian feminine ideal of womanhood was used as a base for a modern identity for the Palestinian woman, who would match the western-educated Palestinian man.

The Palestinian Anglican-educated woman, regardless of religious background, was thus to be a spiritual redeemer in her home, as well as enlightened in her domestic role. Good housewives were, however, only one of several aims for the St Mary's girls. Western nineteenth-century society saw the teaching of children as a neutral role and duty of women. Like other Protestant mission societies, the JEM stressed the importance of educating the girls as teachers, and preparing them, if suitable, for appointments on the staff of one of the missions. Later on the girls were also encouraged to think of nursing, also a 'natural' feminine occupation, as their future work.[73]

A brief account of former students from 1911 gives an insight into the job options for the former St Mary's girls. Some functioned in roles similar to the female Anglican missionaries, as teachers or nurses at the Anglican institutions in Jerusalem and Haifa, and with the Church Mission in Sudan. Ester Abraham, for example, was nursing at the DMS Hospital in Old Cairo, while two girls were probationers at the Beirut American mission hospital. Three former students had gone to England, either to study for an MA degree or to be trained at a missionary college there. One was a teacher at the JEM's girls' school in Cairo, another a junior nurse at St Luke's Hospital, Haifa. Both of these girls worked for several years before they married. The general westernization in the Middle East created a demand for female indigenous teachers outside the mission establishments. Some were teaching music and English in Cairo in private homes. In Palestine and Syria social developments, like the building of the railway in the 1890s, opened up the area to outer influence and created a general demand for European education. Lydia Domet, for example, who left St Mary's at seventeen and went home to Haifa, was teaching a Turkish girl whose fiancé was anxious for her to learn English before he married her.[74]

As this account indicates, some of the girls who attended the Anglican school lived the life of the 'new Christian woman'. This was not achieved without friction with local traditions. Hopwood writes of the Russian mission schools that

> a minor revolution was brought about in the lives of those girls who remained as teachers with the [Russian church's] schools. They had graduated from school at eighteen and by the age of twenty-one were still unmarried in a country where the usual age of marriage was considerably lower.[75]

The training of teachers and nurses as future career missionaries at St Mary's created the same conflicts within the local society. By the time the girls came to their teens, they were wanted as household workers at home, and were also sought after as brides, having increased their worth with a British education. This was contrary to the Home's intentions, since fourteen was just the age at which the girls could be trained for mission work. In order to prevent pupils from leaving the school early, the entrance fee was returned to the girls, with an extra sum for an outfit, if they stayed on until they were seventeen. By then they were found work in other mission-based schools or hospitals in Palestine and other places in the Anglican bishopric.[76] This meant that not only did the teacher or nurse support herself, but she also continued to live separately from her family after finishing her education.

This Anglican vision of a new Christian woman in the Middle East, which was a product of the Evangelical female ideal, also included a social aspect of economic independence. Bishop Blyth, for example, insisted on the St Mary's girl being trained 'to fit her to support herself when she leaves the school'.[77] The idea of a financially independent woman was radical in the Palestinian context. It was, however, growing as a result of the general influence of modernization in the Middle East, which affected all religious communities in Palestine.

Besides St Mary's School, there were two other Evangelical training institutions, both colleges for nurses and teachers, open for women in Palestine and Syria in the same period. The American mission in Beirut started regular nursing training in their hospital, and in 1908 the British Syrian mission opened a department for training women teachers.[78] Other Christian missionary institutions also offered female education, including the training of teachers and health personnel. Besides German and French institutions, the Russian church established a boarding school for girls in 1890, with the aim of training Arab girls to teach in Orthodox schools.[79]

While missionary schools played an important role in establishing girls' schools for higher education in the Middle East, the state authorities to some extent participated. As part of strengthening the country through a modernization process, the state authorities in Egypt as well as the Ottoman Empire had started schools that offered a basic education for women as well as a specialized training of nurses and teachers.[80] Between 1870 and 1900 the gradual increase in the numbers of girls entering secondary schools in the Ottoman Empire made it necessary to establish a women's teacher training school in Istanbul.[81] There were also high schools for girls outside the capital. Under the Young Turks, educational opportunities for women were further extended.

Muslim Girls in Anglican Schools

The Turkish authorities, however, did not encourage education for the Arab population. By 1914 the Ottoman government schools in Palestine, which were mainly Muslim, provided education for only 1,400 girls and 6,848 boys out of a total of 71,933 Arab children of school age. At the same time there were 131 girls (out of a total of 8,705 pupils) at private Muslim schools.[82] Wealthy Muslims, taking advantage of the Ottoman educational system, sent their sons as far as Istanbul, others sent them to the Christian mission school in Jerusalem, 'Ain Tura and Beirut, where they met sons of the wealthier Christian communities.[83] When an increasing number of these Muslim parents wanted to educate their daughters, one of the few alternative institutions acceptable to girls from a traditional Muslim background was the mission schools' segregated female education.

According to George Antonius, the male students of the foreign schools were overwhelmingly Christian, since the Muslims' fear of proselytization made them send their children to less efficient but religiously orthodox schools managed by the state or their own community. This is contradicted by the impression from the JEM source material. Muslim parents did not hesitate to send their girls and boys to the Anglican school. A study of Jordanian women who went to Protestant mission schools supports this impression. Here it was found that Muslim parents were pragmatic in their choice of school. The important factors in deciding where to send children were the reputation of the school, if it was within a convenient distance, and the cost.[84] It has also been shown that in Nablus in the 1930s, the leading Muslim families sent their girls to Christian mission schools without finding it problematic.[85]

According to Billie Melman, Evangelicals had only a limited interest in Muslims. She refers to Albert Hourani, who has pointed out that in Christian cosmology and history there was no place for a third revealed religion, in addition to the fact that proselytizing Muslim Ottoman subjects was prohibited by law and punishable by death. The JEM's educational projects in the Middle East show, however, a considerable number of Muslim pupils in all Anglican schools.[86]

The girls' day school in Jerusalem had, as shown earlier, Muslim students from the very beginning, and there were Muslim boys at St George's. By 1900 the Muslim pupils were between one-third and one-half of the total number of girls at the day school.[87] There were also a few Muslim girls living at the Home. At the JEM's girls' school in Haifa, most of the eighty pupils were Muslim. The inclusion of Muslim children may have seemed a radical move to the home audience, as Deaconess Ruth Berkeley indicates in a speech to the Annual Meeting in London: 'Next to the Jewish work, we have the Mohammedans, and I have often wondered . . . how it is that there seems in England so little interest taken in the Mohammedans'. In Miss Berkeley's experience, Muslim girls did 'not object, but show a keen interest in the (Christian) teaching . . . Not any of their parents have ever withdrawn them from instruction either in Old Testament or New, or in Hymns or in Prayer.' The missionary was quite optimistic: 'a number of these [Muslim] girls tell us that they daily use prayers, and I have no doubt in years to come there will be a great result from that work'.[88]

Despite this optimism and the fact that a relatively high number of Muslim children, girls as well as boys, attended the JEM schools, Muslim converts were a rare phenomenon. There was, however, the long-time value of educating Muslim girls, emphasized by Nina Blyth:

> Few as the actual conversions are, there is a tolerance of Christianity creeping in widely amongst the Moslems, whose children go to mission schools, while the children themselves learn to read and appreciate the Bible. This is the highest work of the schools; here is the brightest hope for the future.[89]

When Turkey entered the war in 1914, British and French schools and hospitals were closed and all building activities were suspended. The British mandate in Palestine from 1918 to 1948 created a new framework for the Anglican schools. The following section will focus on the JEM's female education under a British colonial administration. What role did the Anglican girls' school play in British Palestine?

The Mandate Period

After the British occupation of Jerusalem in 1917, several Anglican mission organizations, through the Syria and Palestine Relief Fund,[90] had established an English high school for girls. This was warmly welcomed by the local population:

> Even to us on the spot the rush of applicants for admission to the temporary British School . . . has been a revelation of startling surprise. The people here are realising by glorious contrast the difference between British civilisation and methods and those which have preceded them . . . feelings . . . are transient, and our British schools must gain their reputation before the desire for what is British passes.[91]

This euphoric mood, as well as a strategic interest in playing a role in future educational work in a British-ruled Palestine, led the three mission organizations, the JEM, CMS and LSJ, to join in a cooperative educational scheme for boys as well as girls: one high school and college for boys and young men, with a training college for teachers attached, and the same for girls.[92] This was done with the full support of the new rulers in Jerusalem, who appreciated the Anglican missionaries' long-time experience and knowledge of local Palestinian conditions. The work of the relief fund had been organized by women like Frances Newton and Mabel Warburton. The former had lived more than twenty years in Palestine, and had a 'very exceptional and intimate knowledge of Syrian conditions and Turkish politics',[93] while Warburton had been the principal of the British Syrian Mission's Girls' Training College in Beirut for several years. Warburton had also impressed the military administration by the way she headed the relief fund's school.

By 1920, it had become clear that the British military occupation of Palestine was to be transformed into an internationally sanctioned mandate rule. Part of the 'colonial burden' of the new rulers was to improve material conditions in Palestine, ideally by creating a western way of life for the population. It was, however, not enough to modernize the infrastructure. If Palestine was to become a modern society, the local population had to be transformed by western education.

The civil administration gave priority to re-establishing primary schools in rural, predominantly Muslim, areas, for both girls and boys, and to higher education for boys and men in urban centres. This limited the scope of the Anglican missionary associations, which led to a concentration on secondary schools in the major towns in Palestine.[94] The 'Government concentrated on the provision of primary education and a normal school . . . deliberately leaving the field open to Western Christian Missions to provide secondary and higher education'.[95] This division suited both parties, and the government's Education Department, and especially the director of education, H. Bowman, gave great support in the secondary educational work.[96]

In 1921 the civil administration under Sir Wyndham Deeds and Hilda Ridler, the long-time head of department for female education, confirmed this in a meeting with Warburton:

> He [Deeds] told me the Government had decided they could not touch secondary education at all for the present; and . . . brought it in our hands. Miss Ridler told me the same, that as far as girls are concerned the Department of Education were prepared to leave the secondary education of girls entirely to us and concentrate on Primary education and training of teachers for primary school.[97]

This was to be the case throughout the whole mandate period, with the Jerusalem Girls' College as the only English educational institution in the region offering education up to university level. While the government held all responsibility for state education, private schools were left in the hands of their governing bodies, as had been the case before the war. This was parallel to the British rule in Egypt, where missionary schools were seen as a necessary part of the educational system. Judith Tucker argues that this was done out of economic considerations, in order to save British taxpayers' money.[98] Economic considerations were certainly present in British policy for Palestine. After 1918, it was difficult to find the means in London for the development of a mandate area, like Palestine, that did not yield any material surplus for the British nation. Private schools (missionary schools and, for the Jewish population, the Zionist schools), were thus a way of establishing educational institutions, with the government financing only a small part of the cost in state support given to all schools.

The Jerusalem Girls' School and College

There was a strong urge among the Anglican establishment in Palestine not only to continue their educational work, but to expand it and thus play a formative role as part of the British colonial rule in the country. The encouragement from the British authorities in Jerusalem and the already established relationship with the parents of Christian, Jewish and Muslim girls were also influential factors in making the Church Missionary Society, the Church's Mission to the Jews and the JEM (as well as the United Free Church of Scotland for a short period) lend teachers and share the expenses.[99]

The school was named the British High School and Training College for Girls, with Miss Warburton as principal. With her thorough knowledge of Palestinian women's conditions, she was the perfect candidate to take responsibility for Anglican education of girls and young women. The fact that she was a woman of personal means, which she was to invest in the High School for Girls in Jerusalem, as well as a brilliant educationalist, made her a crucial person in the realization of the Anglican educational scheme in Jerusalem and the true founder of the school.

The standard of the school was to be equal to that of a secondary school in England, with a small primary department. It was a training college for teachers, as well as an institution that took the students up to Matriculation, opening up the possibility of university study, for example at the Protestant University in Beirut and the Universities of London, Cambridge and Oxford.

The school was divided into two departments: the secondary department for students from fifteen to twenty-four, while in the primary department the ages were from five to fourteen. The kindergarten department lasted for two years, a primary department for seven years and a secondary department for nine years, of which the first two were parallel with the highest classes of the primary and intended as preparatory years for older non-Arabic-speaking girls who did not know sufficient English to enter the first year of the secondary department directly.

In 1919 Miss Warburton's staff consisted of eighteen full-time teachers, eleven being European, six Syrian and one Hebrew Christian, while there were seven visiting language teachers (three or more periods per week), two in Arabic, one in Hebrew, one in Russian, one in Modern Greek, one in

Armenian, one in French. This list of languages and teachers reveals the multinational character of the school. It was open to all denominations, and in 1919 there were 245 pupils, representing ten different nationalities: Syrian, Jewish, Armenian, Russian, Serbian, Montenegrin, Greek, French, American, British. The pupils were divided according to religion, 206 from different Christian sects, twenty-two Jewesses (chiefly in the secondary department) and twelve Muslim girls (chiefly in the primary department).[100] A year later, when the school reopened for its second year, the number of students had increased to 335 girls, fifty-eight of whom were boarders.[101]

The JEM also supported a high school for girls in Haifa, headed by Miss Gardner, who had been teaching at St Mary's School in Jerusalem before the war. In 1919 there were twenty-nine girls, most of them Arabic-speaking, in four classes.[102] Even though Haifa was economically the fastest-growing city in Palestine, the government never opened a school for girls there.[103] The lack of competition meant growth and expansion for the Anglican High School. In 1925 the numbers had more than doubled with seventy-six pupils, including boys under seven who were in the nursery, while five years later there were ninety-seven girls enrolled. During the 1930s the number of pupils was around 150.

The girls' schools in Haifa and Jerusalem were run on a similar basis. In both schools English was the main language for the five top forms, with Arabic taught as the second language. With the exception of Hebrew and Arabic, the subjects taught followed standard English secondary education for girls: Scripture, mathematics, music, physics, chemistry, French, drawing, domestic science and physical education, with special syllabuses for history and regional geography.

The Missionary Aspect of Education Work

On the establishment of the institution in 1919, the missionary aspect of the Jerusalem Girls' High School was stressed by the provisional Joint Committee who promised to 'make it the most efficient school in the mission field'.[104] It was hoped that 'this experiment will justify itself and that the school will become a permanent institution of great value'.[105] The institution was to play a dominant role in higher female education during the mandate period, but the missionary side of the education was not to be as straightforward as it might have seemed in 1918.

The words quoted above were written for JEM supporters in Britain (and the USA), who were potential financial contributors to JEM educational schemes. They clearly expected a more traditional missionary approach, and the official reports in *Bible Lands* did not mention the problematic sides of proselytizing and education in a multi-religious society. In a private letter, Warburton did, however, discuss the problems the school met on the one hand from the instructions of the mandate administration not to proselytize, and on the other hand from the parents. The government approved of the Christian side of the work, as long as there was no active proselytizing. In the words of the headmistress: 'We have promised to keep controversy out of our religious teaching but the Bible itself, Old & New Testament is taught as part of the school curriculum.'[106] This strategy was also eventually accepted by the parents:

> I have had difficulty on this point, but the parents have now accepted my standpoint that this is a *Christian* school and those who come must accept Bible teaching. But in regards to attendance at opening Prayers, I have found it best *not* to make this compulsory for others than Christians, and I feel sure myself that this is the right thing to do, one cannot force Jews and Moslems to join in Christian Prayers, and yet we must be free to make the prayers definitely Christian.[107]

At St George's there were also students belonging to others of the three monotheistic faiths and it was expected that they were interested in religious study in general, and would especially want to learn about the Christian religion. There was, however, no pressure for belief or acceptance, and it was not required of students to attend or join in services of Christian worship. Like the JGC, it was more important to attract and influence non-Christian students: 'We wish the college to be a place where a keen and loyal Moslem or Jew can send his son, knowing quite clearly and openly what is going to be done about the question of religion, and able to accept it.'[108] Openness about this issue in relation to the students was important: 'We wish to "play the game" with absolute fairness and openness towards students who are of other religions.'[109]

The 'League of Nations'

The pattern from Ottoman times, when the different religious communities had provided their own separate schools, continued during the mandate period. From 1918 to 1948 the educational system was characterized by a dual autonomy. The autonomous Zionist schools were independent of the government schools, which were attended by Muslim children. The Anglican girls' schools, as well as St George's, could, however, present themselves as a multinational religious alternative, open to all communities in Palestine: 'We pride ourselves that Arab, Jew, Armenian, Persian, English, German, Russian, Moslem and Christians of many different Churches work peacefully side by side in our classrooms, and live happily together in our Boarding Houses. We rejoice in this League of Nations.'[110]

When looking at the diverse student body of the Anglican schools, the 'League of Nations' image becomes apparent. For example, at the British High School for Girls, Haifa, in November 1930, there were ninety-seven girls.[111] Of these, forty-eight were Arabs, eight Turks, seven Jews (of whom two were Palestinian, two Russian, one French, one Australian, one Bulgarian), six Persians, six Armenians, four Cossacks, one Greek and one Bosnian. Looking at the religious side, there were forty-eight Christian girls, twenty Muslim, seven Jewish and six Baha'i girls. The Christian group consisted of eighteen Greek Orthodox, seven Greek Catholics, four Armenians, two Maronites and seventeen Anglican or western Christians. The same diversity was found in Jerusalem. In the same year, 1930, at the Jerusalem Girls' College, which was twice as large as the Haifa High School, 226 girls were enrolled, of whom 140 were Christians, fifty-three Muslim and thirty-three Jewish. Beside the Palestinians, there were Armenians, Greeks, Cypriots, Turks, Russians, Abyssinians, Germans and English represented. Among the fourteen boarders, there were four Jewesses, three Muslims from Transjordan and seven Christians: five Greek Orthodox, one Armenian from Port Said and one Cypriot.[112]

The dividing elements were not only religion and language, but also nationality. The possibilities of conflict were present, as this example from the JGC shows: '[The first few years the] difference between Jews and Arabs was clearly marked, deputations from either side constantly arriving in the Principal's Office to make complaints against the other.'[113] It was, however, important for the JEM missionary to stress the college's socializing role in creating peaceful coexistence: 'But within three years after the establishment these differences and rivalries had become practically unknown, and Jewish and Arab girls were not only fraternising in class and on the playground, but visiting one another's homes in holiday time.'[114]

The multinational profile survived throughout the political unrest related to Lord Balfour's visit to Palestine in 1922. The government reacted with harsh measures and closed down the Government Training College for the rest of the year because of anti-British, pro-Arab demonstrations among its students. The fact that these students were Palestinian men, with a public political role not expected from Palestinian women at the time, might explain the different situation at the Jerusalem Girls' College where the upper school continued as usual. To the JEM teachers it was a proof of the success of the multinational character of the Anglican schools:

> Our exams are on, and it takes more than Balfour to make them risk a bad place in class next term ... the language exams were that afternoon [of Balfour's arrival], and it was rather comic, that while the town was being patrolled by armoured cars and lancers to keep Jews and Arabs from each other's throats, in every class in school were alternate rows of Jews and Arabs busily engaged in writing Hebrew and Arabic exams, with only one amiable staff there to give out fresh paper.[115]

Even after the riots in 1929, both of the Anglican girls' schools, as well as other missionary institutions, stayed open without apparent hostility among the students. The same was true during the general strike in the late 1930s.

During the 1940s, there was, however, a decline in numbers due to Arab emigration and increased Zionist pressure on all Jewish children to attend the schools run by the Zionist organization.

The multinational character of the Anglican schools was presented as central to the development of a future Palestinian society, thus combining the 'embassy-role' legacy of Blyth's bishopric with British promises to both Jews and Arabs in Palestine. While the Anglican church saw its role as aiming to fulfil the obligations of the mandate, it was critical of the British government's efforts. After the publication of the White Paper in 1930, *Bible Lands* questioned the British government's ability to keep its obligations to the Arab population and to establish peace and prosperity in the country. The solution offered by the Anglican mission, higher education for the local population, was legitimized by referring to the demand by the indigenous population, not only in Palestine, but in all new nations for an educational system based on the English school model.[116] The essence of British education was its Christian character, which was the way to peaceful coexistence and progress in a heterogeneous nation. This applied to boys' as well as girls' schools, and the bishopric pointed to the Jerusalem Girls' College as the ideal example:

> In the work for girls, this college stands pre-eminent as an example of how a Christian College can be an effective power in the eliminating of race preju-dice and the creation of the spirit of fellowship and good-will, and service to the community . . .[117]

Despite the insistence on its multi-ethnic, -national and -religious charac-ter, the percentage of Jewish students at the Anglican schools was never high. In 1935 Jewish children in Christian schools made up only 2 per cent of the students, of whom only 1 per cent were in the eleven Protestant institu-tions.[118] The percentage was higher in the Christian high schools for girls, and the symbolism of children from the three faiths of the Holy Land, learn-ing and living together, was seen as a living proof that the premises of the mandate could function as the base of an Arab–Jewish future of Palestine.

The members of the Peel Commission, who came to Palestine to look at the causes of the Arab riots in 1936, were struck by this image, being impressed with the Anglican schools' successful record of educating children from all communities. The issue of education within the mandate was given thorough attention by the committee, who saw the development of segre-gated schools as deepening the conflict between Arabs and Jews. Why had the Anglican mission institutions managed to create integrated schools following the English education system, while the government had not?, was the question asked.[119]

The bishop and his staff, when explaining the apparent success of the Jerusalem Girls' College, the Girls' High School in Haifa, as well as St George's, focused on the previously mentioned ambassador role. By their living example, the teachers/missionaries would create a Christian tolerance, which would develop a British and Christian character in their students. This was to be the basis for the peaceful coexistence of the different Palestinian communities. Reports back to JEM supporters in Britain emphasized the missionary aspect of the teaching. But in reality the non-proselytizing tradition prevailed. Christian character was taught through practical education, and much emphasis was put on Girl Guides and physical education. The latter introduced team sports, especially netball, which was a novel experience for Palestinian girls. It was compulsory in all the upper classes and evidently gained growing popularity. Its importance as an introduction to 'fair play' was evident: 'girls being chosen without regard to nationality or religion, there being Armenian Christians, Jewesses, Moslem and a Turkish Moslem in the [JGC] team.'[120]

Team sports and popular means to develop the young Christian man and woman in Britain physically as well as spiritually were adopted in educational work among Palestinian girls. One of the teachers at the JGC pointed to the fact that she had experience in Girl Guiding as the most important factor of her being employed by the JEM in the early 1930s. She took her Guides, Jews, Christians and Muslims, on hikes out in the 'wilderness', having obtained permission from all the parents to camp overnight, and giving special attention to the Muslim girls who remained veiled until they were away from the town.[121]

Another activity that was meant to encourage tolerance and 'team spirit' was the Debating Society, which held meetings alternately in Arabic and English. Subjects for debates were non-national/religious in character, with themes like 'As good an education is necessary for a girl as for a boy' and 'Manners are acquired rather than inherited.' The JGC as well as the Haifa High School for Girls even established their own branches of the League of Nations among the older students, representing the very essence of the schools: 'This branch is a little League in itself, being composed of members of six nationalities and all three religions.'[122]

The ideal of tolerance and peaceful coexistence was also encouraged after the pupils had graduated. Both the JGC and the High School in Haifa ran an Old Girls' Association, which published journals and attempted to keep the former students in touch with the school by attending the Debating Society and playing netball and other sports. In this manner a network of 'old girls' was created, whose loyalty to their former schools would create an alternative to the narrow national and religious identities.

The Peel Commission was not only impressed by the JGC and St George's schools, it also recommended that mixed schools (ones with Arab and Jewish pupils, which, besides the Anglican schools, included other western mission institutions) should be given every support. Most of the mixed schools had a high standard of educational achievement, their curriculum was broader than that of the Jewish or Arab schools, their educational methods and ideas were western, and the fact that most of them aimed for a specifically Christian type of character was appreciated.[123] But it was not only the educational standard that impressed the members of the Commission. Their conclusion echoed the ideology behind the Anglican schools. 'Had it been practicable in Palestine, such a system, adopted at the outset and consistently pursued, might have gone far in a generation to break down the barriers between Jews and Arabs and to nourish a sense of common Palestinian citizenship.'[124]

The director of education in Palestine, James Farrell, however, was critical of the Commission's praise of the mixed schools, and this feeling was shared by the Colonial Office. While the Jewish population had a well-developed educational system from nursery up, including university level, less than 50 per cent of the Arab children in Palestine were receiving any education at all. This was one of the chief grievances of the Arab population against the British government. The education authorities in Jerusalem therefore had to give priority to Arab elementary schools, and not secondary institutions on the British model.[125] In view of the hostile political situation in Palestine and plans for a partition of the country, the mixed schools looked like a well-intentioned philanthropical idea, but without much standing in the realpolitik of Arab and Jewish nationalism. Before the war, St Mary's Home had seen nursing and teaching, professions that were closely linked to the missionary role, as the future professions for its students. During the mandate period, these were still the professions acceptable for a Palestinian woman from the middle and upper classes, and the JGC as well as the High School at Haifa encouraged the traditional women's careers in health and education. There was, however, a widening of job possibilities for women during this period. Like the male students at St George's, the Anglican-educated women were employed in government offices and schools. Most of the schools, missionary as well as government, had a majority of Palestinian teachers, and there was a great demand for Arab women teachers.[126]

Some of these girls went on to teachers' colleges or universities abroad, the closest being the American university in Beirut, and others in Europe and the USA. It was important to secure local girls as teachers at the mission schools, and promising candidates were given scholarships to go to England to get further education. One of the Arabic members at the JGC, Miss Ernestine Ghory, was for example sent for one year's training at the Brighton Diocesan Training College for Teachers in 1935.[127] Other students were trained as nurses at mission hospitals and practised in Palestine before eventually starting their own families. An example of JGC students trained as nurses at an Anglican institution, who were active in their profession in Palestine, are the Armenian-English Rose sisters whose story is told by John Melkon Rose in his family biography, *Armenians of Jerusalem*.[128]

A dominant trait of Anglican education was 'character training', instilling a strong sense of social duty in the female students. The motto of the JGC was 'I serve', and the students were encouraged 'to work for the country and to undertake some form of social service when they leave'.[129] Letters from former students show that women did volunteer in their local community, teaching other women childcare and working at infant clinics. The career for most St Mary's girls was still, however, within the home sphere, a fact appreciated by the staff.[130] The college wanted to give both the future mother and wife as well as the teacher at the Jerusalem College 'the best [educational] conditions that we know, both as Englishwomen and as Christians'.[131] Regardless of religious background, most former students got married, and the ideal 'old girl' was expected to use her modern education within the home as well as outside, as an active volunteer, for example, as health visitor or assisting at child welfare centres: 'their letters show that they [the former students] are bringing up their children on modern hygienic lines, while finding time to help their poorer and ignorant neighbours.'[132]

The insistence on obligations to the wider community was intended to result in active humanitarian work in the Christian, missionary tradition. The JGC maxim 'I serve' did, however, have wider political implications for Anglican-educated Palestinian women. In 1930 there were two former JGC girls studying medicine at Beirut University, who would be among the first Arab women to become doctors in Palestine. These women came from Christian families, who traditionally had a much higher percentage of educated girls and women than Muslim society. As seen earlier, the existence of European mission schools since the latter part of the nineteenth century led to a generally higher level of education, male as well as female, compared with the Muslim population.[133] In her work on the Palestinian women's nationalist movement, Allison Wilke shows the involvement of Christian Palestinian women in the cause to improve the standard of life of rural, mainly Muslim women.[134] The above-mentioned 'old girls' at JGC were part of this movement for national improvement. While Miss Coate, the principal of the JGC, was strictly against any activity that could be interpreted as pro-nationalist in any way, the work of these women doctors was very acceptable because it was seen as based on the 'Christian spirit'. 'They are Christians and have entered the course with a view to helping Moslem women in the future.'[135] Ironically the same religious, non-political education could also be the basis for Arab nationalist involvement.

Further research is needed to discover what role the former students of the Jerusalem Girls' College and English High School in Haifa played in mandatory Palestine. What influence did Anglican-educated women have on their local communities as well as across religious and national borders within Palestinian society and after 1948, and also in the Palestinian Diaspora?

Conclusion

During the mandate period, the Anglican girls' schools carried on the tradition of female education initiated by Bishop Blyth and his family in the 1880s. The continuity was reflected in the staff, as well as in the priority given to female education and the stress on the 'embassy' role, which developed into a central idea as an alternative to the mutual exclusiveness of the Arab and Jewish communities.

During the Ottoman period, however, the JEM girls' schools were only a few among the many existing European mission schools in Palestine and Syria, and latecomers at that. After the First World War, the British mandate encouraged the establishment of Anglican institutions of female higher education. The government's low priority given to secondary education in general, and especially to girls' higher education, gave the high schools for girls in Jerusalem and Haifa a unique position. As the only English institutions in Palestine, the Anglican schools' higher education qualified girls for university studies.

Pre-war education had aimed at improving the domestic role of eastern women. The only career options had been the traditional ones of nursing and teaching. However, during the mandate period, the opportunities given to the former students greatly widened, for example with many 'old girls' finding work in government offices and administration. This was not in opposition to family life, which would be the natural choice after some time in gainful employment.

The Anglican girls' schools were acceptable to Muslims, and to some extent to Jewish pupils, as well as to Orthodox Christians, because of their non-proselytizing basis as well as their high educational reputation. The schools' record of a student body representing all religious communities in Palestine gave them a special standing in the religiously and nationally divided country. As the only British educational institutions to hold up the mandate intentions, the Anglican schools aimed at socializing their students for multinational and peaceful coexistence. These institutions also provided Palestinian women with an advanced educational basis that enabled them to be active participants in the social and political changes taking place in Palestinian society as a whole during this period.

Notes

[1] The Jerusalem and East Mission (JEM) was founded by Bishop Blyth in 1888 and was controlled and directed by the bishop in Jerusalem. *Bible Lands* was the JEM's journal aimed at members and supporters in England, and to some extent the USA.
[2] B. Melman, *Women's Orient: English Women and the Middle East, 1718–1918* (London, 1995), 165–234.
[3] A. L. Tibawi, *British Interests in Palestine, 1800–1901: A Study of Religious and Educational Enterprise* (Oxford, 1961); and *American Interests in Syria 1800–1901: A Study of Education, Literary and Religious Work* (Oxford, 1966).
[4] D. Hopwood, *The Russian Presence in Syria and Palestine 1843–1914* (Oxford, 1969), 137–58.
[5] A. Schölch, *Palestine in Transformation 1856–1882: Studies in Social, Economic and Political Development* (Washington, 1993), 48.
[6] Ibid., 49. This political and religious-cultural penetration by Europeans was made possible after Muhammad Ali's conquest of the geographical region of Syria (including Palestine) in 1831, when, in order to secure the goodwill of the European Powers, he

permitted the opening of European consulates, as well as the expansion and institution-alization of religious missionary activities. The Ottomans had to continue this policy after reconquering Syria in 1840, something that resulted in the entrance of other European consulates and religious dignitaries.

[7] Ibid., 97.

[8] Ibid., 50; in 1850 the Protestants were recognized as an official religious community in the Ottoman Empire.

[9] K. Crombie, *For the Love of Zion* (London, 1991), 37–45.

[10] Ibid., 50. See also M. Eliav, *Britain and the Holy Land* (Jerusalem, 1997).

[11] K. Cragg, 'The Anglican Church', in A. J. Arberry (ed.), *Religion in the Middle East Three Religions in Concord and Conflict*, vol. 1: *Judaism and Christianity* (Cambridge, 1969), 482. See also Crombie, *For the Love of Zion*, 20–3.

[12] Ibid., 42.

[13] Ibid., 98.

[14] D. Tsimhoni, *Christian Communities in Jerusalem and the West Bank since 1948: An Historical, Social and Political Study* (Westport, 1993), 138.

[15] Tibawi, *British Interests*, 225.

[16] Ibid., 21 and 158–61.

[17] A. O'Mahony, 'Christianity in the Holy Land: the historical background', *The Month* (December 1993), 469–76.

[18] Tibawi, *British Interests*, 22.

[19] Cragg, 'The Anglican Church', 570–95.

[20] Crombie, *For the Love of Zion*, 122–3.

[21] Cragg, 'The Anglican Church', 578.

[22] JEM papers, IV/1, Middle East Archive, St Antony's College, Oxford.

[23] JEM, LVIII/2.

[24] JEM, IV/4, Bishop Blyth's notes on the foundations at Jerusalem, written end of 1907 or early 1908.

[25] *Bible Lands*, I (1901), 211.

[26] JEM I, VIII/2.

[27] JEM, IV/4, Bishop Blyth's notes on the foundations at Jerusalem.

[28] Melman, *Women's Orient*, 46–7. See also B. Tuckman, *Bible and Sword: How the British Came to Palestine* (London, 1957).

[29] Schölch, *Palestine in Transformation*, 64. See also Crombie, *For the Love of Zion*, 15–30.

[30] See B. Baron, *The Women's Awakening in Egypt* (London, 1994).

[31] Melman, *Women's Orient*, 181.

[32] Ibid.

[33] Crombie, *For the Love of Zion*, 61.

[34] Ibid., 89.

[35] Tibawi, *British Interests*, 261.

[36] *Bible Lands*, I (1903), 3.

[37] A. M. Burton, 'The white woman's burden: British feminists and the "Indian Woman", 1865–1915', in N. Chauduri and M. Strobel (eds), *Western Women and Imperialism: Complicity and Resistance* (Bloomington and Indianapolis, 1992), 139.

[38] *Bible Lands*, I (1901), 88.

[39] See E. Blyth, *When We Lived in Jerusalem* (London, 1927).

[40] *Bible Lands*, I (1913), 85. Article by Bishop Blyth.

[41] Crombie, *For the Love of Zion*, 146.

[42] Melman, *Women's Orient*, 184–8; Tuckman, *Bible and Sword*.

[43] Melman, *Women's Orient*, 208.

[44] Tibawi, *British Interests*, 162.

[45] Melman, *Women's Orient*, 184.

[46] *Bible Lands*, I (1901), 88.

[47] *Bible Lands*, I (1899), 16.

[48] S. Hill Lindley, *You Stept Out of your Place: A History of Women and Religion in America* (Louisville, KY, 1996), 81.
[49] *Bible Lands*, II (1903), 3.
[50] *Bible Lands*, III (1910), 166.
[51] L. A. Flemming, 'A new humanity: American missionaries' ideal for women in North India, 1870–1930', in Chauduri and Strobel (eds), *Western Women*, 197–9.
[52] P. Horn, *The Victorian and Edwardian Schoolchild* (Glouchester, 1989), 27, 79–81.
[53] *Bible Lands*, VI (1913), 150.
[54] *Bible Lands*, I (1899), 16.
[55] *Bible Lands*, II (1904), 63.
[56] *Bible Lands*, II (1906), 183.
[57] *Bible Lands*, I (1899), 16.
[58] Hill Lindley, *You Stept Out of your Place*, 81.
[59] K. Jaywardena: *The White Woman's Other Burden: Western Women and South Asia during British Rule* (London, 1955), 37.
[60] *Bible Lands*, II (1903), 21.
[61] *Bible Lands*, III (1908), 70–3.
[62] Flemming, 'A New Humanity', 198.
[63] Horn, *The Victorian and Edwardian Schoolchild*, 52.
[64] *Bible Lands*, II (1906), 186.
[65] D. Kirkwood, 'Protestant missionary women: wives and spinsters', in Fiona Bowie, Deborah Kirkwood and Shirley Ardener (eds), *Women and Missions: Past and Present, Anthropological and Historical Perceptions* (Providence/Oxford, 1993).
[66] Melman, *Women's Orient*, 167.
[67] *Bible Lands*, IV (1911), 27.
[68] Horn, *The Victorian and Edwardian Schoolchild*, 49–50.
[69] *Bible Lands*, VI (1911), 27.
[70] Ibid.
[71] F. Davies, *The Ottoman Lady: A Social History from 1718 to 1918* (New York, 1986), 51.
[72] *Bible Lands*, IV (1911), 27.
[73] *Bible Lands*, III (1913), 232.
[74] Ibid.
[75] Hopwood, *Russian Presence*, 148.
[76] *Bible Lands*, II (1906), 183.
[77] *Bible Lands*, II (1904), 3.
[78] *Bible Lands*, III (1908), 200; Tibawi, *American Interests*.
[79] Hopwood, *Russian Presence*, 147.
[80] J. Tucker: *Women in Nineteenth Century Egypt* (Cambridge, 1985), 120. See also J. Tucker, 'Taming the West: trends in the writing of modern Arab social history in anglophone academia', in H. Sharabi (ed.), *Theory, Politics and the Arab World* (London, 1990), 198–227.
[81] Davies, *Ottoman Lady*, 51.
[82] A. L. Tibawi, *Arab Education in Mandatory Palestine: A Study of Three Decades of British Administration* (London, 1956), 20. Statistics from 1914.
[83] Ibid., 34.
[84] W. Jansen, *Christian Teaching in an Islamic Context: The Rise of Women's Education in Jordan*, Working Paper for BRISMES, 1997. Quoted with permission from the author.
[85] Annelies Moors referring to her fieldwork in Nablus, Bayt Jala, 4 September 1997.
[86] Crombie, *For the Love of Zion*, 135.
[87] *Bible Lands*, I (1901), 112–13: seventy out of 120–30 children.
[88] *Bible Lands*, I (1901), 112–13.
[89] *Bible Lands*, IV (1911), 26.
[90] Tsimhoni, *Christian Communities*, 139.
[91] *Bible Lands*, VI (1923), 298.

92 *Bible Lands*, VI (1924), 502.
93 JEM, XLI/3, letter from M. Warburton to Bickersteth, 2 October 1921.
94 See Tucker, *Women in Nineteenth Century Egypt*.
95 Emery Papers, DS 113.1, Middle East archives, St Antony's College, Oxford.
96 JEM, XXXIX/1, 1919, 'Britain's place in the educational reconstruction in Palestine'.
97 JEM, XXXI/1, general plan for Union British School and Collge in Jerusalem.
98 See Tucker, *Women in Nineteenth Century Egypt*.
99 *Bible Lands*, V (1919), 365.
100 JEM, XL/4.
101 *Bible Lands*, VI (1920), 4.
102 *Bible Lands*, VII (1925), 614.
103 See M. Seikaly, *Haifa: Transformation of an Arab Society* (London, 1995).
104 *Bible Lands*, V (1919), 365.
105 Ibid.
106 JEM, XL/3, letter to Oldham from M. Warburton, 9 February 1919.
107 Ibid.
108 *Bible Lands*, VI (1921), 100.
109 Ibid.
110 *Bible Lands*, VI (1924), 22–3.
111 Of these sixteen were in the English kindergarten.
112 *Bible Lands*, VI (1924), 23–3.
113 *Bible Lands*, VIII (1932), 184.
114 Ibid.
115 Emery papers, Middle East archive, St Antony's College, Oxford. Letter from S. P. Emery to her mother, dated Jerusalem, 29 March 1922.
116 *Bible Lands*, VIII (1932), 184.
117 Ibid.
118 *Bible Lands*, IX (1936), 697.
119 Bowman papers, 2/2, notes from Palestine Royal Commission. Question raised to the director of education, H. E. Bowman.
120 *Bible Lands*, IX (1936), 697.
121 Ruth Rhoden in interview with the author, January 1996.
122 *Bible Lands*, VI (1924), 506–8.
123 Colonial Office (CO) Archives (PRO, Kew), 733/362/2, dispatch on Royal Commission, 14 March 1938.
124 CO 733/362/2 Royal Commission on Palestine, p. 333, quoted in dispatch by J. Martin 14 March 1938.
125 CO 733/362/2, dispatch by Downie 8 December 1938.
126 *Bible Lands*, VI (1923), 56–7.
127 *Bible Lands*, IX (1935), 650.
128 J. Melkon Rose, *Armenians of Jerusalem* (London, 1993).
129 *Bible Lands*, VI (1925), 303–4.
130 *Bible Lands*, VI (1923), 85–6.
131 *Bible Lands*, VIII (1932), 184.
132 Ibid.
133 On the history of the Christian Arabs in Palestine see for example A. O'Mahony, 'The religious, political and social status of the Christian communities in Palestine, *c*.1800–1930', in A. O'Mahony with Göran Gunner and Kevork Hintlian (eds), *The Christian Heritage in the Holy Land* (London, 1995), 237–65; and *idem*, 'Palestinian Christians: religion, politics and society, *c*.1800–1948', in A. O'Mahony (ed.), *Palestinian Christians: Religion, Politics and Society in the Holy Land* (London, 1999), 9–55.
134 A. Wilke, 'Shoulder to shoulder: women and Palestinian nationalism 1929–39' (unpublished thesis, M.Phil., St Antony's College, Oxford, 1994), 38–48.
135 *Bible Lands*, VIII (1932), 184.

INDEX